TRUE STORIES OF
THE COMMANDOS

ROBIN HUNTER

Also by Robin Hunter

TRUE STORIES OF THE SAS
TRUE STORIES OF THE FOREIGN LEGION
TRUE STORIES OF THE SBS
TRUE STORIES OF THE PARAS

First published in Great Britain by
Virgin Publishing
Thames Wharf Studios
Rainville Road
London W6 9HA

ISNB 978 0 7535 4053 4

Typeset by Galleon Typesetting, Ipswich

The Random House Group Limited supports The Forest Stewardship
Council (FSC®), the leading international forest certification organisation.
Our books carrying the FSC label are printed on FSC® certified paper.
FSC is the only forest certification scheme endorsed by the leading
environmental organisations, including Greenpeace. Our
paper procurement policy can be found at
www.randomhouse.co.uk/environment

MIX
Paper from
responsible sources
FSC® C018072

www.randomhouse.co.uk

Printed and bound in Great Britain by Clays Ltd, St Ives PLC

CONTENTS

INTRODUCTION

'They performed whatsoever the King commanded'

Book of Samuel II
On the Commando Memorial
Westminster Abbey, London

This is the story of the real Commandos, the Army Commandos of the Second World War, the men who gave the word *'commando'* the significance it has never lost, even if terrorists and murderers have attempted to assume and corrupt it in the decades since the war. As the stories in this book will reveal, usually in the words of the Commandos themselves, in accounts extracted from the Rob Neillands archives, Commando soldiering during the war was a hard and difficult business – but one with compensations.

Some time after the Second World War, a Commando soldier, recently returned from Germany, was asked to sum up what Commando soldiering was like. The story goes that he brooded for a moment and then replied, 'Well, it's like a pleasant sort of pain in the neck.' That seems to sum it up exactly: Commando soldiering is hard work and even in the good times is fairly uncomfortable, as indeed is all infantry soldiering. And yet it has something. If I turn my head, I can see, hanging on a peg behind my study door, my faded green beret, earned on a Commando course many years ago. I have a few other trophies of a busy life, but none that means so much to me. Other trophies were given to me; the green beret I had to earn.

Over the years, other Commando soldiers, when confronted with that same question, have agreed that the above description is probably about right. Commando soldiering is easier described by saying what it is not, than by trying to sum up what it is – for the very nature of irregular, or special forces, warfare demands that Commando soldiering might be many things. What it is not, is easy.

However, I recently asked a very distinguished wartime Commando leader, a man with a chestful of decorations and a well-deserved reputation in battle, 'Was it fun?' He gave me what we used to describe as an 'old-fashioned look', and said slowly, 'Yes, as a matter of fact, most of the time it was great fun.' That is also true and the thing that makes it fun is the people you do it with – your 'oppos', your 'mates', or 'muckers', the other blokes in the green berets, those who have been through the same mill that you have, who know the score and will never let you down.

Commando soldiering is dangerous. That is part of the attraction. Even the training is dangerous but that too is the good part; the hard part is the relentless, ongoing grind, the sheer discomfort, the cold and wet and lack of sleep, the carrying of great weights over long distances and terrible ground, the need, the demand, to keep going, keep smiling and keep up. If you can ignore all that, Commando soldiering is indeed great fun.

So, in brief, how do you become a Commando? It helps to be a lunatic but assuming that you have enough common sense to know what you are doing, how can you get a green beret? First of all, the only way to get it is to earn it. It does not come easily and would be without value if it did. So, the first step is to become a soldier and a good one.

Good soldiers come in various guises and the tall, good-looking one, he with the well-pressed trousers and the steely gaze, may not be right for Commando soldiering. You will frequently hear Commando soldiers talking about some acquaintance and running him down happily, discussing his various shortcomings but usually concluding, 'He knows how to soldier, though,' and in these circles that is the ultimate accolade. So, you join, you learn to soldier and you volunteer for Commando training.

If you do, you have to know what you are letting yourself in for . . . at least six weeks of soul-searching, feet-blistering, shoulder-aching, muscle-weary misery – with lots of cold and wet and hunger thrown in. There are even some dangerous bits but those are the good parts, as they take your mind off the misery and fill it with a few seconds of stark terror.

Commando recruits don't get a lot of rest. The training is physical and the hours are long, and much of the training takes place at night, in all weathers. The basic elements consist of trying to find out – or rather helping you to find out – exactly how much more you can do than you think you can; and suprisingly, with the right attitude and a helping hand from the 'oppo' you are helping, you gradually find that you can hack this sort of training, do the runs, cover the ground, scale the cliffs, hit the target – and enjoy it.

Where that enjoyment comes from is hard to say, but there is a definite moment in a Commando's life when it all makes sense, and those tasks that were seemingly impossible a few days or weeks before are now in your gift. You are fit and strong and your head has got the hang of all this and you are now not just a soldier, but a Commando soldier, a very different kind of animal.

That animal is bred at night, on long marches in the rain, in small boats bobbing about on wild seas, on rain-drenched cliffs, snow-caked mountains and most of all by wet nights in damp trenches. Hardship is the breeding ground of the Commando soldier. He is created by assault courses and scramble courses and Tarzan courses, by 'full regains', 'death slides' and 'cat crawls', by weapon training and unarmed combat training and cliff assault training – and the training never stops.

In the end, or at some time in the process of that training, the budding Commando learns that he can do more than he thought he could, that it is indeed 'all in the heart and the mind' – and that mental toughness, the ability to stick it, depends more on attitude than on the ability to do a hundred press-ups.

As for the rewards, the first one is the satisfaction of finishing what you started, of completing the course and getting the green beret. That also admits you to the company of an élite, cheerful, dauntless bunch of rogues, the best friends and comrades anyone could wish for, men who give you all they can and ask in return only that you pull your weight, do your bit – and know how to soldier. The worst thing you can do is let your mates down. And if things get a bit rough, and you break every bone in your body, remember the old Commando saying – 'If you can't take a joke, you shouldn't have joined'. The men whose stories are told in these pages know all about that and I commend them to you.

1

A BRIEF HISTORY OF COMMANDO WARFARE

'If there were a hundred tongues in every head they could not recount or retell or enumerate all we have suffered at the hands of that valiant, wrathful, purely pagan people.'

An Irish monk on the Viking raids
AD 468

The story of the Commando soldiers of the British Army, and the units in which they served during the Second World War cannot be less than inspiring. This is the story of how a small group of men, many of them junior officers, created a force, a special force trained to fight a new kind of war, units that were to carry the war to the enemy, even in the darkest days of defeat, and later play in every campaign of a world war, taking the green beret from the fjords of Norway to the jungles of the Arakan. It is also a tale of official obstruction, wilful misunderstandings and a failure to grasp what these new 'Commando' forces could do – and could not do.

As far as possible this story is told in the words of the original Commando soldiers, covering every aspect of their time from recruitment to disbandment, and many of the conflicts, triumphs, defeats and disasters the Army Commandos encountered during the years between. These soldiers then stayed together in the Commando Association – the Old

Comrades Association of the Army Commandos – and kept up their wartime comradeship in the long dull years of peace; yet the story of the Army Commandos as a fighting force was not over when the wartime units disappeared.

After the Army Commando units were disbanded in 1946, it seemed that they had gone for ever, but today, as the world moves into a new millennium, they live again. Over 1,000 Army Commandos now serve in No. 3 Commando Brigade, Royal Marines, providing many of the services that fighting brigade needs – artillery, engineers, transport and air. These Army Commandos, having taken the All-Arms Commando Course at the Commando Training Centre, Royal Marines, at Lympstone in Devon, and having earned the green beret, serve with Commando units all over the world. They sailed with their comrades of the Royal Marines Commandos – in Nos 40, 42 and 45 Commando – unit survivors of the Second World War, to retake the Falkland Islands from Argentina in 1982.

Nor are Commando units restricted to the British Army and the Royal Marines. Australia has Commando units; and the Belgians retain a Para-Commando Regiment that has its origins in the Belgian Troop of No. 10 (Inter-Allied) Commando, in the Second World War. The United States used Commando units for reconnaissance tasks – Recondo Units – in the Vietnam War. Like all good ideas, the Commando idea has spread.

Besides, in the full context of history, and especially British history, there is nothing new about Commando operations. It is possible to go back to the Old Testament and trace stories that are easily identified as typical exploits for the modern Commando soldier. Small wars – and guerrilla warfare – have a long history, and from the earliest times irregular warfare – ambush, night raids, sudden attacks, cut and run operations – has been the way a small country can keep fighting against a larger or more powerful foe.

This is true of many nations, but especially of the British nation, which has never been heavily populated – or short of enemies. When British history is examined, it seems to be a long series of campaigns where amphibious warfare – Britain being an island – has played a significant part. This being so, it is hardly surprising that Britain's soldiers took naturally to amphibious warfare when the Second World War began in September 1939. It is appropriate, therefore, that this book should begin with a brief historical survey of amphibious assault – striking from the sea – the chosen way of attack for the British Commando soldier.

The written history of Britain could be said to have begun with the Roman seaborne invasion of 55 BC. That invasion was repulsed but the following year a more successful assault was launched and Britain remained a Roman colony for the next five hundred years. The Roman Empire in Britain lasted about 470 years. From the late fifth century, the Britons faced new maritime attacks, this time from the Jutes, Angles and Saxons who came sailing across the North Sea in their narrow ships to loot monasteries and towns, slaughter or enslave the Romanised population and eventually to settle in East Anglia – home of the Angles. Essex and Sussex, once settled by the East and South Saxons, are just two county names that can be dated back to those raiders whose descendants created Anglo-Saxon England and ushered in a brief period of peace.

This interlude did not last long. In the following centuries the Saxons were followed by the Danes – the Northmen – who occupied half the country, and then by the seagoing Normans, who took over the whole Saxon–Danish kingdom. It is clear, therefore, that the British people, often described as a hybrid race, come from a raiding, sea-roving stock.

The British have always had a taste for irregular warfare and, especially around the Celtic fringe, their menfolk seem to have an affinity for it. Indeed such warfare was a feature of daily life for centuries in large areas of the British Isles, for example on the Welsh Marches and the Scottish Border – and any roll call of Britain's irregular and Commando forces is notably full of Celtic names – Lord Lovat and Paddy Mayne, to name but two.

In 1066, William the Conqueror, himself a descendant of Viking raiders who had created a Northman state in Normandy, repeated Caesar's landing and eventually conquered most of the island. This too proved a precedent. Nearly 900 years later, in 1944, armies sailed the other way in a series of combined operations, culminating in the D-Day landings in Normandy of 6 June 1944 – landings in which Britain's Commando soldiers played a leading role. The 'Overlord' Tapestry in the D-Day Museum at Portsmouth mirrors the scenes on the one at Bayeux – with green berets dotted among the steel helmets. A visit to the D-Day Museum formed part of the research for this book.

During the Hundred Years' War, from 1337 to 1453, the French constantly raided the south coast of Britain, paying particular attention to the Cinque Ports of Kent and Sussex, ports charged with supplying ships for the English Navy and with conveying English armies over to France. The English, in turn, raided French towns and returned repeatedly to land armies on the coast of France, notably at Harfleur at the mouth of the Seine, to start the Agincourt campaign of 1415.

In 1588 the English Navy, with the royal galleons in the van, beat off the Spanish Armada of Philip II. King Philip, who dispatched the Armada to destruction, was in no doubt regarding the difficulties of an invasion if contested by English seapower. 'The Kingdom of England is, and must always remain, strong by sea, since on this the safety of the realm chiefly depends,' he wrote during that brief period when he was consort of the English queen, Mary Tudor. The Armada was, in fact, part of a combined operation, a naval force sent to ship an army to England. Had the Duke of Medina Sidonia managed to meet with the armies of Alexander Farnese, the Duke of Parma, in the Low Countries, as was the intention, there would still have remained the complicated task of landing that army on a hostile shore.

English cannon and English weather prevented even that possibility, but the lesson to be drawn from history here is that although navies are ideal for defence, they lack the ability to project their power ashore – unless they possess some amphibious capacity. For a landlocked power this may not matter; for an island kingdom it is essential. The Falklands War of 1982 only underlines that historic lesson and – as in the defeat of the Spanish Armada – that too was a close-run thing, entirely dependent on Britain's small but well-trained amphibious capacity.

In the seventeenth century, with the Royal Navy now officially in existence, a force of infantry was available – though in a rather minor way – for just such an amphibious role. The Duke of York and Albany's Maritime Regiment of Foot, raised in 1664 from the Trained Bands of the City of London, were armed with the new-fangled flintlock musket, a weapon calculated to be more suitable on the wild, wet and windy sea than the usual matchlock musket.

This regiment, which was also known as The Lord Admiral's Regiment, eventually became the Royal Marines – Britain's sea soldiers – a corps of soldiers, trained in amphibious warfare, which was to provide the captains and admirals of the fleet with that capacity to project some force ashore, enable snipers to shoot enemy officers and gunners in close-fought, ship-to-ship engagements and – if the need arose, as it sometimes did – suppress mutiny among the sailors. These Marines were stationed amidships, to prevent mutiny or, as they used to say, 'to stop the sailors and their officers eating each other'. The Marines took part in many great naval engagements, but amphibious operations were not confined to them. The British Army also took to storming ashore and was often at the launch of great campaigns.

The British Empire expanded from the 1750s – a process that often involved a landing operation, most notably in 1759 when General Wolfe's army was ferried up the St Lawrence river in Canada to storm the Heights of Abraham by night, take the city of Quebec and endow the British crown with the vast icy resources of Canada during the Seven Years War. Wolfe's landing below the Heights of Abraham was the blueprint for a dozen major Commando assault landings in the Second World War, and many more such landings were to follow during the ensuing two centuries. This Army–Royal Navy capture of Quebec in 1759 was a classic 'Combined Operation' but only one of many as the Royal Navy pushed across the world and added new territories to the British Empire.

Fifty years after Quebec, during the Napoleonic Wars, the British received first-hand experience of what an irregular force could do in a land campaign – another lesson from history. When Lord Wellington took Britain's only effective field army to fight in Spain, he found that the Spanish Army could achieve very little in open battle against the French, but that the peninsular terrain – a country 'where small armies are defeated and large armies starve' – was ideal for the ambush and snipe activities of the Spanish *guerrilleros*. It was this Spanish campaign, which lasted from 1808 to 1814, that gave us the term guerrilla warfare, from the Spanish *guerra* – war. There were great battles fought by regular troops, at Vittoria, Salamanca, Badajoz and Talavera, but it was the combination of regular and guerrilla troops that wore down the French and forced them out of Spain.

Parties of well-armed irregulars attacked and slaughtered French garrisons, cut the lines of communication, ambushed couriers and generally rendered the French position in Spain completely untenable. Meanwhile, there were coastal raids, when dashing frigate captains – real-life Captain Hornblowers – sent in parties of sailors and Royal Marines from the sea, to cut out ships from well-defended ports. These attacks were not without risk; Admiral Nelson lost his right arm during the amphibious assault on Tenerife.

All this should have added up to something, not least the establishment of an amphibious tradition, yet such forays were still seen as ancillary ventures, mounted as required, with whatever forces came to hand, not the highly specialised operations a later war showed them to be. During the nineteenth and early twentieth centuries, the main conduct of war was left to capital ships – battleships and cruisers – and big battalions; Britain's amphibious forces, never large, almost disappeared.

The small wars, colonial campaigns and conquests of the Victorian era were not greatly concerned with amphibious operations, for by then the Empire was established and needed to be controlled and extended by land campaigns. Even the landing in the Crimea was unopposed and the subsequent campaign was a disaster. As far as the British were concerned, the Royal Navy ruled the waves, while the British

Army could land at will and, protected by the guns of the fleet, could march wherever it wished . . . or so it seemed until the Boer War at the turn of the century. Then the British Army met a new foe, not some ill-equipped tribesman but a resolute irregular, skilled in fieldcraft and equipped with modern weapons he knew how to use.

In the early years of the twentieth century, the scene shifted to South Africa during the South African War of 1899–1902. After some initial successes, the Boer Army found itself quite unable to defeat the ever-increasing power of the British armies in regular engagements. But after the Boers went 'on commando' – the name *commando* being the Boer name for locally raised parties of mounted riflemen – they were able to keep up the war for years, against the full might of the British Empire and its most famous generals, Roberts and Kitchener. The story of the British Commandos of the Second World War and the present day can be traced back directly to the South African War. Indeed, many Second World War commanders cut their soldiering teeth in that long and gruelling campaign.

One Boer commando, Denys Reitz, wrote a book about his life in the Boer commandos – called, inevitably, *Commando* – still in print and an inspiration to British soldiers some forty years later. In *Commando*, Reitz describes how small roving forces of horsemen, equipped with little more than courage, tenacity and high-powered rifles, could beat off the assembled might of an empire, though they took terrible losses and suffered considerable privation. Reitz's account of his departure for the wars would touch the 'get-up-and-go' spirit essential to any Commando soldier:

> In September of 1899, we heard that British troops were moving up to the Transvaal and the Free State, and we were ordered to entrain for the Natal border. The moment we heard of this, we took our rifles, fetched our horses from the stables and within ten minutes had saddled up and mounted . . . little knowing on how long and how difficult a trail this light-hearted enlistment was starting us.

11

One Boer Commando blew up an armoured train. Among the passengers was an officer of the 4th Hussars, serving in South Africa as a war correspondent. His name was Winston Churchill, Britain's Prime Minister in the Second World War and the 'Father of the British Commandos'.

The First World War (1914–18) provides two examples, one disastrous, one successful, of amphibious operations. The first was the landings at Gallipoli in the Turkish Dardanelles Strait on 25 April 1915. These landings, by British, French, Gurkha, Australian and New Zealand forces, were compromised from the start when the Royal Navy attempted to force a passage through the Dardanelles and so alerted the Turks to the coming assault. The landings met with firm resistance, and were soon checked, with great loss. The force maintained itself ashore until the end of 1915, at great cost in lives and to no visible gain, finally being withdrawn under cover of night on 8/9 January 1916. The Gallipoli landings set a temporary blight on the political career of Winston Churchill, who had been in favour of this maritime attempt to outflank the Western Front and drive Turkey out of the war. Nothing at all was achieved and the losses among the troops were considerable: 30,000 killed, 74,000 wounded, 8,000 missing or taken prisoner.

Even worse, no lessons were learned about the conduct of major amphibious operations. Churchill was forced to resign and, from then on, the British military establishment became very wary indeed of amphibious operations. Fortunately, the next amphibious operation, the Zeebrugge raid, if smaller in scale, was much more successful in execution.

On St George's Day, 23 April 1917, a force of Royal Marines, drawn from the 4th Battalion of the Corps, carried out a raid on the Belgian port of Zeebrugge. The port was believed to be a submarine base and the raiders were to block the channel and the docks and destroy the harbour facilities. The raid was carried out with considerable success; the harbour was completely blocked and the Corps gained two Victoria Crosses. It did not stop German submarine operations, for Zeebrugge was only one of several U-boat bases, but this landing was made under the overall command of Captain Roger Keyes RN, later Admiral of the Fleet Sir Roger Keyes, a distinguished naval officer and believer in amphibious warfare who in 1940 became the Director of Combined Operations, in charge of Britain's amphibious and Commando forces.

Peace was forced on the Central Powers at the end of the First World War by a naval blockade, by terrible losses on the Western Front, and by the entry into the war of the United States, which offered the Allies an unlimited supply of cannon fodder should the war of attrition continue (successful strategy having very little to do with it). The war ended on 11 November 1918, and for the next twenty years the military forces of Britain quietly stagnated. Even so, a few of our Commando characters are already on stage, notably Roger Keyes and Winston Churchill, men who had some experience of irregular warfare. Given 2,000 years of history and countless examples of what an amphibious strategy could achieve, it is somewhat surprising that Britain still saw no need for a properly trained and equipped amphibious force – other than the Royal Marines – a force properly equipped for this complicated kind of warfare.

In this book, which covers the Second World War, amphibious warfare falls into two broad areas, small coastal raids and all-out amphibious assaults. Since 1664 Great Britain had maintained a force designed for these two purposes, The Corps of Royal Marines, but by 1918 the Corps had all but lost its amphibious role. The role of the Corps had become more naval than amphibious, its opportunities for shore training were limited, and even its continued existence was often in doubt. If the admirals had been forced to choose between a new battleship and the Royal Marines, the Corps might have vanished.

During the Great War, apart from Zeebrugge, the Corps had manned part of the main armament, the big gun turrets on battleships and cruisers and it had provided some infantry brigades for service with the Royal Naval Division on the Western Front. When the war ended, Corps' strength stood at

55,000 men, divided into two branches, the Royal Marine Artillery and the Royal Marine Light Infantry. This force was swiftly reduced by demobilisation to around 15,000 men, and in 1923 the two arms were amalgamated into a single Corps, the Royal Marines. The functions of this Corps were then defined by the Admiralty as 'to provide detachment for HM ships which, while capable of manning their share of the main armament, are also trained to provide a striking force . . . for amphibious operations such as raids on the enemy coastline, or for the seizure and defence of bases for the use of our own fleet'.

This directive seemed to offer the Corps the chance to develop the role it had demonstrated at Zeebrugge, but there is no further indication of the need to develop amphibious forces or specialised craft and equipment, although the problems of making assault landings had been outlined by a joint Army–Navy Committee as far back as 1913. This committee's findings had been published in *A Handbook of Combined Operations*, which laid out the problems of amphibious warfare very clearly. Analysing the problems, however, was not enough. Money was tight and nothing was done to tackle the problems, to provide the necessary craft or to train men in amphibious techniques. It was thought they could learn on the job; and the British technique of 'muddling through' was to underpin any difficulty.

Although the Corps' amphibious role was raised again by the Madden Committee in 1924, no funds were provided for equipment, training or landing craft, and when war broke out again on 3 September 1939, Britain was, as usual, woefully unprepared. The problems of Combined Operations – which in practice meant large-scale seaborne landings with air and naval support – had by now been under review for about ten years, following the belated appreciation that Great Britain was an island. In 1930 an Inter-Service Training and Development Centre (I-STDC) was established at Fort Cumberland in Portsmouth, commanded by a naval captain, L. E. H. Maund, assisted by a small Inter-Service staff, an RAF Wing Commander, a Royal Artillery major and a then captain of the Royal

Marines, J. Picton-Phillips. Colonel Picton-Phillips was later to be killed at the head of his men, leading No. 40 Commando – then the Royal Marine A Commando – ashore on the Dieppe raid in 1942.

On its formation in 1930, the I-STDC had got hold of three prototype landing craft, which were used to experiment with. The best of these craft had a top speed of five knots and drew four feet of water; none of them could get near a suitable landing beach. In the next ten years the number of landing-craft available expanded to six – but none was of a noticeably better design. On the rare occasions when there were landing exercises, the army was rowed ashore to the beaches in the launches and cutters of the Royal Navy. Nelson would have felt completely at home. Ten years of relentless prodding from the I-STDC failed to convince the War Office that landing craft or amphibious training were necessary and the centre failed to get the necessary funding or manpower.

When war broke out in September 1939 and the British Expeditionary Force departed for France, the I-STDC were given short shrift. Captain Maund sent a signal to his superiors requesting instructions for expansion, and was told that – with the BEF already established on the Continent – there would be no need for amphibious operations of any kind. The I-STDC was therefore to be shut down at once, the equipment put in store or sold, the officers and men returned to their units; the concept of Combined Operations had been dropped . . . then, less than a year later, came Dunkirk. Now that the British had been evicted from the Continent, the need for an amphibious capability became all too obvious – yet none existed.

There is a certain gap in British military thinking. No nation has produced so many innovative soldiers; great generals and officers such as Marlborough, Wolfe, Sir John Moore, Wellington, T. E. Lawrence, Orde Wingate of the Chindits, David Stirling of the SAS – the list is endless and continues. No nation has been so willing to experiment with new methods of warfare: tanks, paratroops, the SAS, the Long Range Desert Group, the SBS, midget submarines, bouncing bombs, jump jet aircraft . . . again, the list continues. But every fighting soldier writes of the sheer weight of bureaucracy and red tape that strangles new or even obvious ideas presented to the military establishment where everything has to be done by the book, where innovation must be resisted or, better still, crushed.

This is not seen as a snag by the 'powers-that-be'; far from it. According to the book, there is, there must be, a place for everything, with everything in its place. But there is no place in the book for people with wild ideas who want to raise private armies and go about at night with blackened faces, killing sentries. Fortunately, nothing concentrates the military mind quite so much as a crushing defeat of the kind experienced by the British Army in 1940.

Between September 1939 and the spring of 1940, Hitler's armies, masters of *blitzkrieg* or 'lightning war', rapidly overran those parts of Europe which had not already been ceded to the Nazis during the years of appeasement. During the 'Phoney War', which occupied the winter of 1939–40 after the defeat of Poland, attention shifted to the northern flank, and in particular to Denmark and Norway which the German Army invaded on 9 April 1940. Denmark, with only one short strip of land to defend against the German *blitzkrieg*, was swiftly overrun, but France and Britain were able to send forces into Norway; this turned into a mixed blessing for the Norwegian campaign was another débâcle.

The German Luftwaffe ruled the skies, and although the Royal Navy scored some successes against the German fleet and transport ships, a shortage of air cover plus the combined effects of the bitter weather swiftly led to a collapse of the Allied effort, and Norway surrendered. This disaster, however, does have two bearings on the Army Commando story. First, as a result of this defeat, Neville Chamberlain was forced to resign and Winston Churchill became Prime Minister. Second, the Independent Companies, the forerunners of the Army Commandos, took the field for the first time.

Five Independent Companies – hastily raised forces from the Territorial regiments – were sent to the Norwegian campaign because the Royal Marines, who might have been rushed north, were busy manning the guns of the fleet or serving in Coastal Artillery, their infantry role seemingly forgotten. A Royal Marines Brigade was being formed, mainly from wartime recruits – Hostilities Only or 'HO' ratings – men considered incapable of grasping the technicalities of naval gunnery; but since this Brigade – which later became a full Division – was still undermanned and quite untrained, the decision was taken to raise a number of small units – to be called Independent Companies – from the various divisions of the Territorial Army.

With the bulk of the Regular Army in France with the BEF, the Territorials provided the Home Army Commands, and they proved a fruitful source of volunteers. Each brigade was directed to furnish a thirty-man platoon for an Independent Company, with every battalion of that brigade providing a ten-man section. Each section was led by a lieutenant or subaltern, and the company was commanded by a major. Ten Independent Companies were eventually formed and among their numbers were some famous Commando soldiers, men like Major Charles Newman, later to win the VC as CO of No. 2 Commando at St Nazaire, Major Thomas Trevor of No. 1 Commando, Major Ronnie Tod, who was to lead No. 9 Commando in Italy, and many more who appear in this book.

Each Independent Company had a strength of 21 officers and 268 men, and the first 5 companies were soon in Norway, where they did sterling service, notably in the heavy fighting around Narvik. The Norway campaign was otherwise a complete disaster. The Anglo-French forces withdrew from Norway on 8 June, the country fell to the Nazis . . . and the disaster at Dunkirk was to follow within weeks. Recruiting for the Independent Companies continued and there was no shortage of volunteers.

Charles Hustwick, a signaller, was one of the early Commando soldiers and joined No. 9 Independent Company:

One morning they called for volunteers who wanted to see some action and I was the first to step forward. We were

17

kitted out in battledress and sent to St Mellons in Herefordshire where we met the rest of the Company, all volunteers from 38 Division. It was a real mix-up, and not all of us were infantry. There were sappers Royal Engineers, sappers Royal Army Medical Corps, medics, Ordnance, Signals, Cavalry, Tank men, you name it, all mixed up together into No. 9 Independent Company, a complete, self-supporting unit, about 250 strong.

I was a Signaller so we also got radio sets but they had been manufactured for the Romanians and all the instructions were in Romanian so needless to say it took us some time to work out how to use them but it was like that in the early days. These sets had to be carried on backpacks, plus our other equipment, rifle, 200 rounds of ammunition, water bottle, gas mask, entrenching tool – and any other odds and ends. When fully loaded with all our kit we couldn't stand upright. Our then OC, Major Siddons DCM, had fought in the battle of Mons in 1914. He had a German sabre scar on his forehead and carried an African club – a knobkerry – as his personal weapon.

The first task was to get fit and we got very fit indeed before embarking at Gourock on the Clyde. The ship had been a cattle boat and was still full of straw and manure, and we had to sweep out the cattle stalls before we could bed down. We were then told our destination – Norway. Our task was to carry out behind-the-lines warfare and interfere with the enemy lines of communication, but as you know the campaign in Norway collapsed and we returned to Glasgow – where for some reason we were greeted as heroes.

This was now the end of June 1940, the time of Dunkirk. Following their return from Norway, certain members of Nos 6, 7, 8, and 9 Independent Companies were sent to Southampton to form No. 11 Independent Company under Major Ronnie Tod. Charles Hustwick again:

We paraded for the first time at Southampton Football Club ground, The Dell, but in August 1940 No. 11 Independent

Company was disbanded and we were returned to our various units. I went back to No. 9 Independent Company which was by then in the Scillies. From there we were sent to man coastal defences at Mounts Bay – it was thought that the Germans were sure to invade and every spare man was manning a position somewhere on the South Coast during the Battle of Britain. Then we heard that No. 9 Independent Company was to be disbanded and we could either return to our parent units or re-volunteer for 'Special Service' – type unspecified. The volunteers from No. 9 joined those from No. 2 Independent Company, who had also been fighting in Norway; and became No. 1 Special Service (SS) Battalion though nobody liked that SS title, for obvious reasons after what the German SS got up to, and it was soon changed. We mustered about 800 all ranks, under Lieutenant-Colonel Bill Glendenning, and Major Tom Trevor was the second-in-command. The CO was a gentleman in every respect. Being too large for a special service unit – most Commandos were 400 strong or less – in about October 1940, No. 1 SS Battalion broke up to form No. 1 and No. 2 Commandos. I went to join the SS Brigade Signals and started a long service in the Commando forces.

It was now late summer of 1940 and Britain was in a perilous situation. The German Army's *blitzkrieg* offensive of May–June had pushed the British Expeditionary Force back to the Channel coast from where, with collapse and surrender imminent, they had had to be evacuated. The Dunkirk evacuation was seen at the time as a miracle and it was at least remarkable. No fewer than 338,000 soldiers, most of them British, had been lifted across the Channel to the elusive safety of Britain. The British people were briefly ecstatic – not least because they could now get on and fight the war without being hindered and harassed by the French – but, as Winston Churchill remarked at the time, 'Wars are not won by evacuations.' Britain had lost her position on the Continent and it would take a major amphibious landing to get back there again.

Geoff Riley, later of No. 5 Commando, remembers being evacuated from France in 1940:

I was on the last boat out of St Nazaire on the 19 or 20 June. My most vivid memory is of a French boy, about fourteen years of age, who was sobbing bitterly as he watched us marched out to the dock. He clung to me, begging me to take him with us. I couldn't do that, of course, but I promised myself that I would be back with the British Army as soon as I could.

Unless they were checked, it was more than likely that the Germans would soon come thrusting across the Channel to invade Britain. If they could mount a landing, there was little to stop them once they got ashore. In the House of Commons, Prime Minister Winston Churchill told the members and the British people bluntly: 'The Battle of France is over and the Battle of Britain is about to begin.'

This could not be a purely defensive battle. Britain must display her fighting spirit and hit back, soon and often, and as hard as possible, for an army that has been soundly defeated will not be left alone to gather strength; the enemy will pursue it, and strike again. That development could only be a matter of time, for Hitler's armies had passed on from Dunkirk to capture Paris. France duly surrendered. Hitler was triumphant and an invasion must follow.

Fortunately, there was the Channel, that invaluable, 24-mile tidal ditch that has stood so often between the British people and a foreign invader. To cross the Channel Hitler must have air cover for his invasion barges, so the fight now spread to the skies where, for a few weeks in that long, hot summer of 1940, the future of Britain and the free world depended on less than 1,500 young men, the trained fighter pilots of the Royal Air Force, the men of the hour, the famous and gallant Few.

In June 1940, Britain was almost alone and her resources were limited. Other than in the Royal Air Force, where pilots from the Dominions were already in the fight, the British

Empire had still to muster. The United States would not enter the war for another year and a half, until the Japanese attacked the US Fleet at Pearl Harbor in December 1941. If the British people were not dismayed, those in the government and in High Command knew how desperate the situation really was; but even in this dark hour the fight back had already started. On 26 June 1940, a day before the French government surrendered their country to the Germans, a small British force made the first Commando raid on the Channel coast of France.

2

EARLY RAIDS,
1940–1

*'The object of Special Service is to have available a
fully trained body of first-class soldiers, ready for
active offensive operations against an enemy in any
part of the world.'*

Lieutenant-Colonel Newman, CO
No. 2 Commando, 1940

The Dunkirk evacuation, which rescued most of the BEF, and
a large number of French soldiers, though not, alas, most of
their equipment, was officially terminated on the afternoon of
4 June 1940. The first feeling, when the news of this successful evacuation was broadcast to the nation, was one of relief.
That feeling was then replaced in some quarters by worry
about what would happen next and how the British Army,
without weapons or transport, could again be brought up to
fighting trim. It was clearly necessary to gain some time, and
show the enemy that Britain was still full of fight – and one
way to do that was by raiding.

The birth of the Commandos can be timed almost pre-
cisely. It occurred at about 19:00 hours on the evening of 4
June 1940, when Lieutenant-Colonel Dudley Clarke, Military
Assistant to General Sir John Dill, Chief of the Imperial General Staff, the man who advised the government on military
matters and relayed official policy to the High Command,

was walking home from the War Office, pondering on the need to find some way to strike back at the German forces now celebrating their victory on the Channel coast. While serving in Palestine, watching the British Army attempting to keep the Arabs and Jews from cutting each other's throats – not always successfully – he had seen how a handful of guerrillas could nullify the strength of an army corps mustering two divisions.

Clarke wondered if what had been done in Palestine could now be attempted here, on the shores of enemy-occupied Europe, where a thousand miles of coast from Norway to the Spanish frontier lay open to the Royal Navy and her amphibious forces. The difficulty was that there *were* no amphibious forces, neither men, nor equipment, nor boats to put them ashore. There was one force, the Royal Marines, who, by tradition, should have filled this raiding role, but they were now hastily manning coastal defence batteries, or serving the main armament on HM ships or – for those newly joined HO ratings – mustering for some sort of as yet unspecified service in the Royal Marines Division. Besides, they were under the Admiralty and the sailors tended to be even more hidebound than the Army Staff; in the circumstances it seemed wise to start with the Army.

That evening Dudley Clarke put his ideas down on one sheet of paper and passed it to his chief. Briefly, the idea harked back to those Boer Commando raids in South Africa at the turn of the century, suggesting that it might well be possible for something similar to be attempted on the coast of France where lightly equipped teams of fighting men, carried across in small fast ships of the Royal Navy, could harass the enemy and give evidence of Britain's willingness to fight on. It would also, Clarke suggested, demonstrate to the public at home that all was not yet lost. The gamble was not excessive, a few men and boats, and the effect might be considerable.

Winston Churchill always had a weakness for irregular warfare and original proposals, and in this case could judge the worth of the suggested enterprise from his own experiences in South Africa. He thought the idea well worth trying and gave his approval. On 6 June – four years before D-Day marked the British return in force to the Continent – General Dill called Clarke into his office and told him that his scheme was accepted. He was to form 'Commando units' – as Churchill wanted them called – and mount a cross-Channel operation at the earliest possible moment.

Some flesh now had to be put on Clarke's brief, original proposal and it was decided to form ten Commando units, each consisting of ten 'troops' or platoons, with a total strength of 500 men – a formation based on recent experience with the Independent Companies. These were to provide a basis for many early Commando units – and a considerable number of the first Commando recruits. A circular letter was sent to the Commanding Officers in all battalions of the various Home Commands, calling for 'Volunteers for Special Service'.

Applicants must be trained soldiers of good physique, physically fit, able to swim and immune from air- or sea-sickness. Personal qualities must include courage, endurance, initiative, activity, marksmanship, self-reliance and an aggressive spirit towards the conduct of the war. Volunteers must be prepared 'for longer hours, more work and less rest than other recruits to HM Forces; and will be trained in the military uses of scouting, able to live off the country, move unseen by night and day, being able to stalk the enemy and report on his activity'.

Such a demand was calculated to produce a fine body of men. Officers would interview prospective candidates and be satisfied that they had the necessary moral and physical attributes for good Commando soldiers. After a little more calculation and discussions with the Navy, the final strength of these all-volunteer Commando units was fixed at 462 men. This gave a Commando about half the establishment of a regular infantry battalion, organised in ten troops of approximately fifty men.

Among the first to apply was an artillery officer, Captain John Durnford Slater, who took the memorandum upstairs to his commanding officer and said, 'This is exactly what I want to do . . . will you release me?' Durnford Slater's colonel went a little further than this and directed him to write the application himself which the colonel would then sign. The letter must have been a good one for it had a surprising effect. Ten days later, the reply stated that, 'Captain J. F. Durnford Slater, RA, is appointed to raise and command No. 3 Commando in the rank of Lieutenant-Colonel. Give every assistance and early release as operational role is imminent.' Nos 1 and 2 Commando had yet to form, so John Durnford Slater became the first Commando soldier of the war.

The practical result of the War Office circular was to raise ten Commando units, drawn from the various Home Commands. Major Leslie Callf recalls that No. 9 was a mixture of Scots and English troops, and when the troops were formed the officers were careful to pick first an Englishman and then a Scot, so as thoroughly to mix the unit. No. 9 Commando always retained a Scots flavour, with a piper for every troop, and a black hackle on every green beret, when that headgear was eventually issued.

No. 10 Commando, which it was hoped the Northern Command would raise, never found sufficient volunteers, but a year or so later, it regained life as No. 10 (Inter-Allied) Commando with troops formed of French, Dutch, Belgian, Norwegian, Polish and Yugoslav soldiers, and even from German Jewish nationals.

The Army Commandos were raised entirely from volunteers, every unit selecting its own men from those who came forward. The COs selected the officers and the officers then travelled about the Home Commands selecting men from among the volunteers. Peter Young, one of the great Commando soldiers of the war, also joined No. 3 Commando by recommending himself. His parent unit, the 2nd Battalion, Bedfordshire and Hertfordshire Regiment, was at Yeovil when Young was summoned for an interview at the HQ of No. 3 Commando, meeting 'a Captain with a high-pitched voice who bore a superficial resemblance to Mr Pickwick'. The interview had gone on for some time before Young realised that the 'Captain' was his future CO, Durnford Slater . . . but he still got accepted. All new officers, like those from the other Commando units, were then dispatched to raise their own troops.

This was not an easy task, even after the War Office directive ordering the battalions to produce Commando volunteers. Many battalion commanders were naturally reluctant to lose their best men, and not all the volunteers were entirely suitable as the request to release men was used to get rid of the sick, lame and lazy. That apart, these amateur recruiting officers had different ideas on exactly how to pick out a potential Commando soldier, as Major Milton of No. 7 Commando recalls:

I was one of the last of the cadets to pass through the RMA Sandhurst before the war and I had a Regular commission. In June 1940 I was stationed in Hounslow, the depot of my regiment, the Royal Fusiliers. It was *intensely* boring. Salvation came soon after Dunkirk with a call for volunteers for either an experimental parachute unit, or a seaborne raiding force. This was a wonderful idea, so I immediately volunteered.

Then I went to the mess for lunch where I met Captain Dudley Lister, who told me that he had just been appointed to command one of the new Commandos. I said, 'I have just volunteered,' and he said, 'In that case, you can be my first officer,' and so I joined 'C' Troop, No. 7 Commando. Quite soon we were sent out to interview hundreds of volunteers in the Eastern Command. I had no idea how to pick men for an enterprise of this sort. We knew that toughness would be essential, but I think that the idea of rigid, strong discipline, which is needed to fight in a co-ordinated manner, escaped us at that time.

We tended to choose the men who stood out for having done something odd in civilian life; there was one who had gone round Cape Horn in a Finnish sailing barque, and another who had fought in Spain in the International Brigade, and another who had been in a razor gang in Glasgow. One of our officers had served in the Gran Chaco War in Paraguay. When No. 7 was finally formed it contained officers and men from no less than *fifty-eight* separate corps and regiments of the British Army – everyone wearing his own head-dress and cap-badge. The green beret did not come in until later.

Peter Young had some very decided ideas about Commando soldiers, ideas he put into practice when putting his own troop together:

Before the war, we had perhaps half a dozen officers in my regiment who would have been accepted as officers in the Commandos. We also had a lot who were either useless or who didn't want to be at war at all, reserve officers who didn't want to go around cutting throats. The officers in the Commandos were quite different . . . maniacs, really. Some of them just loved to fight and craved battle and the soldiers will follow officers like that. The rest of the Army was different, which is hardly surprising when you remember the run down of the Services between the wars. When the war started we had maybe 200 men in the battalion, and 'A' Company, which I was in, had two officers and nineteen men – there should have been well over 100. We were made up with reservists, and your typical reservist would as soon hear the devil as a drum. They had long since settled down to their dull civilian lives, and it is dull, believe me.

So, what makes for a good Commando soldier? Well, a restless nature for a start but they were all different. You had to know the different Troops and play on them like a violin . . . their different ways, how to tweak them into action; every Troop in 3 Commando had its own character and getting them going is an art and great fun. We had wonderful people. I was cut off in Italy for a week once, with only four soldiers, and they looked after me so bloody well, you know? You look after them, with a good plan and all, and they will look after you, relieve you of all fear of ambush or surprise. Those chaps would always get their shot in first. It also helps to be lucky. I am notoriously lucky and I didn't get a lot of soldiers damaged, and the sods like that.

A Commando is like a club and you have to keep up the membership. You mustn't squander soldiers, not at all must you do that. Breed them up into suspicious alertness, never

27

relaxed, always on their toes. Otherwise you are no bloody use to me, as officer or man, or sergeant-major . . . I'll break your back if that's your attitude. I looked for a man who could soldier – absolutely.

As to how to pick them, Lord? You look at them, don't you! You talk to them a bit, make up your mind if he's a bullshitter or has something to contribute . . . you can usually tell after a bit. I was very seldom wrong but I admit to being wrong sometimes. Young soldiers are good and they follow you out of innocence – well, you know that. And a good old soldier is a good soldier but a *bad* old soldier is worse than useless.

Durnford Slater toured the garrison towns of Southern Command to recruit his officers and then gave them four days to select their men and get them to Plymouth. He preferred 'men who didn't talk too much, the quiet type of Englishman, who knew how to laugh and how to work'. According to Peter Young, 'The majority of the men in No. 3 Commando were reservists – men who had seen service, many of them having served seven years with the Colours, mostly in India. Their average age was about twenty-six. They knew their weapons, had seen some fighting and wanted more of it.'

Commando soldiers are usually light years away from the popular gung-ho image of a Special Force soldier. They tend to be small, tough, quietly spoken and humorous, not afraid of hard work and with somewhat happy-go-lucky natures. A typical Commando hardly exists but a good cross-section lies among the following early volunteers.

Stan Weatherall joined No. 6 Commando in 1940:

I was in No. 1 Troop. The Commando was in civilian billets, with civvy ration cards and we were paid 6 shillings (30p) a day billeting allowance. The landladies in Scarborough asked £1. 10s. (£1.50) a week, so the lads benefited by 16s. 8d. (83p) a week, which was not to be sneezed at when a pint of beer was just 6d (2.5p) and the better brands of fags 6d for twenty . . . some brands were even less. At the first parade there was a talk by the Troop Commander who said, 'You will be made to suffer all manner of discomforts. Those who cannot make the grade will be RTUd (returned to units). As you are all volunteers, you can all return to your units at any time at your own request.' Our training was tough, no mistake about it. It largely consisted of forced marches across country and field exercises on the Yorkshire Moors. Every man of the troop was certainly put to the test, but the civvy billets were great.

In spite of the tough training, men of all ages came forward to volunteer, as Cecil Blanch of No. 12 Commando remembers:

I particularly remember a Scotsman, Sergeant Jock Bellamy. His real name was McKenzie and he took the name Bellamy from a book he read while in prison for smuggling whisky, as he was afraid his record would bar him from the Army. How he ever got into the Commando was a mystery, for he was much older than the rest of us and had served in the First World War. I think he had the DCM and the *Croix de Guerre*. Jock was as tough as his native granite, but he had a heart of gold and a great sense of humour. When Lord Louis Mountbatten became Chief of Combined Operations sometime in 1942, he visited 12 Commando, and during the inspection he stopped in front of Jock, took a good look at him and said, 'Another old-timer like myself, I see. How old are you, Sergeant?' Jock replied, 'Thirty-five, Sor.' 'Come on,' said Lord Louis quietly, 'I won't give you away.' Whereupon Jock said, 'Ach, well, I'll take a chance . . . thirty-five-and-a-half, Sor.'

Sidney Dann of No. 6 Commando had to go to a great deal of trouble to get into the Commandos:

When my call-up came I requested an infantry regiment and went to the Essex Regiment but lots of tradesmen were lost in France before Dunkirk and, as I had been a butcher in

Civvy Street, I was sent to the Royal Army Service Corps, then to the Royal Electrical and Mechanical Engineers (of course, just right for a butcher), and finally into the Catering Corps from where I volunteered for everything that would get me out of cooking and into the infantry. COs could veto any application for transfer and although I finally got before a Commando selection board, I had a lot of trouble convincing the officer that a cook could make a good Commando. I was accepted and returned to my unit to await posting, and was at once reduced to the ranks from full Corporal by my CO, who did not want to lose me because I was a good scrounger and kept the Officers' Mess supplied with eggs and chickens.

From the formation of the Commandos in mid-1940 until the Commando Basic Training Centre was opened at Achnacarry in Scotland, most of the initial Commando training was carried out at unit level. Alf Barker joined No. 5 Commando in 1940:

The first task was blancoing my webbing three different colours in as many days. This bull was considered essential to wipe out stories which had appeared in the newspapers about the new 'killer force' full of desperados and criminals. I then went to No. 12 Commando and when No. 12 was broken up later in the war, to No. 6 Commando. Apart from unit training, much of the early training was at Lochailort and at places like Dorlin House, which have never received full credit for all they did in the early days. Achnacarry gained all the kudos as the Commando School. As Heavy Weapons personnel, I remember the training we did at Braemar under Colonel John Hunt, later Sir John Hunt of Everest fame. In addition to ordinary training we did a lot of work with mules, packing the mortars and machine guns over the Highlands.

The advantage of this unit training was that it gave scope for individual initiative. Ideas could be tested at unit level and if they worked they were adopted and passed around. The disadvantage was that there were considerable variations in unit standards which eventually led to the opening, in 1942, of the Basic Training Centre, based at the home of the Cameron of Lochiel, chief of Clan Cameron at Achnacarry House near Spean Bridge in the Western Highlands. Training and exercises at Achnacarry were tough and the training started on arrival, when the men had to jump from the train at Spean Bridge, cross the line, scramble on to the far platform and then make a seven-mile forced march to the camp at Achnacarry.

Fred Musson joined No. 5 Commando at Bridlington, Yorkshire, in July 1940:

> In the early days, most of our training was done in Scotland, in the Loch Fyne and Lochailort areas. It was in Scotland that No. 5 Commando was issued with the Balmoral bonnet as the standard head-dress (until then we had all worn the one of our parent regiment), and on it we wore our own regimental cap-badges, over a green backing, with a gold-coloured hackle. For an arm-badge we had crossed fighting knives with No. 5 on it. There was a lot of weapon training, night work and troop attacks. Every day we did speed marches, carrying platoon weapons, rifles, Brens, ammunition, the lot, covering five miles in fifty minutes. After weeks of training we were fit enough to do our five miles and still be fit to fight.

John Murphy of No. 2 Commando was another early recruit:

> I remember marching from Fort William to Lochailort on an unmade road and that was no joke, despite the fact we were all reasonably fit. I also remember being in the tender care of Captains Sykes and Fairbairn – ex-police officers from the Far East – for unarmed combat. Eventually, No. 3 Independent Company became part of No. 2 Commando.

Cecil Blanch joined No. 12 Commando in 1940:

Life in a Commando was poles apart from that in normal army units. For a start we were in our own billets – it was like living at home. Secondly, there was no pettifogging discipline. It was made plain from the start that self-discipline was the order of the day. You were expected to be perfectly turned out and to keep your weapons in perfect order, and it worked. We were not the thugs some made us out to be and the biggest disgrace that could befall any Commando soldier was to be RTUd – or kicked out – which was the only punishment.

Training was designed to achieve peak physical fitness, self-reliance and skill at arms. Weapons were the .303 Lee-Enfield rifle, the Bren light-machine gun, the .45 Thompson sub-machine gun, issued centrally as required, and later on the Sten-gun. Coshes, knuckle-dusters and the fighting knife made by Wilkinson were also issued. Route marches of up to thirty miles were regular events, and there was plenty of night work. Physical fitness certainly reached a very high level. For example, in the winter of 1940–1 'B' Troop of No. 12 Commando marched from Crumlin to Londonderry, carrying full equipment, and covered the distance of 63 miles in nineteen hours.

Cecil Blanch recalls other exercises:

In November 1941, when 12 Commando were at Ayr, we made a dawn crossing of the River Doon before carrying out an attack on the Carrick Hills. We remained out that night, night patrolling, before marching back to Ayr in the late afternoon of the following day. It was bitterly cold and we were soaking wet, but I do not recall any of us suffering ill effects. Basically our training was similar to that of an infantry unit, but more prolonged and intense. On a march you did not fall out unless you passed out, and at the end of a march or an exercise you were not dismissed but sent over the assault course or for a spot of drill or weapon training. It was all designed to teach you that you *could* keep going and fight at the end of an arduous day, so it toughened you mentally as well.

Commando training could also be dangerous. Over forty men were killed in training exercises at Achnacarry between 1942–5, and Geoff Riley of No. 5 Commando recalls an incident when his troop were training in Cornwall:

We were on the firing range situated on a cliff top, practising grenade throwing. A grenade is primed with either a four-second or a seven-second fuse, the seven-second for the distance throw, and the four-second for street fighting. On this particular day, we were throwing grenades for some forty yards on to a marker post, with the aim of making them explode on contact. To do this meant pulling the pin, letting the plunger strike home and, holding it, counting up to four and throwing. This was to eliminate the situation where an enemy could pick the grenade up and throw it back at you. I was actually very good at this, dropping them on to the stick in one go and we had been at it all day. Then, about 16:30 hours I took up my usual stance, took the pin out, let the plunger click, and after counting four seconds, dropped the grenade at my feet!

Pandemonium! 'Take cover everybody!' Captain Addington yelled, at the same time hurling me to the ground and covering me with his body. The grenade exploded with a crash, covering us both with dirt and rock. Nobody was hurt and the drama was over. Then Captain Addington said, 'Where's Geoffrey?' My Troop OC, Geoff Rees-Jones, was nowhere to be seen. Then we heard a faint cry coming from somewhere below, for Captain Rees-Jones had actually flung himself over the cliff, his fall stopped by a bush some fifty feet down; all we could see was his moustache. It brought a little light relief and Captain Tom said, 'Right, I think we'll call it a day. We're all getting tired now.' No recriminations; it was taken as part of the job in wartime.

33

While all this was going on, the Special Service command structure was being set in place. On 12 June Churchill appointed Lieutenant-General Sir Alan Bourne, Adjutant-General of the Royal Marines, to the post of Head of Combined Operations or 'Offensive Operations', as it was then called. General Bourne held this post for only a month until 17 July 1940, when he was replaced as Director of Combined Operations by Admiral of the Fleet Sir Roger Keyes of Zeebrugge fame, who asked General Bourne to stay on as his deputy.

By then the fledgling Commandos had already tasted action. An official British communiqué of 26 June 1940 states: 'In co-operation with the Royal Air Force, naval and military raiders carried out a reconnaissance of the enemy coast of France. Landings were effected, contact made with German troops and casualties inflicted before our troops withdrew without loss.' This operation was carried out by No. 11 Independent Company under Major R. I. F. Tod. Among the party was Lieutenant-Colonel Dudley Clarke, who had thought up the Commando idea just three weeks previously. Parties landed at four points on the French coast, between Boulogne and Berck Plage. One party advanced inland for a quarter of a mile, found nobody and withdrew.

Another party found itself in a seaplane anchorage and was about to attack a seaplane when, to its considerable annoyance, the plane took off. The third party, landing at Mirlimont Plage near Le Touquet, surprised and killed two German sentries. The last party, which included Major Tod and Lieutenant-Colonel Dudley Clarke, got ashore without trouble but was surprised by the enemy during the withdrawal. In an exchange of fire a bullet struck Lieutenant-Colonel Clarke behind the ear, injuring him slightly. Three weeks later it was the turn of No. 3 Commando to mount a raid, on the island of Guernsey.

This operation was mounted with great speed. John Durnford Slater's appointment to No. 3 Commando came through on 28 June; No. 3 Commando paraded for the first time at Plymouth just seven days later on 5 July, and on 7 July it commenced training for a raid against the enemy-occupied island of Guernsey.

The raiding party, from H Troop of No. 3 Commando under Durnford Slater, and No. 11 Independent Company, commanded by Major Ronnie Tod, embarked at Dartmouth on the destroyers HMS *Scimitar* and *Saladin*, accompanied by seven RAF air-sea rescue launches, or 'crash boats' which, in the absence of proper landing craft, would take the men ashore. H-Hour, the time of landing, was set for 00:50 hours on the night of 14/15 July.

The force sailed from Dartmouth at 18:00 hours on Sunday 14 July, aiming to land on the Jerbourg Peninsula, where No. 3 would attack a machine-gun post and cut a wireless cable, while No. 11 Independent Company attacked the main target, the island's airfield. Matters began to go awry soon after sailing. Two of the RAF launches assigned to No. 11 dropped out with engine trouble and those which continued turned out to be terribly noisy. But by midnight the small force was in station off the south of Guernsey, in the lee of the land, and here the Commandos transhipped into the launches – after which Durnford Slater's launch promptly set off in the wrong direction, towards the coast of Brittany. Once the compass error had been detected, the craft put about and closed the beach on Guernsey by about 01:00 hours, putting the men ashore at high tide in several feet of water, which drenched all the weapons and drowned their radio set. It all made for a noisy landing and was followed by a hard, squelching run up a long flight of steps to the top of the cliffs where the machine-gun post was found, empty and unmanned.

No. 3 Commando wandered about on Guernsey for an hour or so until Durnford Slater fell over and let off his pistol, which produced a burst of machine-gun fire from the enemy. At the re-embarkation point, four men admitted they could not swim and had to be left behind, but the balance of the Commando withdrew by swimming out to the boats through the surf. The Independent Company, coming ashore in two craft, also fitted with faulty compasses, got totally lost, one boat hitting a rock and the other landing the men on the island of Sark. They had done no damage to the enemy but they had learned a few useful lessons, not least that amphibiosity is not half as easy as it looks.

Churchill, who was already having some difficulties with the military hierarchy over the entire Commando concept – which the 'powers-that-be' in Whitehall were anxious to crush – was less than pleased with these initial raids. 'It would be most unwise to disturb the coasts of these countries by the kind of silly fiascos which were perpetrated at Boulogne and Guernsey,' he wrote. 'The idea of working up all these coasts against us by pin-prick raids and fulsome communiqués is one to be strictly avoided.'

Commando operations were plagued throughout the war by problems with landing craft which fouled things up even before the men got ashore. Landing craft broke down, got lost, put their men on the wrong beach, failed to turn up or ran ashore so firmly that they could not get off again. With all their other problems, the lay reader might suppose that these additional difficulties drove the Commando soldiers frantic, but in fact their stories are full of praise and support for their friends and comrades in the landing-craft crews. This is probably because the Commandos knew just how difficult a task the crews had.

On the face of it, getting ashore on to a beach in a flat-bottomed landing craft looks simple – until you consider the situation. Commando soldiers went ashore in a wide variety of craft during the war, from two-man canoes to the large, ocean-going LSTs (Landing Ship Tanks). But, as the war wore on, they increasingly used the LCA (Landing Craft Assault), a flat-bottomed craft, with the steering wheel forward and the engine room aft. She carried a crew of four – a commander, a coxswain (helmsman), a stoker who controlled the engines, and a deckhand – and had a speed of about six knots. Fully loaded, she could carry a platoon of thirty Commando soldiers, who sat on long thwarts below deck level during the run-in to the beach. About fifty metres offshore the craft slowed and the deckhand dropped a kedge anchor over the stern. The craft then grounded and the coxswain dropped the bow ramp; the steel doors to the passenger compartment opened and on the order 'Down Ramp – Out Troops!' the troops streamed ashore, fanning out as they crossed the beach. The LCA crew then pulled the craft off the beach, using the cable to the kedge anchor . . . or at least that was the idea.

After a while the Commandos got very good at rapid disembarkation and the equally vital re-embarkation. At Inveraray in 1941, the thirty men of Algy Forrester's 'F' Troop from No. 3 Commando could get out of their craft and twenty-five yards up the beach, fully equipped with platoon weapons, in ten seconds. Peter Young's troop held the re-embarkation record of fourteen seconds. This rapid embarkation and re-embarkation was crucial, for both craft and men were most vulnerable when beached offshore, within easy range of the enemy defences; constant practice in disembarking was essential.

Getting ashore sounds simple; but consider the difficulties of getting the men ashore, not on a peaceful exercise, but in wartime. The landing will probably be made in the dark; there is probably a sea running. The men in the first wave have to climb out over the rail of the transport vessel into their craft, without lights and without talking, and the craft are then lowered into the sea. Subsequent waves must clamber down scrambling nets. Anyone who falls into the sea, fully loaded with all his kit and ammunition, will almost certainly drown. Once in the water, the LCA is very low and the visibility, even in daylight, is restricted. Dropped five miles or so offshore, the coast may only be visible when the craft rises on a wave and the right beach cannot be spotted.

At night, trying to find the right beach *and* arrive exactly at the right time to fit in with the assault plan, with no lights other than gunfire, can never be an easy task; and perhaps the real surprise is that the landing-craft crews did not get lost or into trouble more often than they did. In an attempt to reduce landing problems, later in the war, Combined Operations established a Beach Pilotage School for landing-craft crews at Tighnabruaich in Scotland, where all landing-craft personnel were trained before being attached to amphibious squadrons.

By the end of July 1940 the Commando organisation was more or less in place, but a certain amount of tinkering then followed. In October the Chiefs of Staff decreed that the Commando and the Independent Companies should be amalgamated into Special Service (SS) Battalions. The letters 'SS', with all their German connotations, found no favour with the Commandos and John Durnford Slater, for one, refused to have anything to do with the name. 'Never let the term "Special Service Battalion" appear on our Orders,' he told his adjutant, Captain Charlie Head.

After a few weeks, the War Office gave up the SS Battalion idea, but the various Commando brigades remained 'Special Service Brigades', at least officially, until the end of 1944. The first brigade was formed in October 1940 under the command of Brigadier I. C. Haydon, DSO, OBE, and by March 1941 this brigade consisted of eleven Commandos.

Their organisation had by then been altered from the unwieldy ten troops to a more handy six troops, each of three officers and 62 men, which fitted neatly into two of the new ALC (Assault Landing Craft – later called LCAs) which were then coming into service.

The unit establishments were not yet homogeneous, although the majority of Commandos were based on the 'fighting troop' or 'rifle troop' organisation and consisted of five 'fighting' troops plus a Heavy Weapons Troop, the latter equipped with 3-inch mortars and Vickers machine guns. Each troop was divided into two sections under a subaltern and each section divided into two subsections, each commanded by a sergeant. Every CO nevertheless had a fairly free hand within his own unit.

One of the great initial attractions of Commando soldiering had been the absence of red tape, but although it was always kept to the minimum, some administrative back-up proved necessary.

'It is the greatest job in the Army,' wrote Geoffrey Appleyard of No. 7 Commando. 'No red tape, no paperwork, just operations.' When Durnford Slater commanded 2 Special Service Brigade in Italy three years later, he recalled in his memoirs that his Brigade Major, Brian Franks, could keep all the brigade paperwork in one trouser pocket of his battle-dress. Nevertheless, someone had to do the administration, see to the pay and the mail, send men on courses, indent for ammunition and supplies. Some units therefore established an Administrative Troop and most units had an Administrative Officer; among the most notable of these was the redoubtable 'Slinger' Martin of No. 8, and later No. 3 Commando, who kept the troops happy and did his share of fighting.

During this period, when most of the Commandos were concentrated in Scotland, on Arran, or around Largs, some units began to develop special sections. No. 6, for example, raised a canoe section, later called 101 Troop and the original No. 2 (Para) Commando became first No. 11 Special Air Service Battalion and later the 1st Battalion, Parachute Regiment. No. 12 Commando was based in Northern Ireland on internal security duties against the IRA threat, while in February 1941 three Commandos, Nos 7, 8 and 11 (Scottish), sailed for the Middle East, where they were brigaded with two small, locally raised Commando units, Nos 50 and 5, the whole unit coming under the command of Colonel Robert Laycock and therefore being known as Layforce.

Too much training with no prospect of action will soon take the edge off any fighting unit, and by the early months of 1941 many of the original volunteers were getting very dis-gruntled, some even applying for return to their parent units. Raids were constantly planned and trained for, but somehow they were all cancelled, often at the last minute. Then, on 4 March 1941 a real raid came along at last, when Nos 3 and 4 Commando were ordered to mount a full-scale operation against the Lofoten Islands off the coast of Norway.

3

LOFOTEN TO VAAGSO, 1941

1941 'It is the first principle of training for war that training is the most important duty of the Army when troops are not engaged on actual operations.'

Training For War
British Army Handbook

The Commando forces began as raiding units and it is as raiding units that their appeal and their usefulness still chiefly depends. To this has to be added the role of spear-heading amphibious assaults, but it is as *raiders* that the Commandos made their mark and are chiefly remembered, and it is *raiders* that most Commando soldiers want to be.

Landing on a hostile shore by night, scaling cliffs in small parties, doing damage and vanishing with the dawn, this is what Commando work is all about – at least in the popular imagination. And, for a while at least, that is how it was in the first days of Commando operations. These raiding operations were few and far between, for as the war continued amphibious assault became more important. Nevertheless, there were raids and the first of them was to Lofoten.

The Lofoten Islands lie just inside the Arctic Circle, a thousand sea miles north of Britain, separated from the Norwegian mainland by the channel of the Vestafjord, opposite Narvik, an area well known to those Commando soldiers who had served with the Independent Companies. In the 1940s the main occupation of the islanders was fishing and the Germans were obtaining valuable supplies of herring and cod-liver oil from processing factories at four of the Lofoten ports: Brettesnes, Henningsvaer, Stamsund and Svolvaer. Combined Operations decided that in this first raid, 'Operation Claymore' as it was called, Nos 3 and 4 Commando should raid these ports, destroy the processing plants, kill Germans, arrest Norwegian traitors and return with German prisoners and volunteers for the Norwegian forces in Britain.

The raiding force, commanded by Brigadier Haydon and escorted by five destroyers, sailed from Scapa Flow on 1 March 1941 on two former cross-Channel ferries, the *Princess Emma* and the *Princess Beatrix* – early versions of the *Norland* which took the Parachute Regiment to the Falkland Islands in 1982 – with LCAs replacing lifeboats in the davits. The force consisted of 500 men drawn equally from the two Commandos, plus demolition teams from the Royal Engineers, together with guides and interpreters drawn from Free Norwegian Forces.

The Lofoten raid was successful but fairly uneventful; the two Commando units received a tumultuous welcome from the local population and the somewhat disappointing news that the islands were not occupied by enemy forces; so there was no fighting, although a number of German prisoners trickled in throughout the day. The oil factories were blown up, 300 Norwegian volunteers were taken out to the landing ships, and the force sailed for home early in the afternoon, cheered on their way by a great deal of flag-waving and not a few tears from the local population. Lofoten proved that large-scale raids were possible, yet no more such raids were mounted until the end of the year.

There were, however, a number of smaller operations – and a great deal of hard training. A young officer of No. 3 Commando, Lieutenant Algy Forrester, introduced the concept of 'rocky landings' – coming ashore in small boats on to rugged rock-strewn shores rather than smooth sandy beaches – plus all-out 'cliff assault' techniques, in which the commandos landed at the very foot of steep cliffs where no conventional soldier would dream of making a landing. All this was added to the Commandos' operational repertoire for, as Algy Forrester pointed out to Durnford Slater, the more obvious landing places, sandy beaches and sheltered areas, would surely be mined, wired and covered by machine-gun and mortar positions; going ashore at the obvious spots was suicide. Whatever the physical difficulties of landing on rockbound coasts, scaling sheer cliffs would probably be safer and provide the vital element of surprise.

Algy Forrester's initiative eventually led to the founding of the Commando Cliff Assault Wing, which then became the Mountain Warfare Training Centre and is now the Mountain and Arctic Warfare Cadre of the Royal Marines, where the Commandos are taught the elements of rock climbing and the basics of cliff assault. Certainly accidents were common in the early days. Men fell and were killed rock climbing on the screes in Cumberland; men falling into the sea wearing full fighting order were drowned, and orders came round that everybody had to be able to swim a few yards in battle order – and it is not easy to swim in battle order.

To acquaint the troops in the necessary survival techniques, most units paraded the men in battle order and forced-marched them to the nearest swimming pool, where the CO led them in single file up the ladder to the top diving board where, hot on his heels, they jumped off into the pool; those who had to be rescued got extra training in swimming – or were sent back to their units.

Joe Edmans, who served in No. 1 Commando, went through one of these early Commando schools:

We came up to Scotland on the landing ship, *Princess Beatrix*, and were sent on a mountaineering course at Glencoe, south of Fort William, no great distance from Achnacarry. My Troop was taught to climb or scramble from scratch, first over small boulders, then on higher cliffs, then abseiling from top to bottom. When we had finished, I stayed on to instruct the other troops when they came up.

Among the Commando instructors at this time were two former officers of the Shanghai police, Captains Fairburn and Sykes, who instructed the volunteers in unarmed combat and knife fighting. For this last purpose the weapon employed was the blackened, razor-sharp, two-edged, Wilkinson dagger or 'fighting knife', which was used held low in the right hand at the point of balance, raising the left hand to create an opening for an upward thrust with the fighting knife, under the rib-cage.

Among other unarmed combat techniques, the troops were taught how to break away from someone holding a pistol in their back, breaking the man's finger in the trigger guard as they turned. How much of all this was actually useful is doubtful, but it gave the volunteers great confidence in hand-to-hand combat, and added to the awesome reputation the Commandos were to acquire. Weapons were in short supply but No. 2 received a present from the mayor of New York: a chest full of 'Tommy-guns' (.45 calibre Thompson sub-machine guns) confiscated from New York gangsters by the city police.

Meanwhile, thanks to the Lofoten raid and the resulting press publicity the units were attracting more volunteers and had to weed out – RTU – the sick, lame and lazy and a great many professional heroes and 'cowboys'. The Commando units were being presented in the press as 'suicide squads' or thugs and 'Dusty' Miller, a Guardsman, recalls how he was recruited for No. 2 Commando in 1941: 'My oppo Reg Tuson and I left the Grenadier Guards at Windsor to join the Commandos and the Senior Drill Sergeant wished us a mournful farewell. "Miller," he said, "goodbye to you, lad . . . I hate to see you die so young." '

Dusty and his friend were billeted in Ayr, where the landlady's son was a keen member of the local Home Guard. Dusty Miller again:

Within a month of being in the Home Guard he was a sergeant. We used to pass on everything we learned and take him for rifle shooting, map and compass work, unarmed combat training, you name it – he must have been the best-trained Home Guard recruit in Britain . . . and like a lot of Home Guard people, a good soldier. Like us, they were all volunteers.

Raids were still rare but the training, that unavoidable part of Commando life, went on relentlessly. Apart from basic field craft the Commando course included demolition and sabotage, and the instructors included Lord Lovat, later of No. 4 Commando, Major Spencer-Chapman, who was cut off in Singapore and lived for three years behind the Japanese lines in Malaya, and Bill Stirling, one of the Stirling brothers of SAS fame. The Lochailort Commando course involved 'survival skills' as it would now be called, a subject then known as 'fieldcraft'.

For the final exercise the troops were given small quantities of light food and obliged to make a long and tactical march across the Scottish mountains, whatever the weather and the midges were doing, performing various tasks on the way. One task was to prepare a supposedly unused railway line for demolition, using fully armed charges. On one occasion, just as the men put in the detonators, a train came along and they had to rush back and disarm the charges before they blew the train – and its unsuspecting passengers – right off the track.

This training was all very well and the men enjoyed it but as Major Milton of No. 7 Commando says, 'Not once did I have the chance to practise or teach any of the things I learned at Lochailort, which I recall as being the best course I ever attended.'

The truth was that Commando operations were not seen as serious operations of war by the Army Staff or higher authority. On 27 October 1941, Sir Roger Keyes stepped down as Chief of Combined Operations, then put on his Admiral of the Fleet uniform to head directly for the House of Commons to tell the assembled MPs: 'Having been frustrated at every turn in every worthwhile offensive operation I have tried to undertake, I must endorse the Prime Minister's comments on the negative power of those who control the war machine in

Whitehall.' Sir Roger was an MP, but that did not daunt the 'powers-that-be' who, in an attempt to silence him, posted him a copy of the Official Secrets Act and sent an officer to impound his private papers.

Sir Roger's problems and frustrations were not untypical. One officer commented: 'The real war, the only war worth fighting with any enthusiasm, is the one between the front line soldier and the Staff.' The Commando units had been at the sharp end of this war since their inception but now it looked as if people in Whitehall were winning. It may seem strange in these peacetime days, but front-line soldiers need action; there is never any shortage of volunteers for hazardous service; the hard thing is actually to find hazardous service, when anything that smacks of risk is avoided by the High Command.

The military hierarchy also dislikes *private armies*, and these new formations, especially Durnford Slater's No. 3 Commando at Plymouth, was viewed with great suspicion by the Army and the Navy as 'Winston Churchill's private army' – an unnecessary, irregular and pointless unit which got a lot of attention and was busy taking all the best men from regular established battalions and teaching them to creep about at night cutting throats, if only they were given half a chance. Since the Commandos could not be simply wished away, they were ignored, and denied facilities such as training areas, and above all active operations against the enemy.

The General Staff deployed passive resistance against the Commando units, a resistance no less effective for being unstated. If a training area was needed, it was not available. If there was brawling in the town between the soldiers and the sailors, the Commandos were blamed and confined to barracks or billets. 'No. 3 Commando left Plymouth thankfully,' writes Durnford Slater. 'No one could have been more kind than the local people, but the continual nagging and obstruction from the Army authorities was really beginning to get us down. We needed more operations, a chance to prove ourselves, or the blokes would start getting fed up and leaving.'

The High Command also dragged its feet over the issuing

of a distinctive headgear to the Commando units. In 1940 and 1941 Commando soldiers wore their own regimental head-dress on parade and for walking out of barracks, and either steel helmets – 'tin hats', as they were called – or the scratchy woollen 'cap-comforter' for battle or training. It looked odd when the whole unit were on parade, and a special headgear was the obvious choice, perhaps, as with the Paratroop units, a coloured beret. When the green beret was proposed, the High Command instantly objected, on the grounds that a variety of head-dress served to increase security and might conceal the fact that a Commando unit had arrived in a coastal port for a raid across the Channel. This was a stupid argument, for an irregular unit would always attract attention, not least on parade. One of the oddities of Commando life was pay parade. Commando units had no regimental status and the men were 'seconded' to Commandos rather than 'posted', with all their records, and pay parades took an interminable amount of time, as the men came from every regiment in the Army and had to be paid on separate payrolls.

This disparity also affected dress. Military conformity was considered irrelevant to Commando discipline – unlike smartness and good behaviour, which was insisted upon – but it was common to see men going out in the evening in Royal Navy roll-neck sweaters, Army leather jerkins and rope-soled boots. If something more formal was required, khaki battle-dress with regimental forage cap fitted the bill. The men were allowed to wear their regimental dress caps, but since no officer could remember which regiments each man belonged to, artistic licence soon crept in.

The 'skull-and-crossbones' badge of the 17th/21st Lancers – motto, '. . . Or Glory' looked well on the dark blue with yellow piping of the RASC dress cap, but overall the men looked a mess on parade, and the green beret replaced this diversity as of 1942 when the objections to the green beret were overruled by the new Chief of Combined Operations, Vice-Admiral Lord Louis Mountbatten, who took up his appointment on 27 October 1941.

Between Lofoten and the next big raid on Vaagso at

Christmas 1941, some small raids were mounted, mostly across the Channel, with varying success. At the end of July, Second Lieutenant Pinkney took a party from No. 12 Commando ashore in France near Ambleteuse, staying for an hour before returning to their boats. Norwegian troops raided Spitzbergen in August, destroying vast quantities of coal and the winding gear for the local coal mines. At the end of August, No. 5 Commando began a series of small cross-Channel raids. Starting on the night of 30 August it landed two parties on the coast of Picardy and the Pas de Calais, one at Hardelot, the other at Merlimont near Boulogne. Neither party encountered any opposition and stayed ashore for only half an hour before withdrawing.

Geoff Riley, who was to go on and serve with No. 5 Commando in Madagascar and Burma, was with one of these parties:

As I recall it, the sea was very rough, choppy, heaving and chucking the landing craft about a lot. We were still fairly fresh at that stage and the raid was more of a probe or a recce rather than a serious operation, but it was good to be doing something and actually getting ashore in enemy territory. Anyway, when we did hit the beach, it was laced with trip-wires and in our inexperience we tripped some and sent flares all over the place, but there was no real contact. When we did make a brief contact with the enemy they shot off out of it, like bats out of hell, and so did we, in the other direction. So we didn't take any prisoners or have a scrap but, as the OC said, 'It'll all do as training, lads,' and he was right.

At the end of September 1941, No. 1 Commando went raiding in France, landing one party from No. 5 Troop under Lieutenant Scaramanga near St Vaast on the Cherbourg peninsula, and another under Captain Davies went ashore near Courseulles, an oyster port in the bay of the Seine, where the Canadians would land on D-Day three years later. This time there was some action for Scaramanga's party cleared the beach and then bumped into a German cycle patrol, which they engaged with Tommy-gun fire, killing three of the enemy before withdrawing. Lieutenant Scaramanga wrote an account of this operation:

This was the only raid that year in which actual contact was made with the enemy and we met the German patrol in the dark. They were on bikes so they came on us swiftly and silently before any plans could be made. Fortunately, I had three men with Tommy-guns in the van of the section, so it was all over in a second. Everything is unpredictable when you land by night on a strange shore, but I am sure the Germans gradually realised that they must be prepared for Commando raids at any time and place on a thousand miles of coast and kept a lot of good men busy on the coast of France they could have used in Russia or in the Western Desert with Rommel.

Meanwhile Captain J. H. Davies and his party were busy at Courseulles:

Our MGB slipped its LCA at 00:55 hours. Land was sighted at 02:10 hours and found to be not Courseulles but the resort town of St Aubin, some miles to the east, in the direction of Luc sur Mer. The men went ashore and as the last few men were leaving the LCA, a loud hail was heard to the left. This was thought by some to be 'Halt', but it was followed immediately by a burst of machine-gun fire, so may have been a fire order. An immediate assault was made upon the machine-gun post but the men were confronted with a ten-foot-high promenade wall surmounted by the usual railings and two coils of barbed wire, one upon the other. As the patrol was climbing this wall a second MG opened fire from the right flank, followed immediately by a blue flare and fire from a third MG, firing at a high rate and apparently of heavier calibre – a Spandau perhaps – from a second-storey window seventy to one hundred yards to the left.

Faced with this heavy opposition and with so little time left, Captain Davies had no option but to withdraw his party to the LCA. The withdrawal was carried out under constant fire from the three MGs while blue flares were sent up continuously. After the bridgehead had been called in, two of our men were seen to be struggling in the water. Sergeant Hewlett, *with complete disregard for his own safety*, immediately dived overboard and, under continuous and accurate fire, brought them back to the LCA. One of them had been wounded.

Meanwhile, all available fire-power from the LCA, including Troop Brens, was brought to bear upon the MG posts. A check-up of numbers then revealed that two men were missing. There were no bodies on the beach and although searching in the water in the dark did not locate them, it must be presumed that they fell in the water and drowned. The LCA then went out fast, being hit repeatedly by MG fire. Flares continued to go up until she was well out to sea and quite out of range. The MGB was found fifteen minutes later and the troops from the LCA transferred into it and we returned across the Channel at high speed. Portsmouth was reached at 09:50 hours 28/9.

These two lively operations ushered in what became known as 'the monthly raid', an attempt to get a Commando force ashore on the enemy-held coast at regular intervals. There was hot competition to mount these raids and during the next months Nos 2, 5, 9 and 12 Commando all mounted raids across the Channel, some being small affairs, some up to troop strength – fifty men – or even larger. The raid mounted by No. 9 Commando in November 1941 was a large affair when ninety men were put ashore to attack a German coastal battery near Houlgate. As was now usual, the party got ashore without trouble or detection, but due to delays and signalling errors had no time to carry out the attack and withdrew without loss, if not without incident. Captain Lucas of No. 9 Commando describes this operation, a witty account of an operation that went completely awry:

Operation *Sunstar* in November 1941 called for a raid by approximately one hundred men of 9 Commando on an enemy-held coastline and Lieutenant-Colonel Saegert, RE, the sapper officer then commanding No. 9 Commando, decided that the task would be carried out by No. 1 Troop, with elements of other Troops including whatever specialists (Signals, Demolitions, Medics, etc.) might be needed. Captain Cyril Suter, OC of 1 Troop, would command the raiding force, though Colonel Saegert would have overall responsibility for planning and expressed his intention of accompanying the raiders.

I had just been appointed to command No. 4 Troop but as I had been Intelligence Officer since March, and as my successor had not yet been appointed, I continued to act as IO for this operation. Therefore the Colonel, Cyril and I went down to London for a briefing by Combined Operations Staff. It was made clear to us that this was to be a modest, but very positive, crack at the Normandy coastline in the area of Ouistreham at the mouth of the River Orne; this was on the left of what became Sword Beach on D-Day in 1944. We would have the support of three or four Motor Gunboats (MGBs), who would engage these strongpoints and enable us to get a foothold, and I had the impression that the Combined Ops people were rather keen on this scheme.

It was not clear, however, what we would do when we got ashore, apart from creating general mayhem among the defenders, and Colonel Saegert preferred another target. A German battery on the high ground behind Houlgate would, he thought, be an ideal objective for a Commando raiding force of this size and type. The maps and photographs suggested that the landing could be made without opposition from anything stronger than patrols; the cliffs here were no more than seventy-five to one hundred feet high, and not very steep.

The battery was no more than about two miles inland, if that, and it was thought that we would have a good chance – within the very narrow time limits imposed by moon, tide and their Lordships of the Admiralty – of reaching the objective, surprising its garrison, and catching the last boat home. We had been very firmly told that crews would have strict orders not to risk beaching their craft on a falling tide. We appreciated this – our getaway vehicles were of some interest to us and to declare a special interest, I was due to be married on 3 December and fully intended to make it to the church on time. We embarked at Jamaica Quay, Glasgow, on 15 November, in the cross-Channel ferry, *Prince Leopold*, one of the first Commando landing ships and after a very rough passage through the Irish Channel we stopped at Falmouth for exercises with the LCAs.

I think this was the occasion when we carried out a landing exercise at night, on a beach about seven miles west of Falmouth; which involved re-embarking a little after high water. As the first troops approached the beach, they saw that the LCAs were apparently still afloat, but about 300 yards out in the bay. They started to wade out to them but even before the first man reached the nearest LCA, all vessels were firmly aground – they even had dry land all round them. This lesson was taken to heart by all concerned and driven home when we marched back all the way to Falmouth just in time for breakfast and another busy day.

We then sailed to Spithead, where final plans were made for the raid. We had a very instructive and interesting session with Naval and RAF planning officers. The plan, which was naturally determined by Naval considerations was for *Leopold* to leave Spithead with the raiding party on board towards dusk on 22 November and steam to a point five miles off the selected beach, where the raiding party would embark in four LCAs and proceed ashore under their own power, while the parent ship returned to Spithead. Having landed the troops, the LCAs would stand-off the beach until shortly before high-water, when they would come in again, pick up the returning raiders and return to Spithead.

All went well until we were about a mile off the beach, when it became clear that one LCA, with the Colonel and a small party on board, was no longer with us. They had lost touch in the darkness and in fact landed some way to the east of us. They took no further part in the operation as planned but had adventures of their own, I understand. Fortunately most of the party, including the Troop Commander, Cyril Suter, were still together and we made a happy landing on the right beach . . . and this was where things began to go really wrong.

With hindsight, I have to admit that I made a serious misjudgement regarding the suitability of the landing place and, given the time restriction, of the Houlgate battery as an achievable objective. Had I taken into account the geological nature of the cliffs and the effect on them of the heavy November rains, I would have given different advice. As it was, the troops attempting to scale the cliffs found themselves sinking knee-deep and more in a wet, heavy clay. It must have taken at least half an hour of our precious time to get all the men – and most of their boots – to the cliff top, where they found another obstacle. The gorse was extremely difficult to penetrate and by the time the whole party assembled on the other side, it was obvious to Cyril that he was not going to be able to carry out his task and return over the same obstacles within the time limit – or anything like it.

He therefore wisely decided to cut his losses and try to find out something about the movement of local patrols, and even perhaps intercept one and bag a prisoner or two. He went to a house and knocked on the door. To the nervous farmer's wife who asked who he was, he replied, 'The British Army,' a statement which, he told me, made quite an impression. He learned from this helpful lady that the OC of the battery was billeted in her house, and was at that time in the Officers' Mess, but was expected back at any time. This sounded promising and Cyril and his men set about preparing a reception for the gentleman. Unfortunately this one was having a late night. Cyril waited as long as he dared – and much longer than was wise – before he gave up and the party returned to the beach.

Meanwhile, I was carrying out my very simple task of examining the beach area as a potential landing place for larger forces, and in trying to discover whether the smallish pillboxes at either end of the beach (about a mile apart) were occupied. As we approached the western one we heard German voices, and I did have a brief dream of glory involving a hand grenade, a quick rush, a prisoner or two and a Victoria Cross for each of us. But we only had a rifle and a pistol between my batman and myself, and we had been ordered not to stir it up, so we went back to the other end of the beach, found the other pillbox empty and returned in time to meet the main body as they struggled back down the cliff, at least half an hour late.

We had seen no sign of the LCAs since we landed and we now waited for them to appear. Cyril had reached the point of discussing with his brother officers whether we should go to Ouistreham and try to seize a fishing boat, or whether the time had come to scatter and try individually or in very small groups to contact the Escape Line – when someone thought he heard engines. I scrambled to the top of the large white rock which had been our chief means of identifying the beach during our approach, and saw the outline of a smallish craft. I flashed with my blued torch the agreed Morse 'Q' signal. No reply, so I tore off the blue paper and tried again.

The agreed reply was flashed back immediately, and in the same instant a machine gun opened fire from the cliff top. I hit the sand about twelve feet below me, and lay for a moment watching the tracer spraying off the rock where I had been standing a moment before. There was nothing we could do; one young officer, under fire for the first time gave the historic order: 'One round, rapid fire,' but neither we nor the German patrol on the cliff top could get at each other, so we set about swimming out to the LCA, now lying about fifty yards off the beach. Some equipment was left behind, and Private Alanach was wounded in the arm –

not seriously, but he was losing quite a lot of blood and so gave us some concern, especially as it was clearly going to be a long time before he received proper attention.

So, we got on the LCA where most of us went to sleep as comfortably as we could, with seventy or more men in a craft designed to carry thirty. I awoke at about 09:00 hours to find the LCA about five miles off Le Havre, in bright sunshine and wallowing in quite a swell, but otherwise motionless. The steering gear had broken down and once more I had visions of my bride waiting at the altar and wondered if Jerry would let me ring her in time to warn the guests. Fortunately, at that moment, we spotted another craft about half a mile away, making towards us. This was one of the other LCAs and her Commander brought her alongside and, after an attempt to tow us in line had been frustrated by the heavy and increasing swell, the two vessels were lashed alongside and we proceeded, slowly but surely, towards Spithead, ninety miles away.

Morale was good, and reached its high point when the promised Spitfires or Hurricanes, I can't remember which, appeared high overhead and proceeded to entertain us with a fine display of aerobatics. We were just enjoying all this when we heard a long burst of cannon and MG fire, and saw the water churned up all around us; a Messerschmitt had come in under our fighter cover, shot a hole through our ensign, and went away with a couple of British fighters on his tail. We discovered weeks later, from a German Air Force report captured at Vaagso, that the pilot had been awarded the Iron Cross for this exploit, so perhaps our journey was not really wasted.

By noon, cloud cover extended from horizon to horizon, our fighters had gone, and we felt rather lonely. Also the wind was rising again, and the seas were now quite big – but not breaking fortunately; though the condition of the LCAs was deteriorating too. There were no fenders on board and the stretchers and other gear we had put between the vessels were soon ground to fragments. Before night-fall the plates were beginning to open, and holes appeared in the sides. These craft were well provided with buoyancy beneath the deck, but they were becoming waterlogged, and we were almost waist-deep in water. Poor Alanach, getting rather weak now, had to be laid on a bed of ammunition boxes built up high enough to keep him above the water. He seemed cheerful enough, but he must have been getting near the end of his tether. Just before darkness was complete, a headland was spotted about five degrees on our starboard bow. 'Culver Cliff,' said our RNVR coxswain. 'That low line you can see to the right is the Spithead Submarine defence boom. With any luck they will have spotted us while it was still light and will send someone to meet us.'

He was to be disappointed. The 'headland' was Beachy Head; the 'boom' was Eastbourne beach, miles from Spithead. The compasses, which had been carefully 'swung' or calibrated for each steel-clad vessel, behaved quite differently when two craft were lashed together and in fact the compass by which we were steering had something like a forty degree error. As the ramps went down the first men out came running back, shouting that we had landed in France. It turned out that the troops holding that part of the coast were French-Canadians and they gave us a wonderful reception.

We had failed and poor Colonel Saegert lost his command, although he was in no sense to blame. I misled him regarding the probable conditions to be expected at the landing place, but I have wondered how many Battalion or Commando IOs would have consulted a geological expert before giving the advice I did, at that stage in the war. Truthfully, no one comes out of this episode with much credit, except perhaps the LCA Commanders who disobeyed orders to come in and get us home, and of course the German pilot for being such a rotten shot. He was the only one who got decorated for his part in the adventure – quite rightly. Private Alanach made a speedy recovery and rejoined 4 Troop within a few weeks and I got married to my bride on 3 December and began many years of great happiness.

This cheery fiasco did not discourage the Commandos at all. It was then the turn of Nos 6 and 12 Commando, who sailed from Scapa Flow in December to attack the town of Floss in Norway. This raid was marred by an accident on board their assault ship, HMS *Prince Charles*, when a primed grenade exploded, killing six men below decks. This raid was accompanied by several press cameramen whose aim was to obtain a record of the operation. They had filmed the usual shipboard scenes – Commandos exercising, chaps in their hammocks, or writing a last letter home – and it was suggested that they should shoot a close-up of the final weapon overhaul and grenade priming on one of the troop decks below.

This was thought a good idea and the cameras began to roll on a scene of intense activity; a hundred men were cleaning all types of weapons, while at a table six men were busy cleaning the Mills bombs – the No. 36 grenade – passing them to the end man, who put the detonator in. One enterprising cameraman, anxious to get things in focus, pulled a handful of grenades nearer, unnoticed by the men busy with their tasks, and so mixed up the primed and unprimed grenades. The first man picked up a grenade, thinking it unprimed, removed the safety pin and so let the striking lever fall on the base plug. To his horror, a small bang denoted that this grenade was primed and the fuse burning. He shouted and made a desperate attempt to hurl the grenade through the open hatch, out on to the empty deck above.

It was a good and gallant effort, but the grenade hit the hatchway combing and fell back. A Norwegian standing below the hatch caught it and hurled it out again; too late, for the four-second delay was up. The hand grenade exploded just opposite his chest, killing six men outright and injuring eleven others. The speed with which the whole thing happened, transforming a happy body of men into a shambles, is a thing one cannot easily describe, but chaos sums it up. Morale on board fell further when the Naval Commander was unable to fix his position, and in the end the raid was abandoned.

What they really needed now was a chance to strike the

enemy a full-blooded blow and that chance finally arrived on Boxing Day 1941, when No. 3 Commando, reinforced by two troops from No. 2 Commando, plus medics and engineers from Nos 4 and 6 Commando, mounted a major raid against the Norwegian port of Vaagso and the offshore island of Maaloy. This raid, 'Operation Archery', was the first to be mounted under the new Director of Combined Operations, Vice-Admiral Lord Louis Mountbatten. Vaagso is also the first example of a truly 'Combined' Operation in the Second World War, a major amphibious landing supported by air and sea forces, the blueprint for other, larger landings in the years ahead.

The naval forces, commanded by Rear-Admiral H. M. Burrough, CB, consisted of the cruiser HMS *Kenya*, flying the admiral's flag, and elements of the 17th Destroyer Flotilla, HMS *Offa*, HMS *Chiddingfold*, HMS *Onslow* and HMS *Oribi*, escorting two of those well-worn Channel ferries, now in use as infantry assault ships, HMS *Prince Charles* and *Prince Leopold*, carrying the landing force, with the submarine HMS/M *Tuna* sailing ahead to mark the approach and lead the force into the Vaagsfjord.

The RAF element consisted of ten Hampden bombers from No. 50 Squadron, tasked with laying smoke to cover the LCAs during their run-in, and bombing coastal defences when they saw a target. Other aircraft were directed to provide fighter protection and bomb the German fighter fields at Herdla. The Vaagso raid was in a different league from all that had gone before, and this difference extended to the opposition. This was no night-time cut-and-run operation; this time the Germans were present in force, in Maaloy and along the Ulvesund strait.

There were German coastal batteries along the shore of the fjord. There were field guns, anti-aircraft batteries and machine-gun posts on Maaloy and heavy guns on the island of Rugsundo, able to bring down fire on the Vaagsfjord. The town of South Vaagso and the island of Maaloy were known to be garrisoned by German troops, and although their numbers were unknown, in view of the artillery defences it was anticipated that the infantry garrison would be large, well equipped and well trained.

The Commando force that was tasked to go ashore and overwhelm all this totalled 51 officers and 525 men drawn from No. 3 Commando, plus two troops of No. 2 Commando which Durnford Slater kept as his floating reserve. The plan required the landing force to approach Vaagso undetected and sail up the Vaagsfjord to the Ulvesund strait which separated South Vaagso from Maaloy. Here the landing force, split into five assault groups, would go ashore in LCAs to capture Maaloy and South Vaagso. Meanwhile, the artillery emplacements would be attacked by bombers and engaged by the 6-inch guns of HMS *Kenya* and the smaller calibre, 4.5-inch guns of her destroyer escort. Once the enemy had been eliminated, the demolition parties would blow up everything of use to the Axis and the force would then withdraw, with their prisoners, Norwegian volunteers for Britain and any wounded. Combined Operations, however, rarely run to plan, and so it was here.

The force sailed from Scapa Flow on Christmas Eve, aiming to land next day, but bad weather forced a change of plan. Charles Hustwick, of the Brigade Signals, was on the Vaagso raid and gives an outline of what happened:

We went to Scapa Flow by way of Invergordon, sailing from there with 3 Commando, on board the *Prince Charles*. We had stuffed hearts for breakfast, not very appetising in a Force Seven gale and it got up to Force Nine, really terrible, when we sailed from Scapa on Christmas Eve. What a terrible trip! Crew and troops were really ill, water and overflow from the heads was everywhere, so we put into Sullom Voe in Shetland for Christmas Day, to clean up, dry out and get pumped out. Here we learned that our destination was Vaagso.

The battle for Vaagso began at 08:48 hours on 27 December, when HMS *Kenya* illuminated Maaloy island with star shells as the bomber aircraft swept in to drop smoke canisters and bombs. HMS *Kenya* and the destroyers then rained fire on the island, pouring more than 400 shells on to the landing area prior to the Commandos sweeping ashore. Fortunately, the gales had convinced the enemy that nothing would happen over Christmas so the German garrison on Maaloy was caught completely unawares and the island fell without difficulty.

The attack was a spirited affair, with 5 and 6 Troops of No. 3 Commando led ashore by its second-in-command, Major Jack Churchill (generally known as 'Mad Jack'), playing the men into battle with the bagpipes. Churchill first piped his men ashore, then put the bagpipes aside, drew his claymore sword – Jack Churchill believed that 'an officer is not properly dressed without his sword' – and led his men to the assault, straight into the heart of the enemy defences. Faced by this fury, the Germans fled, and Maaloy was overrun in eight minutes for the cost of one man killed – Captain Martin Linge of the Norwegian Army – and one man wounded, the redoubtable Major Jack Churchill, who was blown up standing too close to a demolition charge and was carried back to the assault boats, bleeding somewhat and calling loudly for his bagpipes.

South Vaagso is a long, straggling town, running for nearly a mile up the shore of the Ulvesund. Durnford Slater's force had landed at the southern end, first scaling a small cliff, and then began to fight their way from house to house, up the main street. Street fighting eats up infantry and some good men were lost here, in their first big battle. Captain Johnny Giles, OC of 3 Troop, was shot and killed on house-to-house clearing, hit soon after the landing, while 4 Troop lost Arthur Komrower, sent out of battle when he was crushed between a rock and his landing craft. Lieutenant Bill Lloyd was shot through the neck as he stepped ashore. He was to recover but his troop commander, Algy Forrester, the cliff assault expert, was killed attacking the German HQ in the Ulvesund Hotel, about a hundred yards up the main street. Many good NCOs were killed or wounded knocking out a tank, and within twenty minutes of landing Algy Forrester's troop had lost all its officers and senior NCOs, being ably commanded by Corporal White, who gained the DCM for his leadership that day.

The resistance at Vaagso, once aroused, turned out to be much stiffer than anticipated, probably because the German garrison had received a temporary reinforcement of fifty well-trained soldiers. These counter-attacked in the town centre and, as his attack faltered, Durnford Slater sent for his floating reserve and ordered Jack Churchill, who was now back with his troop, to send men over from Maaloy.

Lieutenant Peter Young arrived shortly afterwards with 6 Troop, and with Sergeant George Herbert, another redoubtable soldier at his side, they began to grenade their way up the street. The whole Commando force now began to advance steadily, winkling out enemy machine-gun posts and snipers. By 13:45 hours the battle was over, and an hour later the raiding force withdrew, at the end of a quick and decisive operation.

The Vaagso raid was a great success. No. 3 Commando had achieved all its objectives, dealt the Germans a fierce blow, and returned to the UK with over one hundred prisoners and over seventy recruits to the Norwegian forces. The unit losses had been severe for such a small, closely knit force; twenty men had been killed, including many founder members, and fifty-seven had been wounded. No. 3 Commando would have to recruit more men before it would be ready to fight again.

Vaagso brought 1941, that year of mixed fortunes, to a satisfactory close, at least for those units based in the UK where cross-Channel raiding kept enthusiasm alive. In the Middle East, though, it was a different story; out there the three Commandos which made up Layforce, Nos 7, 8 and 11 (Scottish) were having a much more difficult time.

4

LAYFORCE, 1941

'The object of Commando operations is to harass the enemy.'

Commando Training Notes, 1942

After Dunkirk, from 1940 to 1943, the land battles against the Axis Powers of Germany and Italy took place either in Russia or – for the British and Americans – in the deserts of North Africa. Much of this territory had been annexed by Italy before the war and the British Eighth Army, which contained strong contingents from New Zealand, Australia and South Africa, did very well at first against the Italian forces, inflicting defeat after defeat on them, while managing to divert forces for the overthrow of the Vichy French regime in Syria.

The main problem which faced the army commanders on either side during the Desert War was one of supply. The Desert War was a highly mobile affair, fought out by tanks and lorried infantry, and the armies advanced or withdrew in relation to their ability to bring forward supplies of petrol, food, ammunition and reinforcements from the rear area to the front line. This led to much to-and-fro fighting along the North African coastlines in campaigns which became known to the British, half-ironically, as the Benghazi Handicap. The armies advanced to the limit of their supply lines and were then forced to fall back with the enemy – British or German–Italian – in close pursuit until their supply lines also became over-extended and the process was reversed.

With the desert on one flank and the Mediterranean on the other, there were in fact two flanks open for raiding operations, so in February 1941, Brigadier Robert Laycock embarked in Scotland with Nos 7, 8 and 11 (Scottish) Commando in the infantry assault ships HMS *Glenearn*, *Glenroy* and *Glengyle* and sailed for the Middle East and seaborne raiding operations against the German Afrika Korps.

Lieutenant Milton sailed with No. 7 Commando:

These three ships were fast merchant ships of the Glen Line, with the davits adapted to carry assault landing craft and motor landing craft. The officers were housed in a hold below the waterline in the *Glengyle*. We had been on these three ships for some time, sailing from Gourock to Lamlash Bay on Arran, waiting for some operation which never came off and morale was pretty low until Sir Roger Keyes, the head of Combined Operations at this time, came on board and made a rousing speech.

We were eventually told we were going overseas and embarked at Gourock. I became detached from No. 7 and found myself on the *Glenroy* with a group of officers which included Evelyn Waugh and Randolph Churchill. They seemed to spend most of their time gambling. We sailed at the end of January, spent a day or two in Freetown, sailed on to Capetown, where we were received with incredible kindness and hospitality by the South Africans and then up the East Coast through the Suez Canal to our camp at Genifa on the Bitter Lakes.

This small Commando brigade arrived in Egypt on 7 March where it was joined by two locally raised Commando units, Nos 50 and 52 Commando, the composite formation then being known as Layforce. Layforce promptly fell victim to the Staff and was designated as an infantry brigade in the 6th Division of General Wavell's Desert Army, the Commando units being remustered as battalions. No. 7 became the 'A' Battalion, No. 8 the 'B', No. 11 the 'C', and the now-amalgamated Middle East Commando, the 'D' Battalion. These 'battalions', like the brigade itself, lacked the essential accoutrements of 'heavy' infantry units – engineers, transport, field artillery, signals.

Worst of all, though, the Middle East theatre was on the defensive and the British in Egypt were teetering on the brink of defeat. After a long string of successes against the Italians, the Eighth Army met a much more redoubtable opponent at the end of March 1941, when the German general, Erwin Rommel, landed in Cyrenaica at the head of the Afrika Korps. This mobile, well-trained force, equipped with the latest tanks, struck hard at the Eighth Army and sent it reeling back towards Egypt. As part of this twin-pronged strategic thrust, another German force invaded Greece, where the Greeks had previously given an Italian Army a rough handling.

This time the Greeks too were forced to retreat and the Eighth Army's slender reserves of manpower and equipment were rushed across the Mediterranean to support them. Layforce stayed behind in Egypt, where staff officers, harassed to find reinforcements for front-line units, were soon casting greedy eyes at Laycock's brigade of well-trained infantrymen. This was bad enough, but events were already conspiring to blight the prospects of action for Commando troops in the Middle East.

To begin with, this was an active theatre, where other units were already fighting. The Commandos could not fill the aggressive role they had been created to occupy in the UK. In Greece, Crete and the Western Desert there was enough war for everybody. In addition, the Desert Army was now retreating before Rommel's first offensive, and the three Layforce landing ships – without which the Commandos were immobile – were taken away to ferry Allied troops across the Mediterranean to Greece. Finally, the Allies lacked air superiority, which made raids west along the coast a hazardous affair for the landing ships.

Clearly, a full brigade of trained soldiers could not be kept in idleness at such a time and Brigadier Laycock was swiftly ordered to mount a raid on the enemy-held port of Bardia 300 miles west of Alexandria. After one false start, this raid took place on the night of 19/20 April 1941. It was made by No. 7 Commando carried in HMS *Glengyle*, covered by a powerful escort, including the anti-aircraft cruiser HMS *Coventry*, three destroyers from the Royal Australian Navy and, to carry the canoes of Captain Courtney's SBS Folboat Troop, who would provide the navigation beacons and guide the main force into the port, the submarine HMS/M *Triumph*.

This raid met with an all-too-familiar series of problems. HMS/M *Triumph* was detected and attacked en route by Allied aircraft – which happened with distressing frequency in the Second World War – and was therefore late at the off-loading point. The folboats were damaged, and unable to land and erect the homing beacon, the leading LCA was damaged and landed late; on other LCAs the compasses were faulty and the vessels put the men ashore at the wrong place, and a Commando officer, moving about the beach after the landing, was shot and killed by one of his own men. In spite of all this the force stayed ashore for a short while and managed to destroy four guns before withdrawing – leaving about seventy men behind to be captured by the enemy.

It was not a successful debut for the Commandos in the Middle East. One bright spot in an otherwise gloomy picture was the arrival in the No. 7 Commando ranks of a 71-year-old retired Admiral, Sir Walter Cowan Bt., KCB, DSO, MVO, who had first seen action at the battle of Omdurman in 1898, fighting the Arabs for General Kitchener.

Admiral Cowan was a feisty old gentleman who, bored with life on the retired list and being an old friend of Admiral Keyes, had wangled his way into the Commandos, where Lieutenant Milton takes up the story:

The first plan for Bardia involved 8 Commando as well as 7, with all three landing ships, but this was called off by bad weather and the raid was replanned for 7 Commando alone, in the *Glengyle*. We were divided into two groups –

a smaller group to enter the harbour, land and attack the town's water supply, while the other part landed west of the town to attack a defence battery and do other odd jobs, blow up road bridges and so on.

My job was to take my section into the harbour in the leading LCA, land, ascend a cliff path, then march inland to find and demolish a valve that pumped the town's water supply. This, I was assured, would cut off the water for some time and cause alarm and despondency among the garrison. We were accompanied on this raid by Admiral Sir Walter Cowan, a real fire-eater, about five feet three inches tall who, with Lieutenant Evelyn Waugh, was embarked for the landing in my LCA.

When we arrived off the port and went to Boat Stations, at about 22:00 hours, the sea was quite rough. In those days the first wave of troops climbed into the assault craft in the davits at deck level and were then lowered into the water. For some reason our bow davit lowered quicker than the stern one, and we hit the water bow first, smashed into the side of *Glengyle* and damaged our starboard engine. Therefore, though supposedly the leading craft, we limped ashore slowly, well behind the rest and on one engine. I could see the shore and worked out where we were, but when we were about a hundred yards from the beach we touched the bottom on a sandbar and Admiral Cowan ordered our coxswain, Sub-Lieutenant England, to lower the ramp. He complied and Admiral Cowan and Evelyn Waugh dashed out and disappeared under the water. I held my men back until we scraped over the bar and arrived at the real beach.

We went up the cliff path and towards our objective in complete silence, until I saw figures ahead. These turned out to be a Troop commanded by the unit's second-in-command, Kenneth Wylie, who were going to blow up a bridge. He told me it was too late to go on to the waterpipe and valves, and to recce some buildings nearby; one of these was found to be full of gelignite in a very critical state – the explosive was sweating and looked most unhealthy. I had no means of setting it off, having only short fuses for our pipeline charges, and besides, if that lot had gone off it would have removed 7 Commando and most of Bardia to the middle of the Mediterranean.

I was detailed to act as rearguard and so we embarked late in our damaged craft and went slowly out to sea, having an awful struggle just to get our LCA off the beach. Then we met Wylie's boat again. He had seen signalling onshore, investigated and found two more LCAs stranded. He had taken many on board but even so, some fifty or sixty soldiers from the western party had been left on the beach. Anyway, off they went to the *Glengyle* and we slowly followed, limping behind, but when we got to the RV, the *Glengyle* had gone . . . which was a bit of a blow, frankly.

Sub-Lieutenant England and I decided that the best thing we could do was to sail to Tobruk, sixty miles or so to the west, which was surrounded by the enemy but held by the 9th Australian Division. We made very slow progress and I can't remember much of the night except that it got very rough, and sleeping with my head on my haversack, which contained 808 explosives and gave me a peach of a headache.

At dawn we were not far off the shore but it was still rough. The morning wore on and then a vessel appeared on the horizon flying no flag and guns were turned upon us. As she came closer I asked Sub-Lieutenant England what we should do if she turned out to be Italian, expecting him to say we would have to surrender, but not a bit of it. He was signalling with his lamp and said he would carry on signalling until we got alongside. Then we would board her, capture her and sail her back to Alexandria – he really had the Nelson spirit!

Fortunately, she turned out to be British, a boom defence vessel. We eventually sailed into Tobruk and I was told to report to General Morshead, commanding the 9th Australian Division. On the dockside I found a truck, driven by a very scruffy Australian soldier, who drove me up to Div. HQ, getting thoroughly shelled on the way. There I met the

General, who also looked me up and down and said, 'What you need is a drink.' One of his ADCs went off and returned with half a tumbler of whisky and stood there while I drained it. As I swallowed the last mouthful, he sighed and said, 'You have just drunk the last mouthful of whisky in Tobruk.'

Back in Egypt, Layforce continued to train while awaiting fresh tasks. Lieutenant Ted Galbraith of No. 8 Commando, recalls some of them:

> During the time we were based at Mersa Matruh, a number of officers and guardsmen – including Randolph Churchill – volunteered for the pioneering of aperture parachute dropping. All ranks were most unsuitably attired for parachute jumping, strong winds carried many of them off the drop-zone on to rocky ground, ending up with badly grazed knees and elbows.

Among the more seriously injured men of No. 8 Commando was Lieutenant David Stirling, founder of the SAS, who spent his time in hospital working out the idea for the SAS which took the field a few months later.

As the only body of trained troops not fully committed to one or other of the fronts in Greece or the Western Desert, Layforce was both denied replacements and steadily bled of trained men. This practice was encouraged by the fact that here, as in the UK, the Staff had no real interest in Commando operations and felt, not unreasonably in the circumstances, that trained soldiers would be more useful serving at the front.

Therefore, at the end of May 1941, Layforce began to disintegrate. No. 11 (Scottish) Commando (C Battalion), was sent to Cyprus, while the other units were absorbed into the general army reserve. Then on 20 May, having driven the British from the mainland of Greece, German airborne forces invaded the island of Crete. The situation soon became serious and the garrison began to withdraw from their positions

around Heraklion and retreat across the central mountains t
Suda Bay, where Nos 7, 8 and the Middle East Command
were landed as reinforcements on the night of 26/27 April.

The battle for Crete is a story of great courage against ever
increasing odds. German parachute troops began landing on the
north coast on 20 May and were initially contained by the
defenders and suffered heavy casualties; but the Germans grad
ually won ground around the airfield at Maleme. With this
secured, Junkers transport aircraft began to arrive, bringing in
reinforcements and artillery, while the defenders were kept
under constant air attack from dive bombers, which pounded
their positions and the ships bringing in reinforcements.

Within three days the Germans had landed over 20,000
men at Maleme and the only way to stop more arriving was to
recapture the airfield. This was considered a suitable task for
Layforce but the plan was abandoned on 26 May when the
British front began to crumble and the Layforce units arrived
only to hold the beachhead for an evacuation while the main
forces withdrew into it. Being without heavy weapons, this
was a task for which the Layforce Commandos were badly
equipped.

Private Freeman takes up the tale:

We moved out of the Suda Bay area and dug slit trenches
while the Germans dive-bombed and machine-gunned us
constantly. We had no air support, no planes and we fought
a rearguard action while the New Zealanders and Australians withdrew. After a day or so we withdrew, marching
for half a day through olive groves. There were burned-out
lorries with bodies aboard, and the enemy were around,
even behind us and my mate got a machine-gun burst in the
stomach. The officer said, 'Make him comfortable,' so I
gave him a cigarette and put his small pack behind his head
and we left him for the German medics.

We marched across the island to Sphakia, where the
evacuation had taken place, and hid in caves, but after a
Sunderland flying boat came in and took off some officers,
a German patrol found the caves and took me prisoner of

war. Their front-line troops were not too bad, but I thought I was the only prisoner taken and felt bad. After walking for about an hour with the Germans, we went over a ridge and there were *thousands* of British, New Zealand and Australian POWs. I tried to escape in Greece but was recaptured and sent in a cattle truck to Germany – sixteen days – and a lot of men died on the journey. The man who was shot in the stomach recognised me at the Commando reunion a few years ago. After a lot of beer and saying how I saved his life, he said the Germans were going to shoot him when an English-speaking officer came up and told them to put him with their own wounded.

Layforce had moved inland under heavy air attack and began to dig in while the retreating garrison streamed past them towards the beaches. German ground attacks on the Layforce perimeter began soon after dawn on the 28th, with mortar concentrations and dive-bombing, a bombardment followed by infantry attacks, which No. 7 Commando, assisted by New Zealand infantry and two Matilda tanks, was able to drive off before withdrawing towards the positions of the Middle East Commando.

Then began a leap-frog retreat back across the mountains towards Sphakia. 'An exhausting march, of which the chief features were heat, thirst, hunger and Stukas,' records Major F. C. G. Graham, the Brigade Major. Having taken up a new defensive position, the Brigade IO Captain Evelyn Waugh (No. 8 Commando), was sent to find the garrison commander, General Freyberg, who ordered that Layforce, now reduced to around 400 men, should take up defensive positions around the embarkation beaches and cover the withdrawal, which was completed, in spite of continual German air and ground attacks, on the night of 30/31 May.

The Royal Navy had already lost too many ships in the waters around Crete and stated that any troops not brought off that night must be abandoned. Permission was given for Brigadier Laycock and some of his staff to embark for Egypt, but most of D Battalion (No. 50 Commando), and much of what was left of A Battalion (No. 7 Commando), passed into captivity. Only about half of those who landed returned to Egypt, although some men got away in an abandoned landing craft which they sailed back to North Africa, using blankets as sails when the craft ran out of fuel. Among those on board this craft was Jock Davidson:

Our other choice was to take to the hills but as dawn broke Ron Rogers and I saw an LCM and a ship's longboat lying out about 200–300 yards, left by the *Glengyle*. We stripped off and swam out to it and found we could get one engine going. Just then, Lieutenant Day swam alongside and came aboard with one of his chaps. We went into the beach to pick up Bill Smith and about eight or ten of Lieutenant Day's men and our boys of course. We left quickly as we could hear aircraft becoming active. We landed on a small island, waiting for darkness to avoid detection by German planes and there we found a number of political exiles, living a very basic existence, but they killed two of their goats and cooked them for us, for which we paid well, Greek money being of no further use to us. We also got water from their well.

At dusk we set off, towing the rowing boat behind, heading for Tobruk or, if possible, Sollum. Next afternoon the diesel fuel gave out so we rigged a square sail with a tarpaulin and blanket on a long pole, but obviously it would take many days to make the landfall in North Africa, even with the then favourable wind. It was agreed that Tom Rogers, Bill Smith and I, with Lieutenant Day and two of his men, would go ahead in the longboat to make land as soon as possible and get help for the LCM.

We rigged a rough sail out of groundsheets and set off. The sea had quite a heavy swell and a number were sick. We had one or perhaps two tins of bully and two or three biscuits each, among six or seven of us, and our water bottles. We were three days and three nights, with strong wind and heavy sea at night, and then becalmed during the day, when we took turns rowing. During the day it was scorching, with

70

clear blue sky. About 10:00 hours on the third day we saw on the horizon what appeared to be a long streak. Was this land or just the horizon? Then we thought we saw flashes and wondered if this was Tobruk or the firing line at Sollum. Anyway, our main concern was to get help for the chaps left on the LCM with very little food and water.

Eventually we got ashore, pulled the boat up in case we would have to go back and move along the coast, this being scrubby desert country. After walking for 15 or 20 minutes inland, we saw some dust clouds from vehicles in the distance. A couple of men threw caution to the winds and moved up to the area – and there was an Italian lorry group with machine guns mounted on the back . . . so we really were POWs this time! Anyway, the LCM made it to North Africa under sail and the men in it returned to the British lines, so that was something.

While this little epic adventure was under way, the Commandos had found a new area of attack, in Syria, against the forces of Vichy France. Until well into the Second World War, the French nation was roughly divided into three parts. First, there were the Free French, on the side of the Allies, based in England and commanded by General de Gaulle. Across the Channel, the bulk of the French nation lived reluctantly under German occupation north of the Loire, while in the Unoccupied Zone, or Vichy France, to the south, the rest lived under the collaborationist rule of Marshal Philippe Pétain.

Vichy France, a mildly pro-German – or at least anti-British – regime, was at best neutral in the early years of the war and the Vichy France rule extended to some of the overseas territories of France, most notably Algeria and Syria. Relations between Vichy France and the British had been soured in 1940 when the British fleet invited the French warships, based at Mers-el-Kebir, to scuttle or surrender before they could be taken over by the Germans. When the French fleet refused to surrender, the Royal Navy blockading Mers-el-Kebir opened fire, sinking many French ships with great loss of life. In 1941, problems arose in Vichy-French Syria when, fearing that the Germans would land there and open a third front or obtain the use of the Syrian airfields, the British, urged on by General de Gaulle, invaded from Palestine and Iraq.

On 6 June, the 7th Australian Division, the main force, struck north from Palestine, heading for Damascus and Beirut, while other forces drove west into Syria from Iraq. The advancing Australians soon met with increasing French opposition and were slowed to a halt before the Litani river, south of Beirut where the French troops were known to be well dug-in. It was decided to dislodge the French from this position by landing No. 11 (Scottish) Commando on three beaches north of the river behind the French lines, to seize and hold a crossing over the Litani until the Australian 25th Infantry Brigade could join them.

The Commando landed from HMS *Glengyle* at dawn on 9 June, getting ashore without undue difficulty, but soon running into stiff opposition from the French. Lieutenant Gerald Bryan of No. 7 Commando tells his story of the Litani operation:

On getting ashore I raced madly up the beach and threw myself into the cover formed by a sand dune. The men behind me were still scrambling out of the landing craft and dashing across twenty yards of open beach. Away on the right we could hear the rattle of a machine gun and overhead the whine of the bullets but they seemed fairly high. I was just beside a dry stream bed and so started to walk along it, at the same time trying to untie the lifebelt attached to my rifle. Lieutenant-Colonel Pedder, our CO, was shouting, telling us to push on as quickly as possible. Soon the ditch that I was in became too narrow and there was nothing for it but to climb out into the open.

When I got out into the open I started shouting, ' "A" section – No. 1 Troop', which rounded up my command. Before long we were in pretty good formation, with myself, my batman and a Tommy-gunner in the centre. We came to the main road and saw a trench, showing clearly in the white chalk. It was empty, but behind it were two caves in a little cliff. I fired a rifle shot into the left-hand cave and there were sounds of commotion inside. We stood ready with grenades and Tommy-guns and shouted to them to come out – and seven sleepy Frenchmen emerged, in pyjamas and vests.

It was now quite light, about 04:45 hours. The rest of the section had pushed on, so I followed, and found the section held up and under fire from snipers. Also, which was more to the point, they had found a 75mm gun. It was about thirty yards away and being fired fairly rapidly. We flung some grenades and it stopped. However, we had three casualties, which wasn't so good. A corporal was shot through the wrist and was cursing every Frenchman ever born. As he couldn't use a rifle I gave him my Colt automatic pistol and he carried on. We crawled through some scrub to get closer to the gun. Here we met 'B' section officer, Alastair Coade, and a few men also attacking the gun position, so we joined forces. The gun itself was deserted, the crew being in a slit-trench. We bunged a few grenades at them and then went in ourselves with the bayonet and it was rather bloody.

My section contained a lot of RA blokes who knew how to handle the gun, and in a few minutes the sergeant had discovered which fuses to use from one of the original gun crew. This gun was the right-hand gun of a battery of four, the others were still firing. Our gun was pointing away from the battery, so we grabbed the tail piece and heaved it right round so that it was pointing towards the nearest gun. The sergeant took over command of the gun, shoved a shell in, sighted over open sights and fired.

The result was amazing. There was one hell of an explosion in the other gun site and the gun was flung up into the air like a toy. We must have hit their ammo dump. No time to waste. The sergeant traversed on to the next gun, sighted rapidly and fired. There was a pause – where had that shell gone? Then there was a flash and puff of smoke in the

73

dome of a chapel about half a mile up the hillside. The sergeant hurriedly lowered the elevation and fired again, this time a bit low. However, the gun crew started to run away and our Bren opened up and did good work. It did not take long to get a good hit on each of the two remaining guns. The sergeant then broke off the firing pin of our gun with the butt of a rifle. We had to cross about 300 yards of open ground to reach the Colonel, so we just ran like hell, and although there were a few bullets flying around, I don't think we had a single casualty up to this point.

I arrived at Commando HQ and reported to the Colonel. He explained that he was pushing in some men and wanted our section to support them and pick off snipers. We took up what positions we could but there wasn't much cover. I left the Colonel and went over to a Bren-gun post about fifty yards away but it took me a good ten minutes to get there as I had to crawl the whole way. The French had spotted us and were putting down a lot of accurate small arms fire. The whole time bullets spat past my head and sounded very close. It was very unpleasant and hard to think correctly and when I reached the Bren posts, they were stuck. Every time they tried to fire, an MG opened up and they couldn't spot it. Suddenly the 'B' section officer said he had spotted it and grabbed a rifle, but as he was taking aim he was shot in the chest and went down, coughing blood. Then the sergeant was shot in the shoulder, from a different direction which meant that we were being fired on from two sides; I crawled back to Commando HQ but when I was about ten yards away, I heard someone shout, 'The Colonel's hit. Get the medical orderly.'

I shouted to the Adjutant and he replied that the Colonel was dead and that he was going to withdraw the attack and try his luck elsewhere. So I shouted to my men to make for some scrub about a hundred yards away and started crawling towards it. All the time bullets were flitting past, much too close for comfort and we kept very low. The sergeant, who had been wounded, decided to run for it, but a

74

machine gun got him and he fell with his face covered with blood . . . and then I was hit.

I suddenly felt a tremendous bang on the head and knew I had been hit. However, when I opened my eyes I saw that it was in the legs and decided not to die. I dragged myself into a bit of a dip and tried to get fairly comfortable, but every time I moved they opened up on us. I could hear an NCO yelling to me to keep down or I would be killed so I kept down. After a time – when the initial shock had worn off – the pain in my legs became hellish. My right calf was shot off and was bleeding badly, but I could do nothing about it, and the left leg had gone rigid.

By now the sun was well up and it was very hot lying there. I was damned thirsty but could not get a drink as I had to expose myself to get my water bottle, and each time I tried I got about twenty rounds all to myself, so I put up with the thirst and lay there, hoping I would lose consciousness. After about two hours, a lot of fire came down and the next thing was twenty-five French advancing out of the scrub with fixed bayonets. The four men left from my section were captured. I raised my arm and one of the French came over and gave me a nasty look. I was carrying a French automatic pistol that my sergeant had given me in exchange for my rifle. It had jammed at the first shot but like a fool I had held on to it. Anyway, he just looked at me for a while and away he went and I was left alone. I had one hell of a drink and felt better. About half an hour later my four men were back with a stretcher, under a French guard. Both the Colonel and 'B' Section officer were dead, so they got me on to the stretcher and carried me down to a dressing station, where a British medical orderly gave me a shot of morphia.

While we were lying there, a machine gun opened up and the French medical fellows dived into a cave, but the bullets were right above our heads and they were obviously firing at something else. Some time later an ambulance turned up, and we were taken to a hospital in Beirut. In the ambulance were two wounded French, two sergeants from our side, and myself and we remained there as prisoners of war until the British entered the town six weeks later.

Lieutenant Bryan lost his leg and later left the Commando to work as an explosives expert with the Special Operations Executive (SOE). The central force, commanded by Lieutenant-Colonel Dick Pedder, headed directly for the Kaffa Badr bridge but – as described – met increasing resistance from a redoubt guarding the crossing, and was brought to a halt, Pedder being killed and all his officers wounded. RSM Fraser then took command of the centre force and captured a French barracks. Unfortunately, the southern or right-flank party, commanded by the unit second-in-command, Major Geoffrey Keyes, son of the then Director of Combined Operations, Admiral Sir Roger Keyes, had landed by mistake on the south side of the river.

Keyes soon found a boat and ferried some troops across the river to join the central force, and there, under heavy attack, they managed to hold on while the rest of Keyes's force captured a position on the south side of the river. The French eventually succeeded in blowing up the Kaffa Badr bridge just before the Australians arrived. The Commandos held out north of the river, covering the crossing until a pontoon bridge could be slung across, and after a night attack by the Australians, the French surrendered, Captain More's captors laying down their arms and surrendering to him. In spite of all the difficulties, No. 11 Commando had done well, but at the cost of a quarter of its strength. Major Keyes took command and the much depleted unit returned to Cyprus.

Layforce now hardly existed as an effective force and in August 1941, after barely nine months' existence, it was formally disbanded. Those men, like Lieutenant Milton, who had battalions of their parent units serving in the Middle East, were sent to join them. Some men from No. 7 Commando went on to Burma, while many of the others joined 'L' Detachment of the Special Air Service, a new force established by Lieutenant David Stirling of the Scots Guards, who had gone out to the Middle East with No. 8 Commando.

Layforce was unlucky. It had arrived in the Middle East as a complete Commando formation, carried in proper assault ships, but at a time when the military situation in the Middle East was in a constant state of flux. No one at a high level of command had either the time or the inclination to bother with this new-fangled kind of infantry unit, and Layforce found itself caught between two stools, without the orders or craft for a Commando role, and without the transport, artillery or engineer 'tail' necessary for a normal infantry brigade. It was frittered away on too-little-too-late operations, but when it was given a chance to fight, as at the Litani, it fought well.

Winston Churchill was less than pleased when word reached Whitehall that yet another Commando force had been wasted. He at once issued a minute to the Chiefs-of-Staff that the Middle East Commando was to be reformed and commanded not by a committee but by a local Director of Combined Operations – say Laycock – reporting not to the Army Staff, but to the naval officer commanding in the Mediterranean, Admiral Cunningham. Churchill added one final cutting comment on the fate of Layforce. 'Middle East Command has indeed maltreated and thrown away this valuable force.'

Brigadier Robert Laycock returned to the Middle East, but in spite of Churchill's orders, the last unit, No. 11 (Scottish) Commando, was disbanded on 1 September 1941. The force was then reconstructed and a 'new' Middle East Commando was formed from 'L' Detachment, SAS, which was designated as 2 Troop; remnants of the Palestinian soldiers who had served in No. 51 Commando as 4 and 5 Troops; 6 Troop formed from the SBS under Roger Courtney, and 3 Troop from all that was left of No. 11 Commando under Major Geoffrey Keyes.

This troop, of sixty men, insisted on calling itself No. 11 Commando, while the other troops, giving only lip service, if that, to the new 'Middle East Commando' simply went about their own affairs. Then, in November 1941, No. 11 Commando took on a final and most dramatic task.

During much of 1941 and 1942, the Eighth Army had a propaganda and morale problem. Ever since his arrival in North

Africa, German General Erwin Rommel was generally recognised as the finest professional general on either side. In the words of one Australian infantryman: 'We all thought Rommel was a bloody good bloke.' When Brigadier Desmond Young wrote his biography of Field Marshal Rommel after the war, British Field Marshal Sir Claude Auchinleck wrote a foreword praising Rommel's 'resilience, resourcefulness and mental agility. I salute him as a soldier and a man, as a brave, able and scrupulous opponent.'

This was generous and well-deserved praise, but in 1941 Rommel was the enemy and his influence on the Allied troops was seen as pernicious. Telling the battalion commanders not to let their men marvel at Rommel was one way to combat his appeal but the No. 11 (Scottish) Commando was ordered to try another way. It was ordered to kill him.

In October 1941, at the outset of General Auchinleck's counter-offensive – Operation Crusader – against the Afrika Korps, Rommel was believed to be living in a house at Beda Littoria, near the headquarters of the Italian forces in North Africa. Rommel's HQ was only about twenty miles from the sea so No. 11 Commando, now just sixty strong, was ordered to land from submarines on the coast nearby, attack the Italian HQ, destroy telephone and telegraph connections and, above all, kill or capture General Rommel. The raid was scheduled for the night of 18/19 November.

The raiding force, commanded by Major Keyes but under the overall direction of the old Layforce Commander, Robert Laycock, sailed from Alexandria on 10 November in the submarines HMS/M *Torbay* and *Talisman*, arriving off Beda Littoria on the 14th. That night some of the raiders made contact on shore with an Intelligence officer, Colonel Haselden. He had been carried through the enemy lines by the LRDG – the Long Range Desert Group – to carry out some preliminary reconnaissance, and gave them details of the HQ at Beda Littoria.

The main Commando force, under Laycock and Keyes, then came ashore in rubber dinghies. Due to rough weather only Laycock and seven men got ashore from HMS/M *Talisman*, which reduced the size of the raiding force and necessitated a change of plan. Keyes was ordered to attack Rommel's house and HQ while the rest, under Haselden and Lieutenant Cook of No. 11 Commando, were to ambush the roads round about. Laycock meanwhile remained with a small reserve at the beach, hoping that the balance of his party would come ashore the next night from HMS/M *Talisman*. Information then arrived from friendly Arabs that Rommel was not at his HQ, but living with his staff in a house at Sidi Rafa, near Beda Littoria, so once again the plans were changed.

Keyes took seventeen men and entered Sidi Rafa just after midnight, slipping past the grain silos and a hotel in torrential rain, up to the two-storey house where Rommel was said to live. All was in darkness. After deploying his men around the grounds and quietly trying the locked back doors and windows, Keyes, accompanied by Captain Campbell and Sergeant Jack Terry, decided on the direct approach. He marched up to the front door, pounding on the panels while Captain Campbell called loudly in German for admission. The door was opened by a sentry, whom they tried to overpower but he resisted, shouting warnings, until Campbell shot him with his revolver. This shot roused the house, the sentries and the entire vicinity.

Sergeant Terry entered the house and Tommy-gunned two Germans who came rushing down the stairs from the first floor, while the men outside engaged and shot German sentries now running towards the house. That done, Keyes and Campbell began to clear the downstairs rooms with grenades until, flinging open one door, Keyes was hit by a burst of Schmeisser fire from within and fell, mortally wounded. His attacker was killed by Tommy-gun fire from Sergeant Terry and a grenade from Captain Campbell. They then started to carry Keyes from the house but a bullet hit Campbell in the calf and broke his leg. With firing now coming at the raiders from both inside and outside the house, Captain Campbell ordered Sergeant Terry to round up the party and withdraw, though not before lobbing all their spare grenades into the house.

Geoffrey Keyes died shortly after this and Campbell then

ordered Terry to leave him and withdraw. Sergeant Terry and most of the raiders managed to rejoin Laycock at the beach, and on the evening of the 18th, HMS/M *Torbay* surfaced offshore and closed the beach, but the weather was still too rough to permit the boats to come ashore to get them off. HMS/M *Torbay* withdrew and dived, returning again on the following night, but yet again, heavy surf prevented the force withdrawing. The party was finally located by the Germans on the afternoon of the following day and soon came under fire. At dusk, Laycock ordered the survivors to break out in small parties and Laycock, accompanied by Sergeant Terry, finally got back to the British lines on Christmas Eve, after walking for 41 days across the desert.

The rest of the raiding force were either captured, or murdered by Arabs. Later Sergeant Terry, DCM, recalled this operation:

I joined the Royal Artillery in 1938, and went to the Middle East in No. 1 Troop of 11 Commando, with Lieutenant Bryan and Lieutenant Coade, who was killed as soon as we got ashore at the Litani river. On the Rommel raid, I was on HMS/M *Torbay*. It was only about twenty miles as the crow flies from the beach to Beda Littoria, but as it walks, up and down the jebel, over the escarpment, it took until the third night.

Killing Rommel was just one of the jobs we had to do. We had an Italian HQ to attack and a radio post by a crossroads as well. We went in after midnight, very dark. Keyes posted men about the place, and we went in through the back. I wouldn't have known Rommel from anyone else, but the idea was that we would kidnap him. But if someone fires at you, you kill them, don't you?

Captain Campbell was taken prisoner and lost his leg. We took about a day to march back to the rendezvous at the beach. I nearly fell over the escarpment and lost my Tommy-gun. At the beach, the sea was still very rough, although the sub floated in a dinghy with food, but we couldn't get off, and then the Italians found us. We could see Germans up on the escarpment and had two choices; to head for the alternative beach or go inland to find an LRDG patrol. Lieutenant Pryor tried a recce and got wounded, so we left the wounded in a cave and broke out in small parties. I went with Colonel Laycock and we tried the alternative beach first, but we heard German voices, so they must have found maps or been told of our intentions. Then we tried the LRDG patrol position, but no luck so in the end we walked back.

It took 41 days and I went down to nine stone. We lived on berries and sometimes a goat. We had Italian money and could tap-up any lone Arabs for assistance, but not groups; they didn't trust each other. When we got back to our lines the Town Mayor at Cyrene gave us some rations and passed us on to General Ritchie's HQ, and we were flown back to Cairo.

No one else got away, they were all killed or taken prisoner. Sergeant Terry joined David Stirling's SAS and served with them in the desert and Italy, before returning to the UK for D-Day, after which he fought in France with the Maquis near Dijon.

Rommel was not at Sidi Rafa, nor at Beda Littoria that night; his HQ was actually much deeper in the desert, close to the front line. But when the raiders splashed ashore on the 15th, Rommel was not even in Africa. He was in Rome with his wife, celebrating his birthday (which fell on 16 November) and consulting with his Italian allies on future strategy.

So, like so many of their best-laid plans, this last Layforce operation was unsuccessful. It was still a classic little raid, a milestone in Commando history and for his part in leading it, Lieutenant-Colonel Geoffrey Keyes was awarded a posthumous Victoria Cross, the first VC awarded to a Commando soldier – but not the last.

5

THE ST NAZAIRE RAID, 1942

'If a unit is not trained, equipped and motivated for immediate action, it will not survive the first contact with the enemy.'

Commando Training Notes, 1942

The Second World War began to swing in favour of the Allies in 1942, a year that saw many changes and considerable expansion in the Commando forces. The first indication of change came when the first of the Royal Marines Commandos, the 'A' Commando, was formed in February 1942. In the same month, it was decided to centralise all Commando training at the Commando Basic Training Centre which was opened at Achnacarry House, the home of the Cameron of Lochiel, seven miles from Spean Bridge in the Western Highlands of Scotland.

Before training was centralised at Achnacarry, each Commando had recruited and trained its own men, but with the rapid expansion of Combined Operations under Mountbatten, this ad hoc system had to change. Major Charles Vaughan of The Buffs and No. 4 Commando, became Commandant of Achnacarry, and from then on all potential recruits, and even entire units, would have to pass the Achnacarry Commando course before receiving the green beret.

They would then pass on to the Holding Operational

Commando at Wrexham for further specialist training before being posted to their units. Achnacarry training was extremely hard and made such an impression on those who endured it that one very experienced Commando soldier told me he was not a 'real' Commando 'because I had not been to Achnacarry'. The only exceptions to this Achnacarry training were volunteers for the Commando units serving in the Middle East and Italy, who were forced to recruit and train their own men, although they too received periodic drafts from the Holding Operational Commando.

Achnacarry training was tough, physically and mentally. It was not enough to finish an assault course or a training exercise. It was necessary to complete the task smiling and ready for more. Exercises used live ammunition and the instructors were told that provided no more than ten per cent of the recruits were injured on any course, no questions were asked. The basic lessons were driven home by some (empty) graves by the main gate, each one with a notice giving the cause of demise. 'He forgot to wet his toggle-rope'; 'He ran in front of the Bren gun', and so on.

The Commando course lasted six weeks and consisted of plenty of PT, rock climbing, cross-country runs and exercises, landing rehearsals from boats on the loch, night schemes, cliff climbing and abseiling – this last down the walls of the castle – unarmed combat, knife-fighting, weapon training and forced marches. All ex-Achnacarry Commandos remember the relentless pace and pressure of the training, the drenching Highland weather, and the hard slog of the 'speed-marches'.

Speed-marches required the troops to march and run long distances carrying full equipment with platoon weapons, covering a mile in ten minutes, whatever the terrain. The pass-out speed-march covered fifteen miles, down to Spean Bridge and back. All the training was on a 'me-and-my-pal' basis, where two men teamed up to work together – digging trenches, building a bivouac; whatever one man did, his pal, his 'oppo' or 'mucker' did as well.

Achnacarry training aimed to do more than simply toughen

up the men for action. It aimed to prove that a fit, trained Commando soldier could always do more if he had the right attitude. 'It's all in the heart and the mind' became one famous Commando saying. Another was, 'If you can't take a joke, you shouldn't have joined' – a remark commonly addressed to someone rolling about in agony.

Charles Vaughan expected a high standard of drill and turnout at all times. Even when exhausted, squads returning to camp had to tighten their rifle slings and march into barracks at the slope, marching in for a little arms drill or a practice shoot on the range. Those who passed through Achnacarry felt that they could do anything and got their green berets. Those who fell by the wayside were 'RTUd' – returned to unit. That was, and remained, the only Commando punishment. If you weren't good enough, or gave up, or misbehaved, you had to go.

By the spring of 1942, the Commando organisation was roughly as follows: under Combined Operations HQ came the Special Service Brigade HQ. This headquarters had under command the Army Commando units Nos 1 to 12, plus the Royal Marines Commando units. In addition, there was the Basic Training Centre at Achnacarry and the Holding Operational Commando at Wrexham. Meanwhile, the raiding went on, beginning on the night of 27/28 March 1942 with 'The Greatest Raid of All' on the graving dock in the French port of St Nazaire.

The port of St Nazaire lies in Brittany, six miles from the mouth of the Loire. The great feature of St Nazaire was – and is – a huge dry dock, the Forme Ecluse, then the largest dry dock in Europe and the only one capable of holding and repairing large battleships of up to 85,000 tons. This fact was of particular interest to the Royal Navy. Since 1939 they had been obliged to keep units of the fleet based at Scapa Flow to check any foray into the North Atlantic by German battleships, and in particular the mighty *Tirpitz*. Without the security of St Nazaire and the possibility of repairs there, the likelihood that *Tirpitz* would break out into the Atlantic convoys was considerably reduced.

Bombing this dock was not considered possible, not least because any attempt to do so would certainly cause heavy casualties among the French population; so it was decided to mount a raid, to destroy the dock and the harbour installations – a task entrusted to Lieutenant-Colonel A. C. Newman of No. 2 Commando.

The main force would consist of 100 men from No. 2 Commando, who would attack gun positions and provide the covering parties for demolition patrols drawn from all the other Commando units, Nos 1, 3, 4, 5, 6 and 12. Since they would certainly resist large amounts of explosives, the gates of the Forme Ecluse would first be rammed by a destroyer, the bows of which had been packed with explosives. This destroyer would carry part of the landing force, while the rest would be conveyed to the attack in motor launches. Lieutenant-Colonel Newman would command the landing parties, while the naval contingent would be led by Commander R. E. D. (Red) Ryder.

St Nazaire had a large German garrison who, apart from manning the ships and submarines, also controlled searchlights and coastal batteries and maintained tight security in and around the port. Attacking St Nazaire would stir up a hornet's nest and it was conceded that while Newman's force might get in and do the job, their chances of getting out again were slim. 'There's certainly a VC in it,' said one senior officer. In the end there were five.

Newman's and Ryder's plan called for a bold approach, straight up the river with no firing at all unless detected until the destroyer rammed the gates of the Forme Ecluse. Then the landing parties would swarm ashore from the destroyer and the motor launches to carry out their tasks, and with luck withdraw to the Old Mole, which lay slightly downstream from the Forme Ecluse, re-embark there and head back to sea. The plan was approved by the Chiefs of Staff on 3 March, and the raid, codenamed Operation Chariot, took place 23 days later.

While the demolition teams and Newman's protection parties began to train – though without knowing for what – the search began for a suitable and expendable destroyer. The ship finally selected was one of the fifty old American destroyers sent to Britain in exchange for bases in Bermuda, the four-stacker USS *Buchanan*, renamed HMS *Campbeltown*. HMS *Campbeltown*, under the command of Lieutenant-Commander S. H. Beattie, RN, was first stripped of as much equipment as possible to reduce her draught. Her four funnels were reduced to two, both of them cut and altered to resemble those of the German *Mowe*-class frigates which were known to be based at St Nazaire. This weight loss was balanced by the tons of explosives packed into her forecastle, and by special steel bulwarks welded along the decks to give some protection to the Commandos lying there as HMS *Campbeltown* surged in to ram the dock gates.

Corporal Arthur Woodiwiss from No. 2 Commando went in on *Campbeltown*:

> We had plans of the dock area which we had to draw and re-draw and a wonderful scale model, which we could study in different light to help us identify our targets. As an assault group commander I rehearsed street fighting to the gun positions I had to demolish. Our full dress rehearsal at Devonport against the Home Guard was an absolute disaster and the Home Guard were delighted but we knew it would be all right on the night. If you have to make mistakes it is best to make them in training.

Demolition teams also visited the King George V Dock at Southampton, which had gates similar to those at St Nazaire. The dimensions of the gates give some idea of the scale of the task, for each was 167 feet long, 54 feet high – and 35 feet thick. The destruction of the gates depended on *Campbeltown* ramming them fair and square before detonating her main charge. The Commando demolition teams were preparing charges to destroy the nearby pumping machines and learning how to run about at night while carrying rucksacks filled with 90 lbs of high explosive. These teams would be covered by the Protection Parties from No. 2 Commando which were also busy rehearsing their street-fighting role. The entire force assembled at Falmouth on an ominous date, Friday, 13 March 1942.

The first task facing the naval forces was to get the troops to St Nazaire. The ships had to sail up six miles of constantly narrowing and heavily defended estuary before even reaching the dock gates. The tides had to be just right, so keeping to the timings was crucial. Then air photographs revealed a new snag. In addition to an anti-aircraft 'flakship' moored permanently near the dock, four German *Mowe*-class frigates had recently arrived at St Nazaire, were now berthed close to the landing area and showed no signs of leaving.

There was also a problem with the supporting bombing operation mounted by the RAF. Colonel Newman rightly predicted that the bombing plan would not work, and would indeed alert the Germans to the fact that something else was in progress and should be cancelled, but he was overruled.

Escorted by two Hunt-class destroyers, the Operation Chariot force, totalling 630 soldiers and sailors – 277 of them Commandos – sailed on the afternoon of 26 March, the troops embarked on HMS *Campbeltown* and sixteen Fairmile launches supplied by Coastal Forces. These were wooden launches with a maximum speed of sixteen knots, armed with machine guns and newly fitted Oerlikon cannon. In addition to their normal fuel tanks, each carried long-range 50-gallon petrol tanks strapped on the upper deck and were floating bombs, very vulnerable to enemy fire. The last two craft in this little fleet were MGB 314 and MTB 74. The latter craft carried delayed action torpedoes which would be fired at the dock gates if HMS *Campbeltown* was sunk on the way in.

The force first headed west into the Atlantic, in the hope that any German aircraft or submarine which saw them would report them as an anti-submarine force on a sweep. A German submarine was sighted on the second day and promptly engaged by the destroyer HMS *Tynedale*. At 22:00 hours that night the convoy sighted the beacon of the submarine HMS/M *Sturgeon*, which was marking the entrance to the Loire, and with *Campbeltown* in the van, the force entered the river and forged up the six-mile passage to the docks.

The RAF bombing raid began at about 23:30 hours, but the strange behaviour of the aircraft soon alerted the defenders. This was no rain of incendiaries and high explosives to indicate a proper raid. Instead the bombers cruised about over the estuary, dropping one bomb at a time. After about half an hour, Captain Mecke, the German officer commanding the anti-aircraft defences around St Nazaire, sent a warning order round his command posts – 'Conduct of enemy aircraft inexplicable . . . suspicion of parachute landing.'

On receipt of this signal, one of his subordinates turned his attention to the estuary and saw a force of small ships forging upstream. This was reported back to the Harbour Commander who confirmed that no convoys were expected, and at 01:20 hours on Saturday, 28 March, Captain Mecke sent another signal: 'Beware landing.' When that signal reached the defending batteries, HMS *Campbeltown* was within two miles of the dock gates and working up to full speed.

The first sign of enemy alertness came when a big searchlight snapped on, combing the river to illuminate HMS *Campbeltown* and her supporting craft. Two German signal stations at once challenged the convoy and one or two gun positions fired warning shots. On Commander Ryder's instructions *Campbeltown* signalled back, slowly, in German, using codes discovered on the Vaagso raid: 'Proceeding up harbour in accordance with orders . . .' and this seemed to do the trick. The firing stopped and the searchlight snapped out. The force had gained a precious few minutes and the dock gates were now in sight.

There was then another brief exchange of signals, and in reply Ryder fired a red recognition flare; although the colour was not the right shade, it held the enemy at bay for a few more precious seconds. Then, at 01:27 hours, with the dock gates looming ever closer, HMS *Campbeltown* hauled down the German colours and hoisted her battle ensigns – and every gun in the Chariot force opened up on the defending batteries.

'For about five minutes the sight was staggering,' wrote Ryder, 'both sides loosing off with everything they had. The air was full of tracer, flying horizontally and at close range.'

HMS *Campbeltown* struck the dock gates at 01:34 hours, ramming her bow deep into the caisson. The troops swarmed ashore, joining the five assault and demolition parties now landing at various points around the harbour, and infantry weapons, rifles and Bren guns added their weight to the fire, punctuated by the thud of grenades.

Corporal Woodiwiss remembers the run-in to the dock:

When the German searchlight picked up HMS *Campbeltown* it first shone on the German flag at the masthead, which confused them. When the Germans finally engaged us, the swastika flag was pulled down and cut into pieces for souvenirs. Captain Roy had a piece sewn on his beret for the rest of the war. When we hit, the *Campbeltown* rode much higher up the caisson than we expected and my assault ladder did not reach the dock, so I had to jump down to attack the nearest gun position which was raking us with enfilade fire. Pausing to get my bearings, I saw a potato-masher grenade flying towards me. I kicked this, luckily hitting the handle. It went back where it had come from and sorted out the group who had hurled it.

I eliminated the sentries, forced my way into the gun position and sprayed the crew with my Tommy-gun. I then wrapped my prepared explosive charge around the breech and destroyed the gun. I returned to my assault group and we attacked all the remaining gun positions then placed our incendiary charges in the oil storage tanks. Lieutenant Roderick then ordered our withdrawal. I covered this so that our survivors could recross to the ship and regroup. A large group of Germans were forming to cross the open area we had just left. Lying abandoned on deck behind the shrapnel shields were Brens with 100-round magazines which had been fired as we sailed up the Loire. I set up three of these behind the shields and began firing each in turn to prevent their advance and forced them to withdraw.

The fuses in the six tons of ammonal below had already been activated, and I was lying feet above the charge so decided to leave. I dropped all the spare weapons I could find into the Loire, collected all the Tommy magazines I could carry, rejoined my section and shared out the ammo. When we ran out of ammunition and had gathered a large number of seriously wounded we were forced to surrender. We were then questioned about what we were doing but the interrogation was terminated when a tremendous explosion heralded *Campbeltown*'s completion of our task, taking about one hundred and fifty Germans with it.

For his gallantry at St Nazaire, Corporal Woodiwiss was awarded the Military Medal.

Fighting in small groups scattered across the dockyard, the Commandos soon took it over and formed a defensive perimeter. Every soldier there has a story to tell, but just two tales must serve to illustrate the many actions of the St Nazaire raid. Lieutenant Stuart Chant of No. 5 Commando had the task of destroying the pumps which filled and emptied the dock basin. Though wounded on the way in, Chant and his demolition team of four sergeants came ashore from HMS *Campbeltown*, following the soldiers of Lieutenant Roy's troop across the dock, only to find the entrance to the pumping room barred by a steel door.

They blew it open and, with Chant leading, they slipped inside. Leaving Sergeant Chamberlain, who had also been wounded, to guard the door, Chant led the others down the steel stairs to the pumping station 40 feet below. Here they quickly placed their charges, 150 pounds of explosive, pulled the igniters and ran back up the stairs to the open dock, the wounded Chant now limping heavily. Out in the dockyard, bullets and tracer fire were lancing in every direction, the scene lit up by gun flashes and the many blazing motor launches drifting out on the river. Chant's party ran for cover behind a wall and two minutes later their charges exploded. Chant then made his way to Lieutenant-Colonel Newman's command post at the Old Mole and reported his task complete.

The time was now about 02:30 hours, time for the force to withdraw, but out on the river another battle was raging between the motor launches and the shore defences, the crews using Tommy-guns and Brens as well as their 20mm Oerlikon cannon against German artillery, cannon and heavy machine guns.

ML 192 was hit by shellfire off the Old Mole, caught fire and was well ablaze as she attempted to put her troops ashore; only five men made it. ML 262 forged up the river, was pinned by searchlights and under heavy fire from 20mm cannon as it swept past ML 177, tied up to HMS *Campbeltown*. Here the captain put the troops ashore, while his stoker gave covering fire with his Lewis gun. ML 268 was set ablaze by tracer and blew up, with only one man surviving.

MLs were now drifting all across the river in pools of blazing petrol, being steadily shot to pieces, but those which could manoeuvre still came in to land, taking it in turns to pour fire into a German flakship which was raking the dockside with her cannon. The five German *Mowe* frigates were at sea that night. In all, seven MLs, with many of their commandos and crews, were lost on the way in. Others were destroyed during the landing, or while waiting to re-embark the troops or during the withdrawal. The story of one of these, ML 306, must stand here for all the rest of the little craft and their gallant crews.

ML 306, commanded by Lieutenant I. B. Henderson, RNVR, withdrew from St Nazaire at about 02:30 hours. She had twenty-eight men on board, fourteen of them soldiers from No. 1 and No. 2 Commando including Sergeant Tom Durrant of No. 1 Commando. At 05:30 hours, when they were well out to sea and looking forward to the return to England, ML 306 ran into the five *Mowe* frigates of the German 5th Flotilla, now returning to port. Two of the German ships passed them by in the dark, but the third, the *Jaguar*, detected the darkened ML, illuminated it with a searchlight and then opened fire.

The ML crew and the embarked troops promptly replied with Lewis and Tommy-guns, the two ships engaging each other at close range, circling about with the German ship trying to ram the wooden ML and bringing her heavy machine guns to bear. This went on until twenty of the British were dead or wounded. The *Jaguar* then stood off, stopped firing and asked Lieutenant Henderson to surrender. Henderson declined.

Sergeant Durrant, who was manning a twin-Lewis gun on the stern of the ML, had already been wounded three times, but called for more ammunition as the German ship moved back in, the captain still calling on the British to surrender. Durrant, now hanging in the harness of the Lewis guns, opened fire again, putting one burst right across the chart table in the German wheel-house. The *Jaguar* withdrew until her main guns could bear and open fire again, killing Lieutenant Henderson and riddling Durrant with bullets. It was now broad daylight and when the *Jaguar* once again came alongside the now-sinking launch, Lieutenant Swayne of No. 1 Commando, the only unwounded man on board, stood up among the bodies and called out apologetically, 'I'm afraid we can't go on.'

ML 306 had fought the *Jaguar* frigate for nearly an hour. The ML sank as the surviving British were helped on board the *Jaguar*, where they were well looked after. 'You had no chance,' said Kapitan Paul of the *Jaguar* to Lieutenant Swayne. 'But I must compliment you on a brave fight.' Paul also asked for the name of the army sergeant who had manned the twin-Lewis.

Some weeks later, an officer from *Jaguar* called on Colonel Newman in the prison camp at Rennes, told him about the battle with ML 306, and in particular about the fight put up by Sergeant Durrant, describing it in some detail, 'as you may wish to recommend this man for a high decoration'. Sergeant Durrant was later awarded a posthumous VC, the first ever awarded to a soldier for a naval action, and on the recommendation of an enemy officer.

Four other VCs were awarded for the great fight at St Nazaire, to Lieutenant Commander Beattie of HMS *Campbeltown*, to Lieutenant-Colonel Newman of No. 2 Commando, to

Lieutenant-Commander Ryder and posthumously to Able Seaman Savage of the RNVR. Only 270 of the 630 soldiers and sailors who took part returned to England. Twenty-five per cent of the participants were killed. Of the nineteen ships which entered the river, only four returned to England, but the Forme Ecluse was not repaired until some years after the end of the war.

6

DIEPPE and MADAGASCAR, 1942

'The battle of D-Day was won on the beaches of Dieppe.'

Admiral Lord Louis Mountbatten,
Chief of Combined Operations, 1942

Five months after the St Nazaire raid, Combined Operations mounted yet another attack on the enemy-held coast of France, when the 2nd Canadian Division, supported by three Commandos, Nos 3, 4 and the recently formed Royal Marines 'A' Commando – later to become 40 (Royal Marine) Commando – assaulted the port of Dieppe. Opinions vary as to whether the Dieppe raid was a total disaster or a necessary prelude to D-Day, and Lord Louis's well-known claim for the Dieppe raid is widely contested.

The raid may have been useful, but it was certainly a chapter of accidents, and the main objective, to seize Dieppe, land tanks and proceed inland for a number of miles before withdrawing, was never achieved . . . and if it had been achieved, what then? The raid is instructive in teaching lessons about what could not be done in the face of a skilled and determined enemy, but the cost of learning that lesson was high.

The Canadians were checked on the beaches and suffered terrible casualties. The Royal Regiment of Canada, landing at Puits, was machine-gunned on the beach and cut to pieces in five minutes, losing all its officers and 496 of the 523 men who got ashore. On the other flank, at Pourville, the South Saskatchewan Regiment landed and crossed the river, where their CO won the VC for gallantry under fire. The battalion was then forced to withdraw, linking with the follow-up battalion from the Queen's Own Cameron Highlanders of Canada. These two battalions, totally isolated and unable to withdraw, fought on until they ran out of ammunition, the South Saskatchewans losing 19 officers and 498 men, the Queen's Own Highlanders of Canada 24 officers and 322 men.

The main assault, across the esplanade at Dieppe, never got off the beach. Three fine Canadian battalions, the Essex Scottish, the Royal Hamilton Light Infantry and the Fusiliers Mount Royal, plus the tanks of the Calgary Regiment, were decimated in the attempt to get into the town. The Royal Marine Commando was sent in at 08:30 hours and met a murderous fire as soon as they emerged from the smoke screen, 200 yards from the beach. Their commanding officer, Lieutenant-Colonel Picton-Phillips, was killed, standing up in his LCM to wave the follow-up craft away; this saved the Commando from total destruction, but their casualties were still severe. Only the Army Commando part of the operation went to plan.

The original plan for the Dieppe raid, Operation Rutter, called for parachute landings on the coast, east and west of Dieppe, to knock out heavy coastal defence batteries that would otherwise deal severely with the ships and landing craft offshore. This plan was eventually abandoned and a second plan, Operation Jubilee, was drawn up with the parachute troops replaced by Commandos; No. 3 Commando was to land at Petit Berneval and attack the battery at Belleville, while No. 4 would land west of Dieppe at Varengeville and deal with a six-gun battery in the woods behind the cliffs there.

Matters began to go wrong at 04:00 hours on 19 August 1942, when No. 3 Commando, sailing to the attack in Eureka assault boats and escorted by steam gun-boat SGB 5, ran into a German coastal convoy. Charles Hustwick of SS Brigade

Signals was attached to No. 3 Commando for the Dieppe operation:

The passage through the minefield, which had been cleared by the Navy, was uneventful until we got near the French coast, when a star-shell went up and we were bathed in glorious light. Then all hell let loose.

We had been caught by armed trawlers who were escorting a convoy into Dieppe. We had not been told of our destination until we had been at sea for an hour but we had been told that we had to get ashore at all costs. Our flotilla was now scattered over a wide area of sea; smoke and the smell of cordite was everywhere, dawn was breaking and a heavy curtain of fire was coming from the shore where the enemy had been alerted . . . we were sitting ducks.

After some argument between the Adjutant and the Coxswain, we made our way back to the steam gunboat which was supposed to be protecting us; she was a grim spectacle and full of holes, like a colander. The bridge had been destroyed, the steering had gone and only one gun was still firing. We were hoisted aboard and the Adjutant and the CO of 3 Commando, Lieutenant-Colonel Durnford Slater, got into our landing craft to try to find the HQ ship, HMS *Calpe*. We had no means of letting the Commander know what a disaster our effort had been.

The radio on board the gunboat had been destroyed, and with no steering, the gunboat was now going round in circles. We were eventually taken on board an RAF rescue launch and after picking up a fighter-pilot from the water, arrived back at Newhaven around 13:30 hours. I don't really know what the survival figures of 3 Commando were, but at breakfast the following morning there were treble helpings for all.

Six of the surviving No. 3 Commando landing craft put their men ashore on Yellow Beach 1 near Belleville, where they were promptly engaged by the enemy. Pressing on inland, the Commandos headed for the enemy batteries until they could go no further and only one man of those who landed returned to England; over one hundred were killed, wounded or taken prisoner.

The final No. 3 Commando craft, carrying Major Peter Young and eighteen men from 6 Troop, landed without opposition on Yellow Beach 2 near Belleville, and climbed the cliff, inching along a gully choked with wire. At the top they set off to attack the battery, which they could now hear firing on the offshore shipping. They managed to keep the battery under fire from their rifles and Bren guns until all their ammunition was exhausted and they had to withdraw, rejoining their patiently waiting craft just after 08:00 hours – Peter Young being dragged behind the Eureka on a lifeline until they were out of rifle range. Brigadier Peter Young, as he became, who won three MCs and the DSO during the Second World War, regarded Dieppe as one of his best exploits: 'I took eighteen men ashore, did the job we had to do, and brought eighteen men back.'

The last Commando unit on the raid, No. 4 Commando, commanded by Lieutenant-Colonel The Lord Lovat, MC, landed from LCAs, having been carried to within ten miles of France in the landing ship HMS *Prince Albert*. Lovat split his force into two parts, of which the first, under Major Derek Mills-Roberts, would land on Orange Beach 1 below the Pointe d'Ailly lighthouse, climb a narrow gully and advance to the edge of Varengeville to give covering fire, while the second, Group 2, commanded by Lovat himself, landing a little further south on Orange 2, would assault the battery, which lay about one kilometre inland from the beach. This battery consisted of six 150mm guns, protected by infantry, machine guns and barbed wire.

Mills-Roberts's party landed exactly on time, only to be startled by the tremendous noise as the battery opened fire on the offshore shipping long before Lovat's assault party could be in position. Mills-Roberts received a report from the beach that the Dieppe convoys were already in sight and apparently within range of the battery. Mills-Roberts therefore decided to attack the battery at once and, forcing its way up another wire-choked gully fringed by mines, his party made its way to a point overlooking the battery, and began to engage and distract the enemy gunners with rifle, Brens and mortar fire.

Half an hour later Lovat's group began to mount its attack from the right flank. The garrison, now alert, opened a heavy fire on the assault wave, killing two officers and wounding several men. The fighting on the battery perimeter now became hand-to-hand, with Captain Pat Porteous killing one German with his pistol before leading a bayonet charge through the wire and right on to the guns. Porteous stayed at the head of his men as they shot and bayoneted their way through the position, until he finally fell into one of the gun-pits, shot through the thighs. For his gallantry that day, Captain Porteous received the Victoria Cross.

No. 4 Commando captured and destroyed the Varengeville battery at the cost of twelve men killed, twenty wounded and thirteen missing before withdrawing to the beaches without further loss and returning to England.

The Dieppe raid was a success for the Commando element in the landing force, and apart from No. 3 and No. 4, introduced another raiding unit to the war – the American Rangers – who supplied fifty men, and some men from a curious unit, No. 10 (Inter-Allied) Commando, which had been formed in June 1942 under Lieutenant-Colonel Dudley Lister, formerly of No. 7 Commando. No. 10 (I-A) was made up of troops from many nations, French, Dutch, Yugoslav, Polish, Norwegian, even Germans, these last enlisting under assumed British names. No. 10 Commando never fought as a complete unit, but sent the troops to serve with other Commando units in theatres where their linguistic skills would prove as useful as their fighting abilities.

Dr Anthony Hodges served with No. 10 from the early days:

I had already spent a year and a half at Lochailort, and was promoted to Lieutenant-Colonel to train Army medical officers in living off the land under very hard conditions. I gave them hell, of course, but I couldn't see myself as a

Lieutenant-Colonel sitting at a desk, so I asked for demotion to Captain and transfer to a Commando. Everyone thought I was a complete idiot! I was then sent to Harlech, North Wales, to No. 10 Commando, which was then being formed – an amazing unit. Some of the German Jews who arrived to join X troop were in very bad condition, many having endured some time in concentration camps. They confided very little to me and all took British surnames.

Among the French was Philippe Keiffer, who led the French troops of No. 4 Commando later. The Norwegians were a magnificent lot and I often went up to Shetland where they frequently arrived after sailing or rowing from Norway – many were fishermen. The Dutch were also remarkably good Commandos and after the war the Belgian troop became the nucleus of the Belgian Para-Commando Regiment, which exists to this day.

Not all the raids of 1942 took place across the English Channel. In early 1942 No. 5 Commando sailed to the Indian Ocean with a large Expeditionary Force charged with occupying the Vichy-French outpost, the island of Madagascar, in the Indian Ocean off the east coast of Africa. Japanese submarines had started to operate in the Indian Ocean, and this led directly to the British invasion.

Brigadier Eric Holt, then a major in No. 5 Commando, carries on the story:

The Chiefs of Staff in London considered that the French Vichy Government might well offer the Japanese the excellent facilities of the magnificent harbour at Diego Suarez at the north-east tip of Madagascar. From there these submarines would seriously imperil the Allied convoys sailing up from the Cape to East Africa and more particularly to India, so it was decided that the British would mount an amphibious operation, sailing from the UK to seize the harbour – 9,000 miles away – and thus deny it to the Japanese.

The principal assault formation was 29 Infantry Brigade

with 5 Commando under command for the operation. The Commander was Brigadier Francis Festing, who was later to become Chief of the General Staff and a Field Marshal. The Force Commander, Admiral Syfret, flew his flag in the ageing battleship HMS *Ramilles*, and the air support was provided by naval aircraft in the fleet carriers *Illustrious* and *Indomitable*. There were also two cruisers, nine destroyers and six minesweepers. The assault force was embarked in the civilian transports, the SSs *Winchester Castle*, *Keren* and *Karania*, with assault landing craft replacing the lifeboats in the davits. The plan was that 29 Brigade would land on 5 May on two selected beaches on the north-west coast of the island and then move across country to seize Diego Suarez from the south-west.

Overlooking and dominating these beaches were two French artillery batteries and their neutralisation was the task of 5 Commando, who made a silent landing before dawn, before the Brigade hit the beaches a few miles south. This landing went according to plan, complete surprise was achieved and the two batteries surrendered after a brief fight during which the Commando suffered only light casualties but took over 300 prisoners-of-war.

Geoff Riley recalls his part in the Madagascar campaign:

We totalled only 365 men, part of a force which included the 29th Independent Brigade and the 13th Brigade. We carried French Intelligence Officers on board and therefore guessed our destination was a Vichy-administered colony.

On 5 May, we landed at Courrier Bay on the north-west coast of Madagascar, some eleven miles from Diego Suarez. We were in LCAs and went in down a channel swept of mines by corvettes. There was no opposition. We caught them completely unawares, because of a triumph of seamanship by the Royal Navy and Merchant Navy who penetrated coral reefs believed impassable to ships this size.

Above us on cliffs fifty feet high was a battery of 6-inch

guns. We climbed the cliffs and caught the Vichy gunners asleep. There were French Officers, NCOs and Malagasy and Senegalese troops, who were herded together and guarded but at first light the Vichy counter-attack began. On our flank, forty colonial troops with two NCOs charged up the hill towards us. We carried out a bayonet charge and the NCOs were killed. Their men then gave up and threw down their weapons, our casualties being pretty light.

Captain 'Chips' Heron went forward to take the surrender of a separate party of battery observers on the hill nearby. As they came forward to surrender, some grenades were lobbed over from their rear, wounding Captain Heron and others. They did not get the chance to surrender again.

In sweltering heat, loaded like pack mules with ammo and grenades, we marched against a hot wind across the eighteen-mile isthmus to Cap Diego. There was a bit of a fracas with a troop of Foreign Legionnaires. We shot them up a bit before they surrendered and there were about fifty wounded. We carried out mopping-up operations against colonial troops while the two Infantry Brigades took the town of Antisrane with heavy casualties.

Actually it was a manoeuvre by fifty Royal Marines off the battleship which saved the day. They came off HMS *Ramilles* in Courrier Bay and boarded the destroyer HMS *Anthony*, which then entered the harbour at 22:00 hours, in pitch darkness and under fire from every gun which could be brought to bear. She ran alongside the wharf with the Royal Marines tumbling over the side and rushing ashore. Their orders were to attack everything except the barracks and the magazine, which were strongly held, but in half an hour they were in possession of both of them. They had accomplished everything with one casualty. They prevented much street fighting and damage to the town. The official report quotes: 'These fifty Royal Marines created a disturbance in the town out of all proportion to their numbers' – and they did really well.

We then sailed to Mombasa to rehearse our role in the next show, which consisted of leaping off destroyers as they came along a quayside at thirty knots. We then set out to take Majunga, the largest port on the west coast of Madagascar. The plan was to land right in the docks but the operation went wrong. The landing craft broke down and instead of landing before dawn, we had to go in broad daylight. They opened up on us with four machine guns but we had good cover from the Royal Navy and that kept our casualties down; we didn't need scaling ladders – we went up that quayside like scuttling rats! I could see our chaps going down like ninepins out of the corner of my eye. Our first objective was the Post Office, to cut communications with Tananarive, the capital. The second objective was the Residency, to capture the Governor and raise the Union Jack.

We took both places and it was here that I had my first close-hand encounter. We had swept into the courtyard and I took up a position at the bottom of the stairs and my chum Matt Bolton was opposite, against the other wall. A few yards to my left was the rusting bulk of a car. I chatted to Matt and turned my head to spot a rifle barrel coming into view, followed by a fez from behind the car. As the man stood straight up, dodging to the right, I fired from the hip, killing him. French casualties were heavy. We re-embarked back at Diego Suarez and sailed for Tamatave, the largest port on the east coast of Madagascar.

The plan was to arrive at dawn, the Navy would form a semicircle half a mile from the port and *Warspite* and *Illustrious* would be ten miles out. We would then send in an envoy under a white flag to demand unconditional surrender. If he was refused or fired on there was to be a 55-minute bombardment by the destroyers and *Warspite*'s 15-inch guns; HMS *Illustrious* would send in Seafires and Swordfish aircraft to bomb and strafe. After this, our destroyers would ram the boom at thirty knots, pull hard against the quay and we would leap off and do the business with the bayonet.

The envoy went in, then signalled he was being fired on. Immediately there was a salvo from HMS *Birmingham*, the signal for the general bombardment. This lasted three minutes, during which time a few hundred shells made contact with the French positions and white flags went up everywhere. Our destroyers steamed in with the boom opened for us by the subdued French. We then chased the remnants of the French southwards and in October the whole island surrendered with the French troops signing up for de Gaulle. We embarked for home, arriving just in time for a spot of Christmas leave.

Fred Musson fills in the story of Madagascar:

Majunga, on the Mozambique Channel side of the island, was our first objective. No. 2 Troop were taken by Eurekas up the river to cut off any Vichy forces retreating from Majunga. As we travelled up the river the tide began to go out and we began to run aground on sandbanks. The river was full of crocodiles, so before we could get into the water to lighten the craft and push them off the sandbanks, hand grenades were thrown into the river to keep the crocodiles at bay. Eventually, we reached our destination, but there were no retreating French. We learned later the main force of the Commando had overcome all opposition with some fierce machine-gun fire.

Major Holt:

After spasmodic street fighting the garrison of Majunga surrendered. The formal surrender of the Government at the city of Tamatave took place a few days later. However, this operation was not completed until several determined groups of French soldiers in the area of Antisrane had been overcome. The second-in-command of the Commando, with some sixty officers and soldiers, many of whom were mounted on locally procured horses, moved south, and after a series of dawn ambushes and fighting patrols, this detachment rounded up the French soldiers. There was no further resistance to the British occupation, and shortly afterwards, No. 5 re-embarked on its ships and sailed back to the UK, before being sent out to the Far East.

These Commando raids were clearly causing considerable vexation to the enemy. Apart from the major operations listed in this chapter, small parties were crossing the Channel almost every night and these small raids continued into the autumn, when No. 2 Commando attacked a Norwegian power station in November and did a lot of damage before withdrawing. A month earlier, on the night of 3/4 October, the Small Scale Raiding Force and some men of No. 12 Commando went ashore on the island of Sark in the Channel Islands, an operation which had some far-reaching effects.

A number of distinguished Commando officers took part in this raid: Captain Ogden-Smith, later to recce the Normandy invasion beaches with the Combined Operations Pilotage party (COPP); Captains Pinkney, Appleyard and Dudgeon and the fighting Dane, Anders Lassen, who was to win a posthumous VC at Lake Comacchio in 1945. This small force broke into the Dixcart Hotel on Sark, then a German command post, and took five prisoners, tying their hands and leading them to the beach. On the way the five attempted to escape, and four were shot down.

The discovery of their bodies, hands tied, gave Hitler the excuse to issue the infamous 'Commando Order', instructing his commanders that 'all Commando soldiers were to be hunted down and killed, that no prisoners were to be taken and if any were taken they were not to be sent to the usual prison camps but handed over to the SD – the Gestapo – for interrogation and execution.

When this order was distributed throughout the Wehrmacht, General Jodl, the overall commander, added a note: 'This order is intended for senior commanders only and is on no account to fall into the hands of the enemy.' Even so, news of the 'Commando Order' soon became known to the Commandos. It made no difference to their operations, which continued with mounting intensity. The 'Commando Order' was invoked to shoot the Royal Marines taken prisoner after Operation Frankton, the canoe raid on Bordeaux, and from October 1942 until the end of the war, many Commando and SAS soldiers were executed under its provisions.

For example, Captain Graham Hayes of the Small Scale Raiding Force, captured on an SSRF raid in September 1942, managed to escape to Spain, only to be arrested there, handed back to the Germans and shot, in July 1943. Two other soldiers captured on this operation, Sergeant Williams and Private Leonard, were shot the day after they surrendered. The SSRF suffered heavy casualties; almost all the founder officers, Captain Peter Pinkney, Gus March-Phillips, Anders Lassen VC and many others failed to survive the war.

7

TORCH AND TUNISIA, 1942

'The essence of war is violence; moderation in war is imbecility.'

Lord Macaulay, 1831

Operation Torch, the Allied landings on the west and north coasts of Africa in November 1942, was designed to sandwich the German forces between the British Eighth advancing from El Alamein and First Army coming from the west. Torch was originally envisaged as a purely American affair. The Vichy government were still hostile to the British but it was hoped that if an American force came ashore in North Africa, Vichy French resistance to the landings would be slight.

Two of the landings, at Casablanca and Oran, were made by American forces only, the troops convoyed directly from the USA. The third landing, at Algiers, was made by a mixed force of British and American troops. Apart from British Commandos, from Nos 1 and 6 Commando, the force included American Rangers, the US equivalent of the Commandos, some of whom had participated in the Dieppe raid, and many US Ranger units had trained at Achnacarry.

The British Algiers force was composed of two British Commando units, No. 1, commanded by Lieutenant-Colonel Tom Trevor, and No. 6 Commando under Lieutenant-Colonel

I. F. McAlpine, who embarked for this operation at Belfast and began to go ashore at Algiers early on the morning of 8 November 1942. No. 6 Commando sailed as a complete unit but No. 1 Commando was divided into two parts for Operation Torch; one half under Lieutenant-Colonel Trevor sailed on the SS *Otranto*, the other on an American ship, the USS *Leedstown*. CSM Henry Brown of No. 1 Commando, remembers the *Leedstown* well:

> As a warrant officer I was allowed to eat in the Officers' Mess. Although a good sailor, I was not feeling all that brilliant as the ship was rolling about, but I thought I could manage bacon and eggs. A US Colonel asked me to pass him the molasses which he promptly poured over his bacon and eggs. I was up on my feet and moving much quicker, to find the nearest spot on the deck-rail.

CSM Edmans of No. 1 Commando remembers the landing:

> We boarded at Larne, sailed after some days and when we got to our destination we boarded our LCAs and went ashore, with shells coming over our heads. Later on, when the Navy were shelling the fort, we were too near and got hit by our own naval gunfire, which caused casualties. To maintain the fiction that this was a purely American affair, the British troops wore American helmets, carried Garand rifles and were brigaded with the US 168th Regimental Combat Team.

No. 1's plan for the Algiers landing called for the CO, Lieutenant-Colonel Trevor, to take half the unit and land on the right flank at Cap Sidi Ferruch, ten miles west of Algiers, and capture a fort. This they achieved without a shot being fired, capturing, among other notables, the German ambassador to the Vichy government in North Africa and his family. With that achieved, Tom Trevor took his half Commando off to capture the airfield at Blida.

The other half of No. 1, under the unit's second-in-command, Major Ken Trevor, were not so lucky. Their task was to capture the Fort d'Estres, on the left flank of the landing area, and a coastal defence battery, the Batterie de Lazerete. They landed in a heavy onshore swell and in the wrong place, and the French forces defending the fort and the battery put up a stiff fight. At 11:00 hours Major Trevor called for naval gunfire support which came swiftly from a destroyer, but the shell salvos fell by error on the Commando positions, causing many casualties. The fort was finally dive-bombed by the Fleet Air Arm in the early afternoon and only after that did the garrison surrender.

Landing on the wrong beach was an all-too-common problem, and one that Commando units were to endure for much of the war. This was not always the Navy's fault: visibility from an LCA is very restricted, most landings were made at night, compasses could be faulty and the crews were not always well trained. In an attempt to reduce the number of errors, navigation beacons were often provided, sometimes by submarine, sometimes by canoe parties, who went in ahead of the main assault to mark the beaches. Commandos of 101 Troop, No. 6 Commando, carried out just such a task here for the American Rangers landing at Oran.

No. 6 Commando barely had time to celebrate the successful conclusion of a rather mixed first day when it was called back to the beach and, together with a force of US Rangers, embarked on two British destroyers and sent to seize airfields near the port of Bone, 250 miles east of Algiers, in an attempt to forestall German intervention from Tunisia. No. 6 Commando reached Bone on 11 November and marched on to the airfield just as the first troops of 3 Para, from the British 1st Airborne Brigade, landed on the airfield, having flown in from Gibraltar.

The Allied build-up around Bone continued, with No. 1 Commando arriving on 18 November. Four days later, Stuka dive-bombers arrived over Bone and the expected German counter-attack began, so No. 6 Commando advanced to meet the approaching enemy near Tabarka, 60 miles farther east, in Tunisia. It travelled to Tabarka by train, being strafed twice by enemy fighters on the way, and suffering nearly 50 casualties, before detraining and moving into the hills near Sedjenane and digging in.

C. L. G. Bryen remembers this journey and noted the event in his diary:

22 November, Sunday. Making good headway. Stopped at Morris, where we made tea and picked oranges from the groves. Spitfire escort from Bone with us, but forced to return to refuel every half hour. At 10:15 hours two FW 190s flew very low down the length of the train firing machine guns and cannon. The train pulled up but men jumped out while it was still in motion, many being dragged beneath the wheels and mangled. Grenades which were packed on open wagons were detonated by the cannon shells. Result: eleven men killed and twenty-five badly injured, twenty-two less seriously hurt.

T. S. M. Barlow, like several other men, had been cut to ribbons on falling beneath the wheels. The Arab driver took to the hills and did not return. Troops lay up at El Tarf until dusk, when two Troops went on to La Calle by train, one of our lance-corporals driving, to attack an enemy tank harbour, holding up the advance of First Army. The rest of the Commando marched eighteen miles to La Calle which we reached in a pretty tired condition and slept in a school. A day to be remembered.

It was now the end of November and the North African weather was atrocious, with very cold nights and continuous torrential rain. During this period the First Army, led by the 78th Division, was moving towards Tunis, and the leading Battalion, the 8th Argyll & Sutherland Highlanders, clashed with the German defenders ten miles east of Sedjenane, the enemy being entrenched here astride the road on two features, Bald Hill and Green Hill, where the Argylls suffered heavy casualties in attempting to force a passage.

On 30 November, No. 6 Commando was ordered up to attack the German positions on Green Hill, while another infantry battalion went for Bald Hill. Four troops attacked Green Hill at 04:00 hours on the 30th, and met with fierce resistance from an enemy well equipped with heavy and medium machine guns. After repeated attempts to consolidate its small advances, the Commando withdrew, with the loss of another eighty men, which forced the unit to reorganise into four small rifle troops.

C. L. G. Bryen's diary again:

29 November, Sunday. Warned in the afternoon that MG nests were holding up the 36th Brigade at Green Hill, Jaffna. Four troops of Commando ordered to attack and capture the hill. Made a hurriedly formed plan without a good recce. Did not take American steel helmets owing to their resemblance to German ones. Moved forward by MT in the evening; debussed a mile from Green Hill and crept into position at 20:00 hours. Plan was for 5 Troop to put in a feint attack at 04:00 hours, while 3, 4, and 6 Troops came up over the top of the hill, and dealt with the MG nests.

Dead Argylls lying everywhere, with British equipment and rifles, etc. Going pretty hard, across several ploughed fields and Arab villages. Troop in position by 22:00 hours and waited for zero hour.

30 November, Monday. Zero hour 04:00 hours, and no sign of any enemy, so opened up with LMG and rifle and mortar fire. This, we learnt later, only had the effect of waking up the enemy, who then opened fire with the machine guns on their fixed lines. Nos 3 and 4 Troops came over the hill, but were unable to penetrate the deadly fire of the machine guns and lost several men in the attempt. When day came, several more attempts on the hill, but we were forced back every time, the enemy changing his position constantly. The Buffs, who were attacking Bald Hill at the same time, were meeting with better success, and the Royal West Kents were pushing on.

11:00 hours. My section were sent to the north side of the hill to cut off any enemy who might try and withdraw during the attacks. Royal Artillery came up and gave us supporting barrage, but enemy so well dug in that the shells had no effect on them. Captain Mayne recalled all Commando to top of hill at 13:00 hours in an attempt to capture the hill by following creeping barrage, but the section were ambushed by Afrika Korps soldiers disguised as Arabs, and we split up, only five men reaching the top of Green Hill. Attack was pushed in, with five men of 5 Troop in reserve, 67 men in all making the attack. Artillery ammunition ran very low and Captain Mayne forced to withdraw his men to foot of hill.

Captain Scott shot through the head while taking on a machine gun. Heavy rain came on, and force withdrew to Brigade HQ to re-form, carrying several wounded, but leaving dead and badly wounded. Could not contact Z Section, 5 Troop, so were forced to leave them out. Hot meal at Brigade HQ and back to Sedjenane by MT. Troops very exhausted, having had no rest.

Frank Barton continues this story:

The Germans seemed to be using numerous Spandaus against us, and were firing just above our heads on what appeared to be fixed lines. We couldn't get anywhere near them without being mowed down and in the end we had to withdraw. We made another assault in the afternoon but again with no success. In the two attacks we lost 80 men and were reduced to four troops. Then Lieutenant-Colonel McAlpine was taken ill and replaced by Lieutenant-Colonel Mills-Roberts. After this came the battle at Steam-roller Farm, where I was taken prisoner.

Sergeant Blackburn of No. 6 Commando saw the attack on Green Hill:

For the last attempt on Green Hill (which never fell, in spite of several attempts by our Commando and the main force) our troop was given the task of occupying a neighbouring feature – I think it was called Sugarloaf – from

111

where we could see and hear the main attack on Green Hill. That attempt also failed and we were ordered to withdraw under cover of darkness. Unfortunately, we had wounded men who could not make the journey out, so our section stretcher bearer volunteered to remain with them and be taken prisoner, a very noble and brave act. This stretcher bearer was to return to 6 Commando later, under curious circumstances.

In early January, the unit attacked Green Hill yet again, losing its CO, Lieutenant-Colonel McAlpine. No. 6 Commando, much reduced, was re-formed into four depleted troops under a new CO, Major McLeod, who led the unit until Lieutenant-Colonel Derek Mills-Roberts arrived from the UK after scrounging lifts on various aircraft through Gibraltar and Algiers, hitching lifts on trucks, finally reaching his Commando HQ, which was established in a railway tunnel, on foot.

While No. 6 Commando was fighting for Green Hill, No. 1 Commando, with four American infantry companies under command, had been brought forward for a raid behind the enemy lines, with the task of cutting the enemy communications and feeding men forward to the rear of the German lines around Green Hill.

Charles Hustwick was now serving with the HQ of No. 1 Commando:

We went on to landing craft for Tabarka. The town had been knocked about quite a bit. First Army had now ground to a halt but were anxious to capture the port at Bizerta, so it was decided to send 1 Commando in along the coast, to cut inland, sit on the main road and cut the supply line to the enemy forward troops. We had donkeys on this operation, to carry the 3-inch mortars, but they were last seen swimming out to sea; not one made it to the beach anyway.

We waited all day for the Army to come up, but no joy – and wireless communication was impossible. The enemy discovered our existence and some right tussles took place,

112

causing a lot of casualties for the Commando but on the other hand we took a lot of prisoners. We eventually withdrew to our own lines, spending two days and nights on the march with almost no food. We lived off the land, with a slaughtered stray sheep or two to keep us going . . . and so back to Tabarka.

For this operation No. 1 Commando landed at 03:00 hours on the morning of 1 December, and divided into two, as at Algiers, under the CO and second-in-command, Ken and Tom Trevor. It advanced five miles inland behind the enemy lines without encountering any opposition. By first light the men were astride the main inland road from Bizerta to Tabarka, which they held shut for the next three days, shooting up any enemy transport that came along, beating off attacks by local forces, dominating over one hundred square miles of enemy-held territory with fighting patrols, but at a price; No. 1 lost 60 men, the Americans 74 men, before withdrawing to their own lines.

During December No. 1 Commando, previously in ten troops, with their American allies on the unit strength, reorganised into six troops and spent time serving in the line as ordinary infantry, a role for which lightly equipped Commando units are not well suited.

Charles Hustwick again:

We were then used as infantry of the line. It was very hard work for our numbers were getting less and less and when our American friends had finally been withdrawn, we had a problem holding our line. We spent Christmas in the line and the weather was terrible – very cold, and raining all the time, not a bit like the Africa you read about at school.

CSM Edmans, now with 6 Troop of No. 1 Commando, recalls one sharp little fight during this period in the line:

We were deployed, facing down a track with 2 Troop on our left. After a while we saw Afrika Korps troops jumping

113

across the track right to left, too far to shoot, so we waited patiently – Felmingham and Freddie Witton, the Bren-gun team, Fusilier Wales with a Garand rifle, myself with a Tommy-gun. Suddenly someone shouted 'Enemy left' and there, coming through the bushes, was a German. He fired a burst, hitting Freddie in the stomach, Sergeant Smith in the back, and Lance-Sergeant Sims in the knee, before Felmingham turned and killed him.

We reckoned they had got behind us, so Sergeant Smith said, 'Get out, more are coming!' So we got out, running back through the smoke, with enemy bullets helping us on our way. Freddie was in great pain, but we reached HQ and gave our report. Then, leaving a rearguard, we walked seven miles to a hospital. Freddie walked those seven miles with a stomach wound, sucking a wet handkerchief and gripping hard on his Colt .45. You could see he was in great pain but we could not let him sit down.

No. 1 Commando was joined in its endeavours here by a reinforcement of sixty-five American soldiers who had all been with the Commando on Operation Bizerta and volunteered to stay with No. 1 during the campaign. No. 1 and No. 6 Commando stayed in North Africa until the end of April 1941, returning to the line again and again, and becoming notably skilled at fighting patrols.

Lieutenant-Colonel Derek Mills-Roberts's No. 6 Commando was attached to the 78th Division in mid-January 1943 and he decided to dominate its part of the line by aggressive patrolling, having first established the unit – now reduced to about 250 men – in strongpoints. On one occasion, a No. 6 Commando patrol bumped into a strong patrol from the Hermann Goering Jaeger Parachute Regiment. The two patrols became heavily engaged with both sides feeding in men to bolster their front lines and the battle ended when No. 6 Commando forced the German regiment to withdraw after a five-hour battle, most of it at very close quarters.

Frank Barton was captured at this battle, known to the Commando history as the battle of Steamroller Farm:

There was a steamroller in the farmyard, so hence the name. Lieutenant Bonnin was badly injured there and I was captured while tending him. I was eventually sent to Italy and to Campo 66 near Capua where I met my brother who had been captured in 1942 near Tobruk. In September 1943, after the Italians surrendered, we managed to escape and reached the Allied lines, walking mostly by night in a southerly direction, but also slightly east to get inland a little – it took two months but we made it.

We got a rough direction by the stars, finding the Plough and then the North Star. The Italians helped us as much as they could with food and we found plenty of mushrooms, which we roasted. In November we knew we were getting somewhere near the front line from the amount of Germans we had to hide from. We had one narrow escape when a German came looking along the hedge bottom where we were hiding. Anyway, after about two-and-a-half months' walking, we reached the British lines, and eventually we were repatriated back to England where, after leave and a lot of persuasion, I managed to rejoin 6 Commando who were then at Brighton. I had first landed with them in North Africa and then I landed with them on D-Day and served right through to the end of the war in 1945, so really I did not miss many of 6 Commando's actions.

No. 6 Commando lost forty per cent of its men in the Steamroller Farm engagement, but severely mauled two battalions of the enemy and forced them to a halt, until the enemy were driven back to their own lines by battalions from the Coldstream Guards and the Royal Sussex Regiment. For this action Mills-Roberts was awarded the DSO.

In North Africa, as previously in Crete, the Commandos were used as line infantry, a role for which they lacked both the manpower and the necessary equipment. Their problems were compounded by the fact that they received no reinforcements and were steadily reduced in numbers until, in early April 1943, they were taken out of the line, and after a few days' rest in Algiers finally embarked for the United Kingdom.

Corporal Hustwick sums up the end of the Tunisian campaign:

From the railhead at Souk-el-Arbaive both Commandos went in horse trucks back to Algiers. On arrival there, we camped in a wood about eight miles south of the city and had some lively nights out in Algiers before embarking. We came home to Liverpool in six days, unescorted, getting bombed by Focke-Wulf Condors off the coast of Ireland. Incidentally, before leaving Algiers we scoured all the hospitals for our men and made sure that all our wounded who could move discharged themselves and came home with us – and then we all got fourteen days' leave.

8

SICILY AND ITALY, 1943

'All the business of war is to endeavour to find out what you don't know by what you do . . . that's what I call "guessing what's on the other side of the hill".'

The Duke of Wellington, 1815

With the opening of the Italian campaign in 1943, which began with landings in Sicily, the Commandos were to take on two roles which would occupy them for the rest of the war, landing in the van of major invasions and serving in the line alongside other larger infantry units. Much of this work took the form of pushing ahead of the advancing allied armies, to see what opposition lay behind the beaches or the range of coastal hills.

In Italy the Army Commandos also found themselves brigaded for the first time with the Royal Marine Commando units, and the Commando units now assembling for the campaigns in Sicily and Italy consisted of Nos 2, 3 and (later) 9 Army Commando, and Nos 40, 41 and (later) 43 (Royal Marine) Commando.

A number of contributors to this book have stressed that while all Army Commandos were composed of volunteers, the Royal Marine Commando units were mostly Royal Marine battalions made over into Commando units. This is only partly true. No. 40 Commando was an all-volunteer unit and no Army Commando has a bad word to say about those Marines with whom he was brigaded in the field. For their part, the Marines have nothing but praise for their Army Commando comrades and the Army units.

Nos 41 and 43 (Royal Marine) Commando fought alongside Army Commando units in Italy, notably at Salerno and in the Adriatic, and both were largely volunteer units. The Royal Marine Commando units which formed later were indeed 'made-over' battalions, but the men in them still had to undergo training at Achnacarry, and the RTU was swiftly applied to those who failed to meet the exacting Commando standard. The Corps of Royal Marines expanded to a strength of 80,000 men during the Second World War, and had plenty of vacant posts for men who had no taste for Commando soldiering.

No. 2 Commando now had a new CO in Jack Churchill. One of his officers was Captain R. I. Bavister, who volunteered for Commando service in 1942:

I was interviewed by the CO, second-in-command and Adjutant and was accepted subject to dropping to my substantive rank, given a set of black-and-white '2 Commando' shoulder-flashes and sent on leave. The Commando had black-and-white flashes until the Combined Operations' red-and-blue flashes replaced them. The daily routine was weapon training and physical fitness, with lots of route marching.

Unlike many others, I never did the course at Achnacarry. The Commando had a distinctly Lancashire flavour about it when I joined, a hangover from the old Independent Company days. We had a number of exercises in the Highlands in the vicinity of Loch Fyne, acting as enemy to American troops training for the North African landing.

I missed these by being sent on a three-inch mortar course and being in hospital. I also got friendly with a Royal Marines officer – the next time I met him was when he was in charge of the assault craft taking my section into

Scaletta in Italy – the first time I fired or directed a mortar shoot. The CO was, of course, 'Mad Jack' Churchill, a striking-looking man of thirty-five or so, with very fair hair, moustache and eyebrows. When the Commando was issued with the green beret in the winter of 1943, they wore it like a Scottish bonnet, pulled forward rather than over to the side as prescribed by the War Office.

No. 3 Commando's task during the invasion of Sicily was to land from HMS *Prince Albert* south of Syracuse and capture a battery of coastal artillery at Avola, three miles inland, near the town of Cassibile. The assault began at midnight on 10 July after managing to avoid landing on the wrong beach. 'I am more than ever certain,' wrote Laycock afterwards, 'that we can never expect to land where we wish.' Although there was some machine-gun fire, No. 3 got ashore dry and without loss and captured the battery without trouble. The two Royal Marine Commando units also carried out their tasks successfully, killing some fifty Italians and taking many prisoners.

No. 3's next operation was a raid on 13 July. This did not go so smoothly, for the Commando encountered fierce opposition from élite German forces. No. 3's task was to land at Agnone, several miles behind the enemy front line, and then push inland to the Punta dei Milati bridge over the Leonardo river, seven miles from the sea. At around the same time a parachute force would seize another bridge at Primasole. If both these bridges could be held, then the advancing Allied army could make a rapid advance towards Catania.

Durnford Slater was given just *three hours* to plan this operation and on the quayside at Syracuse, he had been informed that the landing beaches and the bridge were held by Italian troops. Durnford Slater was not so sure. He felt that if the bridge was worth taking it was worth guarding, and his plan called for a landing in two flights, the first of 1, 2, 3 and 4 Troops, the second of 5 and 6 Troops. The unit was then to advance and seize the bridge while one Troop went north to contact the paratroopers at Primasole and another went south to contact 50 Division who were to reach the bridge by first light next day. In fact the area was held by the 1st German Parachute Division and this time No. 3 Commando was up against opponents worthy of their steel.

No. 3 Commando began to land at 22:00 hours, meeting opposition from machine-gun posts before it even got ashore. Abandoning all hope of surprise, No. 3's Brens and the landing-craft guns engaged the defences and the troops went ashore under fire. Some confusion on the beach was rapidly sorted out by Major Peter Young and Lieutenant George Herbert, and the unit reached the bridge at about 03:00 hours, bumping on the way into a section of paratroops, dropped well wide of their mark.

No. 3 was already taking casualties, including Walter Skrine, shot in the leg, and Captain Leese of 1 Troop, shot in the eye. The pillboxes at either end of the bridge were manned by Italians, too busy talking to hear the stealthy approach of the Commandos, and they were quickly disposed of by grenades. No. 3 Commando was then deployed about the bridge, either in the pillboxes or in the surrounding orange groves and ravines, where the men constructed small defensive 'sangars' with rocks, as the ground was too hard for digging in. Then they sat down, ten miles behind the enemy lines, to await events – or 50 Division. There were perhaps 350 men in all, armed only with platoon weapons: rifles, pistols, sten guns, Bren light machine guns and grenades.

Until dawn No. 3 Commando had a great time, shooting up everything which came along, until the approaches to the bridge were littered with overturned or burning vehicles; but the Germans began to mortar their positions heavily and soon brought up a Tiger tank, which began to flay the Commando positions with its 88mm gun, while staying sensibly beyond the range of their only anti-tank weapon, the infantry PIAT. A party sent to stalk the tank could not get close enough over the open ground, and German paratroopers were moving up to 'box-in' the troops, causing a steady stream of casualties.

By 04:30 hours, with no sign of 50 Division, the Commando position was becoming untenable. It had many wounded, its positions in the open valley were enfiladed, enemy infantry were arriving in ever-increasing numbers and the tank kept appearing at regular intervals to put down more fire. Eventually Durnford Slater gave the order to split into small parties and withdraw, leaving their wounded behind, to be well looked after by the men of the Hermann Goering Parachute Division – a kindness the Commando was able to repay at Termoli a few weeks later. No. 3 Commando lost a lot of men on this operation; 5 officers and 23 men killed, 4 officers and 62 men wounded, and 8 officers and 51 men missing, although some of these came in later.

A week later, No. 2 Commando arrived in Sicily, and while Brigadier Laycock went to North Africa, Durnford Slater took command of No. 2 SS Brigade, which now consisted of Nos 2, 3, 40 (Royal Marine) and 41 (Royal Marine) Commando, and the Special Raiding Squadron under Major Paddy Mayne. No. 2 Commando's first operation was a landing at Scaletta which Ted Kelly recalls:

> I wish I could record that it was a successful demonstration of a combined operation. What it cost I shudder to think, but the fact is we landed on the wrong beach and far too late to catch the forces we were supposed to contain. What we encountered were two truckloads of German Army personnel, the tail-enders. These luckless few had us all to themselves, including the nightmarish sight of Colonel 'Mad Jack' Churchill's claymore, waved in their faces with suitable oaths. At daybreak we assembled for the task of chasing the Germans and after a quiet start met German mortar fire and we knew that our war had now really started.

Once Sicily had fallen, all the units prepared for the attack on the Italian mainland. For this operation No. 2 SS Brigade was split between the two invasion forces. Nos 3 and 40 were to cross the Straits of Messina with 13th Corps of the British Eighth Army while No. 2 and No. 41 were to join 10th Corps of the American Fifth Army for the assault on Salerno.

The British 13th Corps, with Nos 3 and 40 Commando and Paddy Mayne's Special Raiding Squadron, crossed the Straits

on the night of 3 September 1943, and made rapid progress ↑
Vibo Valentia which they took on 9 September. At 03:3↑
hours, the US Fifth Army, consisting of the British 10th an↑
the American 7th Corps, began to land at Salerno, whe↑
No. 2 Commando and No. 41 Commando found themselve↑
involved in one of the toughest battles of the entire Italia↑
campaign.

The Germans had anticipated a landing at Salerno an↑
were dug in on the hills above the beaches when the Fift↑
Army came ashore. For the Fifth Army to get off the landin↑
beaches and capture Naples, they must first take a gap in th↑
encircling hills, called the pass of La Molina. No. 2 Com↑
mando came ashore in the first wave, to clear the beaches an↑
secure the bridgehead. Then No. 41 and Brigade Headquar↑
ters landed and this force pushed on to La Molina with th↑
task of taking the pass. No. 2 and Brigade HQ moved into th↑
village of Vietri at the seaward end of the pass while No. 4↑
advanced into the pass itself. Two troops of No. 2 Com↑
mando, one commanded by Captain the Duke of Wellington↑
occupied the northern suburbs of Salerno, where they soor↑
met enemy tanks and infantry.

Meanwhile the rest of the landing was not going at all well↑
The beaches were under heavy shellfire and the Luftwaffe↑
appeared to bomb and strafe the offshore shipping. The↑
bombing and shelling intensified and before long the Ger-↑
mans were attacking the beach perimeter with tanks and↑
infantry. German counter-attacks, supported by artillery and↑
tanks, began to develop all around the bridgehead and heavy↑
mortar fire was soon falling on the No. 2 Commando posi-↑
tions at Vietri. These attacks continued throughout the day↑
with a major counter-offensive clearly building around the↑
beachhead.

Ken McAllister of No. 2 Commando took part in this↑
landing:

It would take a big fat book to relate our experiences at↑
Salerno. It was sixteen days of pure hell and both 2 Com-↑
mando and 41 suffered heavily. The name Commando and

our reputation seemed to convey to the commanders that we were to be used wherever the enemy looked like breaking through. I think it is a wonder any of us lived to tell the tale.

Dudley Cooper, MM, saw action at Salerno:

After landing we went up into the hills. The fighting round Vietri was hard, German mortars, 88s and Spandaus made things difficult, and part of one troop was behind the German lines at one time. They made their way out and back to reform and hold. Day and night became as one, and when we had held and settled the battle, we were withdrawn further south and allowed a night's sleep, except for those on guard duty, which I was on. I sat on a balcony and listened to the fighting all round us going on all night, but most of the men slept through it, they were so tired.

Next day we were lined up on each side of a valley where the Germans had thrown back and mauled the Ox and Bucks Light Infantry. Moving off from the start line under the hills, we went up the valley until it came out at Pigoletti, where the men on the south side crept into the village and captured the Germans and their Commandant in a short, sharp battle. We dug in at the top of the hill, overlooking the road to Naples, listening to traffic below. During the next hour we were shelled with air bursts at the trees and lost two men from our section. It was unanimously decided that things were too hot, so we moved into a position on our right.

We were grabbing a little shut-eye on a patio, when the hill above us was shelled. It later turned out to be our own 25-pounder guns which were firing on the wrong hill. As there was no sleep to be had, we rounded the patio wall to find six of our lads had been killed by one shell. We watched the attack of 2 Troop and noted a particular position of two German machine guns. Next morning, while things were quiet, three of us went up to the first floor of a house and, with binoculars, pinpointed a position where we believed the machine guns to be. We set up a Bren and fired on the position and could see bullets raking the parapet – we had no trouble from them again; Willy Neild saw a German get up and run across the hill and at an estimated range of 800 yards he downed him with a rifle shot.

To prove it was no fluke he later hit another on the road below at the same distance. This got him the job of sniper, and he hated being anything other than a rifleman in a troop with his mates. In the afternoon, noise was heard coming up the hill and a Tiger tank came over, moving in the direction of Pigoletti. Those of us in the house were looking straight down the barrel of the tank's gun, when we heard our mortars fire. The first shot landed right on top of the turret and stopped it dead. By the time the Salerno fighting ended there had been eleven days' constant action, but the beachhead was stable.

At La Molina, No. 41 Commando stood off repeated attacks on their positions, infantry assaults interspersed with heavy shelling and mortaring. A direct hit on the Commando HQ wounded the CO, Lieutenant-Colonel Bertie Lumsden, and attacks on No. 41 continued throughout the day, the last being driven off by a 'Q' Troop counter-attack. No. 2 Commando endured infiltration attacks, with machine-gunning, mortaring and shelling, until at midnight on the 10th both units were relieved and withdrew to the shore for a brief rest – just eight hours – and then they went back in again.

While the Germans pounded the beachhead with artillery, both Commandos returned to their old sangars and trenches at Vietri and La Molina and held them without rest until the dawn of 13 September, when the enemy bombarded No. 2 for an hour and put in a strong infantry attack against both flanks. By now, No. 2 had been fighting for four days and been reduced to no more than 300 very weary men, and No. 41 Commando had already lost eleven officers, including the CO, and 74 men. The enemy managed to force their way past Vietri and were in position to take the commanding feature on Dragone Hill in the Commando's rear, when they were checked by artillery fire and a counter-attack from the brigade reserve, which consisted of one troop each from Nos 2 and 41 Commando – about 100 men. The reserve's advance proved sufficient to halt the enemy and the Germans retreated again into the La Molina pass while the Commandos were again withdrawn back to the beach. This time they were out of the line for a whole day.

The two units were called back to the line on the 15th, and sent to assault the village of Pigoletti, overlooking the landing beaches. Pigoletti is a hilltop village dominated by two other hills, with another high crag to the east. No. 41 Commando attacked and took this crag, naming it 41 Commando Hill, while No. 2 Commando advanced up the steep valley to Pigoletti itself, led by Colonel Jack, sword in hand. The colonel eventually got so far ahead of his Commando, who were clearing enemy positions, that he entered Pigoletti accompanied by just one man, Corporal Ruffell. The two of them overran a German mortar position and, taking one of the prisoners with him as interpreter, Colonel Jack went on to clear the village by himself, sending forty prisoners back into the arms of 6 Troop. By that night No. 2 had captured 136 prisoners and Colonel Jack received the DSO to add to his Military Cross.

No. 2 was then tasked to advance through Pigoletti again, and seize a hill behind it, known as 'The Pimple'. This attack was led by Captain the Duke of Wellington, but it was met with a hail of machine-gun fire and grenades which decimated the advancing troops and killed the Duke. W. G. Bleach remembers the Duke:

He was OC 2 Troop, at Vietri and later at the Pimple. His batman, Tommy Tombs, Syd Crane the signaller, and I were once pinned down in a cave opposite the viaduct at Vietri, and stuck there for two days. Syd got out to try and find some food and returned unsuccessful, so the Duke got out the last tin of 'K' rations from his pouch and passed it to Tommy to share out. Tommy cut it into four pieces, but the Duke said, 'No, not for me, I'm not hungry' . . . and he said it with such conviction that we all believed him.

Next morning, No. 2 linked up with No. 41, still clinging to their hill on the flank. Both units were then heavily shelled, first by German 88s, then by their own artillery, which put down a concentration on No. 41 Commando just as it was about to put in its attack against the Pimple. This barrage cost the life of 41's new CO, Major Edwards, its second commanding officer in three days. No. 41 managed to get one troop on to the Pimple and they held it for twenty-four hours, until the last six men still alive and unwounded were withdrawn.

Ted Kelly recalls Salerno:

The night before the landing was due we heard of the Italian surrender on the radio. We thought that this called for a celebration in preparation for the hysterical welcome we would surely receive, so we ate the hard chocolate and sweets which constituted our emergency ration. Our landing at Vietri was on schedule but the Germans were waiting for us and we were quite hungry when supplies started to come through two days later. Early in the landing we were on a hill above Salerno overlooking a valley. German tanks could be seen far below. One of our men opened up with a Bren gun, which seemed to me to be a noble but fairly useless gesture and as a result our position came under fire from the tanks' 80mm guns. A tank shell burst above us not more than fifteen feet away. I saw the actual burst. It was like those artists' impressions of Great War shellbursts – a fiery centre with shrapnel radiating from it. Both my mates, Stan and Tim were hit. Tim lost an arm, Stan died. I didn't even get dust in my eyes.

At the height of the German counter-attack, we were in close combat and under severe pressure. Support was requested from the Navy and was quickly forthcoming. The gunfire was accurate and shells landed among us. Nothing the Germans threw at us was ever like this. Naval shells exploding a few feet away lifted me bodily out of my trench. To paraphrase – I don't know what it did to the Germans, but it scared the hell out of me! On the fourteenth day of the action I went down with malaria and was removed to hospital, where I remained when No. 2 Commando were withdrawn. I fretted to rejoin them and managed to do so at Bari.

The Salerno battle was a very close-run thing and at one point General Mark Clark, the US commanding general, was seriously considering an evacuation. Nos 2 and 41 Commando played an outstanding part in holding the line while the German positions were pounded by the guns of the fleet. The British Eighth Army finally linked up with the American Fifth Army on 20 September, and Naples fell ten days later.

Landing operations along the Italian coast had this much in common; it was usually possible to get ashore undetected, or in the face of slight opposition – Salerno being the notable exception – but then, after a short delay of anything from a few hours to a day, the Germans would hit back.

'I've fought a lot of people in my time,' says Brigadier Peter Young, 'but if you haven't fought Germans you don't know what fighting is. However hard they were pressed, they usually found something to sling at you.' This fact was borne out in the next two battles in which the Commandos took part after John Durnford Slater was promoted to brigadier and took over command for the landing at Termoli.

Termoli is a small port at the mouth of the Bifurno river on the east coast of Italy, ten miles behind the enemy lines and in front of the Eighth Army units which were now advancing up the east side of Italy at a smart clip. Italy is a country where the terrain favours defence, and one of the finest defensive lines available lay along the Bifurno. To prevent the German Army digging in behind the river, General Montgomery decided to send Durnford Slater's force, No. 3 Commando, No. 40 Commando and the SRS to take Termoli and hold it until the Eighth Army came up.

This operation was codenamed Devon, and the assault force sailed from Manfredonia at 11:30 hours on 2 October 1943. Intelligence information was scanty, but No. 3 Commando was intrigued to learn that its most likely opponents would be men from the German parachute unit it had met at the Punta dei Milati. The force went ashore some time after midnight, No. 3 getting a dry landing, No. 40 meeting a deep gully behind a 'false beach' offshore, drowning all their radio sets as they waded in through the deep water beyond. Some of the SRS even had to swim. Nevertheless, in the face of light opposition, they soon overran the town and were in their positions by 08:00 hours, having taken some 500 prisoners, most of them – ominously – from the 4th German Parachute Brigade.

By 09:30 hours No. 40 Commando was in position astride a road outside the town, happily shooting up enemy transport; No. 3 Commando was in the town; and the SRS had already made contact with a battalion of Lancashire Fusiliers from the Eighth Army. Reinforcements from 78 Division crossed the Bifurno and moved into the town throughout the next day and all the next night. Then, about noon on 4 October, after a quiet morning, the Germans hit back – hard.

Durnford Slater was having lunch when one of his officers, John Pooley, reported 'dozens' of enemy tanks approaching, and put his men on full alert. The pressure on the Termoli perimeter became intense when the constant rain raised the level of the Bifurno and carried away the only bridge linking the garrison with the Eighth Army. The Germans were now on the offensive and tanks from a fresh German armoured formation, the 6th Panzer Division, came up to assault the town. This assault began at dawn on the 5th and opened with a bombing and strafing attack by the Luftwaffe. Then artillery concentrations fell in the town, followed by infantry attacks with tank support. By 14:00 hours all the flank units defending Termoli had been overrun and the town's defence was reduced to a core of two infantry battalions and Durnford Slater's small force. A number of units started to fall back and Peter Young, arriving from hospital, and Captain Peter Hellings of No. 40 Commando, had to force some fleeing troops back into position and fire their artillery pieces at the enemy tanks.

'That was about all I did actually,' says Peter Young,

the early days, Commandos paraded wearing items of uniform
i headgear from the individual soldiers' original units. It was
ie time before the distinctive green beret and the Commando
ige were adopted.

Above Lieutenant Colonel The Lord Lovat photographed with his men on their return from the Dieppe raid.

Right Captain Patrick Porteous, shot through the thighs after leading a bayonet charge on a gun position during the Dieppe raid, was awarded the Victoria Cross.

Left No. 45 Commando is inspected by General Laycock, after whom the North African Layforce (7, 8, 11 and the locally raised 50 and 52 Commandos) was named.

Below Monty inspects No. 40 Commando in Italy prior to them going into action during the Lake Commacchio operation.

Above Twice wounded during the D-Day landings, Lieutenant Colonel Dawson is decorated by Monty before rejoining his unit for the assault on Walcheren.

Right Commandos raising their standard in Osnabrück in April 1945. Nos 3 and 45 Commandos launched a night attack and had taken the town, and over 400 prisoners, by dawn.

By the end of the war, the Commandos had roamed as far afield as the Far East and Hong Kong, where they accepted the surrender of countless Japanese.

'because I was in hospital and not at the landing. Arthur Komrower commanded 3 Commando, "Pops" Manners ran 40 Commando, and that huge Irishman, Paddy Mayne, had the SRS . . . and between them they took care of things.'

The enemy thrust hard against the Termoli perimeter, raining mortar fire on the town, and by dusk had moved tanks to within a hundred yards of No. 3 Commando lines to the west of the town and had more infantry even closer to the unit's HQ. No. 3 Commando quietly disengaged and withdrew into Termoli, from where it prepared to fight it out in the streets.

Meanwhile, No. 40 Commando and the SRS were still holding their section of the perimeter and the Commandos continued to hold it until the bridge across the Bifurno was repaired by sappers and the 38th Irish Brigade advanced into the town. No. 40 Commando beat off another tank and infantry attack through the town cemetery on the morning of 6 October and the battle of Termoli was over. 'In the course of numerous actions during the war,' wrote Durnford Slater, 'this was the only time I really thought we might be defeated.'

At the end of October, Nos 3 and 41 Commando and the SRS returned to England to train for D-Day, and their places in 2 SS Brigade were taken by No. 9 Commando and No. 43 (Royal Marine) Commando. In early November 1943, Brigadier Tom Churchill, brother of Jack Churchill, took command of 2 Special Service Brigade, and the brigade was based at Casteliamare, with its HQ at Molfetta.

Brigadier Churchill wanted his new units, No. 9 (Lieutenant-Colonel Ronnie Tod) and the IA Commando troops to gain operational experience as soon as possible, so the Belgians and Poles were attached to infantry units along the line of the River Sangro, where they carried out night patrols, until heavy snowfalls made foot patrols impossible. While they were still in the line, No. 9 Commando opened its batting with a raid across the Garigliano river near the town of Cassino.

The Commando's task was to land from the sea, thus outflanking enemy positions north of the Garigliano, then march inland and destroy a river bridge. This attack had to be made under cover of night, and the attack went in on the beaches on the north side of the river on the night of 29/30 December 1943. Operation Partridge is well described by those who took part and in extracts from the Unit History:

In the previous three years, almost every operation planned for the Commando had been cancelled. In the next three months almost every one planned took place. Fifth Army had now reached the Garigliano, and was held up by a strongly entrenched enemy in the mountains north of the river and further east at Cassino. Three weeks were spent training for the operation, and a full-scale rehearsal was carried out from the LSLs *Princess Beatrix* and *Royal Ulsterman*.

The operation started badly as the Commando were landed 1,000 yards from the correct beach and an hour and a half late. Once ashore, the Commando split into three parties, X, Y and Z, although X was a boatload short as one craft broke down and failed to arrive at the beachhead. Even so, all the attacks went in, Force X sustaining five casualties overrunning an enemy position at the mouth of the Garigliano.

Captain McNeil led Force Y to attack German positions on a hill north of the landing beach where, although suffering casualties from mines on the way, they overran the enemy positions and destroyed a tank. Force Z found that the low country behind the beach was flooded, threaded with wire and sewn with mines, but pushed on to assault the German positions in and around a Roman amphitheatre. After this attack, the troops withdrew to a spot a mile inland from the sea, where a ruined bridge lay across the river, and Captain Mike Long began to guide them across to the British bank.

In Mike Long's words:

The next problem was to get back across the river to our own lines. The total number of our troops was about 90, plus the POWs. The river was about thirty yards wide, but when the bridge was blown, some of the girders fell into the water and we could use those for eight or nine yards. There was then a gap of say fifteen yards, where some other girders showed just above the water, but then a gap of eight yards before the British bank. We could make out the girders in the middle of the river, which was fairly fast and very cold. We had brought ropes, and I reported to Major Cameron and said I thought that it was possible to swim to the girders in the middle and that I would attempt this.

I swam across and attached my rope to the girders. The next man across was a private, with another rope, and he swam his rope from the girder to a tree on the British bank. We had Mae Wests, which were inflated before the men crossed. The next man across was wearing a rucksack. He jumped into the water upstream from the rope, was swept under it and drowned; we never saw him again. The others got in downstream of the rope, and gripped it to pull themselves across. The first light of dawn was about 06:00 hours, when our artillery opened up with smoke and HE, and the Germans opened fire on our crossing point with mortars and artillery. Fortunately, the ground was very soft and although we were hit by clods of earth, no one was hurt and by 08:00 hours we were all across.

The main body of No. 9 Commando returned in landing craft from the mouth of the Garigliano. The Commando suffered some thirty casualties on Partridge, including nine killed. It achieved its objectives, killed sixteen of the enemy and brought back twenty-six prisoners. Operation Partridge had been a brilliantly successful operation, and No. 9 Commando thoroughly deserved the praise bestowed on it by the Higher Command. Unfortunately this satisfaction was marred by an event which caused some ill feeling. Lieutenant-Colonel Tod was ordered to send out a patrol to bring in some dead who had been left on the river bank. The bodies were not found, the area had been remined, and a very popular sergeant had his foot blown off.

After Christmas, with the Allied armies stalled in front of Cassino, No. 2 Commando was ordered to prepare for operations with the Yugoslav Partisans in the Dalmatian Islands. No. 40 Commando went into the line with the 56th Division, while Nos 9 and 43 Commando went north to prepare for the Anzio landings, far behind the German lines.

9

ANZIO, 1944

'All delays are dangerous in war.'

John Dryden, 1649

The landings at Anzio, on the coast close to Rome, were an attempt to outflank the Gustav Line and force the German Army to withdraw from the positions around Cassino, where it had stood for months, defeating attack after attack and inflicting great loss on the Allied armies. In the event, Anzio itself became another beleaguered beachhead, and the battle there went on for months until the Gustav Line itself finally collapsed.

The Anzio landing – Operation Shingle – was a repetition of other Italian operations. The Allied troops got ashore almost undetected and were able to make some ground before the Germans hit back and contained them. The failure at Anzio came in the first day, when the troops failed to push inland, while there was no opposition, and extend the bridgehead. Once the Germans realised they were there and hit back, this 'containment' led to a bloody battle that lasted from 21 January 1944 until the end of May, during which time the Allied forces suffered severe casualties. At the beginning, however, it all seemed easy.

Captain Lucas of No. 9 Commando:

Some time early in January, officers of 9 Commando learned that the unit was to take part in a seaborne landing, followed by a dash to a major city which, or parts of which, they would have to hold until a larger force arrived to relieve them. The Commando would be armed with special automatic weapons (Vickers K MGs with an exceptionally high firing rate, of a type used to arm fighter aircraft). These were issued and training soon began. The whole unit was to be landed, and then conveyed in jeeps to the objective. The mouth of a major river was mentioned, and it did not need much imagination to guess that the city was Rome and the river the Tiber. 'Theirs is not to reason why', but most of us were not sorry to learn that this harebrained scheme – even for Commandos – had been abandoned, and that we were not to be the first troops to make a battleground of the Eternal City.

We were briefed for a seaborne landing by a 'Considerable Allied force' on the beaches north of Anzio, with the object of threatening the German lines of communication behind the Gustav Line at Cassino, and assisting the main armies now attacking across the Garigliano. The 1st British Infantry Division would land in the first wave, and would form a perimeter on the high ground about a quarter of a mile from the beach. No. 9 and No. 43 (RM) Commando would land in the second wave, pass through the perimeter held at that point by the Scots Guards to seize a hill feature about seven miles away, on the main road to Rome, at a point about five miles north of Anzio, and hold it until the beachhead had been extended to include our position. We would then be relieved, and return to our base. Initial resistance was not expected to be heavy, but fairly prompt reaction by the enemy was likely – and hoped for, since this was the object of the operation.

The Commandos embarked in SS *Derbyshire* on 21 January and landed shortly before dawn next day, virtually unopposed. There was a slight hiccup when the LCAs carrying all except Brigade HQ and 9 Commando's No. 3 (Heavy Weapons) Troop grounded on a bank some way offshore and the Brigadier found himself ashore without the greater part of his command for something like an hour but 3 Troop were not complaining – we had the Guards between us and the enemy, and we also had very heavy loads to carry, and were glad of the chance to get ahead of the assault troops. There was only one enemy gun (an 88mm) in action, firing an occasional shell in our direction. I met the Brigadier just after his servant had been wounded by this gun, and he agreed that I should move my troop up to the perimeter and await our friends there.

The plan was for 3 Troop, with our 3-inch mortars, our Vickers MMGs and ammunition conveyed in steel-framed canvas handcarts, to follow a track which ran north for a few hundred yards, then inland to the top of the higher ground where the Guards were digging in, to meet another track running south, parallel to the shore. I told Lieutenant David Balls, commanding the Mortar Section, that I, with my batman Ted Healey, would go and identify the track through the forest, while he brought the troop round by the longer route as planned.

Healey and I set off passing a sandbagged gun emplacement, found the beginning of the forest track, had a word with one or two Guardsmen, and sat down to have a cigarette and watch our comrades coming ashore. As we smoked and chatted away, Healey said, 'No more from that 88mm then.' Before I could answer, thirteen German gunners climbed out of the emplacement we had passed, threw down their weapons, and surrendered to us, muttering something about their duty. By this time the leading troop of 9 Commando was almost up to us. 3 Troop arrived at about the same time, so I handed my prisoners over to the Guards and we all went on our way.

The Commando moved through the woodland in an 'advance to contact' formation, with flanking parties as well as forward points to avoid being surprised. 3 Troop found the going very hard as the small wheels sank into the sandy track. After about an hour, as we were passing a small farm, David spotted, and commandeered a bullock cart, which speeded things up a great deal. No. 43 (RM) Command meanwhile had branched off to the right to attack the objective frontally, while we were moving round to take it from the rear. Everything was very quiet until, as the leading section approached a road, we heard a motorcycle and several short bursts of automatic fire as this section intercepted and dealt with an enemy motorcyclist. A brave fellow – after being knocked off his machine by the first burst he had made a very determined attempt to get away, which cost him his life. Eventually we recognised our objective away to the right, and were soon in position to attack. The 3-inch mortars were sighted and prepared to support an attack with either HE or smoke; the MMGs were sighted to cover the left flank of the advance, which was thought to be the more likely threat.

My guns were laid on the area round a group of farm buildings. I had gone to Commando HQ to say that we were ready, when I was called back to the guns by the sergeant, pointing to our target, which was about 2,000 yards away, where there was movement, something red and white – a woman hanging out her washing. It was really rather unreal, finding ourselves in a peaceful countryside, the inhabitants totally oblivious of our presence, much less our intention to wage war in their midst. As I turned to look again at our objective, I saw a number of Germans move down the slope towards us with their hands up. They all looked very young and apprehensive but it seemed that they were running away from the Marines, only to find us waiting for them.

During the next 48 hours, the rapid build-up of men and equipment went on. Field and medium batteries of artillery, tanks, self-propelled guns, anti-aircraft guns, ammunition, stores, casualty clearing stations and field hospitals – everything an army needs in the field, poured into the bridgehead. We were relieved and moved back to Anzio town on the third day, and thence by sea to Bacoli. A number of small incidents stick in my mind. On the first morning we chatted to tank crews returning from a patrol into the outskirts of Rome. 'Anzio Archie', German gun on a railway mounting, sent enormous shells screaming over our heads at regular intervals on their way to Anzio. While we were in the town square waiting to re-embark, he gave us a shell all to ourselves, but no harm done. An awful, inexplicable feeling of doom assailed me just before we were relieved – as if I had a premonition of all that was to be suffered in that place during the following weeks – a feeling which disappeared as quickly as it came, fortunately.

Nos 9 and 43 Commando had landed at Anzio at 05:30 hours on 21 January, advanced towards the foot of the Alban Hills, keeping in contact with the 3rd Battalion, US Rangers, met little opposition, and were withdrawn on the 24th to their base at Bacoli, north of Naples. 'The Commando never carried more ammunition and fired less,' says No. 9 Commando history.

Three days later they were sent out to support the 46th Division which had crossed the Garigliano and was fighting its way slowly through the mountain country north of the river. Although 46 Division had seized two peaks, Monte Turlito and Monte Fuga, these were overlooked by two even higher mountains, Monte Ornito, which has two peaks (Ornito itself and Point 711), while Monte Faito dominated the entire range. No. 9 Commando had to clear the way past these obstacles and the task would not be easy.

The Brigade Commander decided to move his forces round Mt Fuga and to attack Faito and Ornito from the north-east. This meant moving through the valley due north of Mt Fuga, in which they might encounter some resistance, but the units would also avoid the heavy defensive fire already encountered on the ridge of Mt Fuga and Mt Turlito and in the valley beyond. No. 43 (Royal Marine) Commando was therefore directed to move from Mt Turlito and go round behind Mt Fuga to its north-east side, then north-westwards to a position immediately north of Mt Ornito, then on to Ornito itself.

After the capture of Mt Ornito, No. 43 Commando was to exploit south-westwards to Point 711. Leslie Callf was a lieutenant in No. 9 Commando and takes up the story:

This was an unwieldy, two-Commando attack, with no chance of surprise, especially for the furthest objective, Mt Faito, and information about these objectives was limited, to say the least. In the event, neither was defended in any strength but there were many well-sighted machine-gun posts covering the approaches, especially to Mt Faito. Most importantly, there were several enemy observation posts, which could, and did, call for stonks of artillery and heavy mortars in a most concentrated manner.

So, No. 43 put in their attack and took Ornito with little opposition, while No. 9 followed on, meeting several isolated posts to the north of Ornito. No. 4 Troop, supported by 1 and 2 Troops, attacked these and took captured prisoners. The Commando was now strung out on two very rocky promontories joined by a saddle, to the north-east of our objective, Faito. 5 and 6 Troops took over the lead for the final attack. During most of our advance round the east side of Ornito, the whole column had been continually shelled and mortared. As 5 and 6 Troops moved forward an extremely heavy 'stonk' covered the area and seemed to continue for ages. 5 and 6 Troops were moving, while the remainder of the Commando were trying to scratch some cover in the rocky ground. I don't know which was better, but I prefer to keep moving as fast as possible.

This was the most vivid picture of the war, which remains very clearly in my memory. The shells and mortars were exploding on the rocks which covered every foot of the ground. The sight of the almost horizontal flashes with tearing pieces of rock and shrapnel, and the cries of the wounded, was horrifying. At the same time, two machine-gun positions sited in derelict stone houses or huts to the front and to the right were firing tracer into the Commando column.

5 Troop (or what was left of us) attacked the front post, taking two prisoners. 6 Troop sustained one killed and two wounded before they silenced a very determined enemy in the right-hand post. A very depleted 5 and 6 Troops now

pushed on to the lower slopes of Mt Faito and the assault team advanced further up the hill as forward patrol. Due to the heavy casualties, now about fifty per cent, including the CO and the second-in-command, the order was given to withdraw and consolidate on the slopes of Mt Ornito. Mt Faito was not finally captured until 12 May, that is, three and a half months later, by the *goumiers* of the French Moroccan Mountain Division.

Captain Harry Lucas gives another account of the Ornito battle:

We were armed with two Vickers MMGs and two three-inch mortars, all of which together constituted at least ten heavy man-loads. The mortar bombs weighed 10 lbs each and were carried three to a case, two cases to a man – a 60 lb load. The MMG ammunition was also heavy and the gun was a thirsty fighter – about 250 rounds a minute, or one belt, normal firing. All this, in addition to the normal equipment and personal weapons, constituted a very heavy load to be moved by a total of 36 all ranks. This factor really made it impossible to employ us on short raids, which had been the original role of Commandos – we had been left out of Operation Partridge, for example.

So far, it is true, we had been relieved of most of our load-carrying problems by the provision of a mule train but this created further problems. These mules were not used to gunfire, and one of them bolted carrying a mortar base-plate and was never seen again – which rendered one of my two mortars useless. In any case, from now on, no mules would be available, and everything would have to be humped. I had another reason for anxiety. The medium machine guns and the three-inch mortar were very useful weapons in attack provided their fire could be controlled by officers in a position to observe the fall of the shot and the position of our own troops.

Otherwise they could be very dangerous to our own troops. In our present situation with a night attack over extremely tough and mountainous country, without reconnaissance, these dangers and difficulties would be magnified. Francis Clark, second-in-command of 9 Commando, a machine-gunner and experienced in handling mortars, understood this. Colonel Tod also said that we would make such a bloody row that the essential element of surprise would be lost.

Around 20:00 hours Commando HQ and the rifle Troops passed through 3 Troop's positions and advanced to the attack, with much badinage between 3 Troop and the rest. Good old 3 Troop, dodging it again, etc., but we were very anxious. It was thought that the enemy held these hills with relatively few troops on the ground, but had massive concentrations of artillery fire, so all depended on quick success and digging in before the enemy could react.

Visits were made to Brigade HQ for news but radio silence was solid and there was little to hear but occasional shellfire, some of it quite heavy. Then the first POWs came in as Ornito was taken. I climbed the flank of Fuga to see whether there was any sign of activity towards Faito. On arriving at the forward edge of Fuga, we observed, through a gap between Point 711 and Ornito, an exceptionally heavy bombardment, lasting several minutes, on the far side of the valley leading north-west to the lower slopes of Faito, through which 9 Commando would pass.

Continuous gunfire, hundreds of shells or mortar bombs (probably multiple-barrel mortars as well as 88s) – clearly, 9 Commando had not achieved surprise. We learned later that this stonk killed or wounded more than half the members of HQ and the four Troops caught in it, including the CO, second-in-command, Intelligence Officer and at least four other officers and several senior NCOs.

Mike Allen was on the mountain at this time.

I remember being heavily shelled by our own artillery as the Commando was licking its wounds on the forward slope of Monte Ornito, after having endured similar and devastating enemy shelling during an approach. This mistake by our artillery arose from a faulty map reference signalled to his gun lines by an FOO. He was soon persuaded to correct the error of his ways.

Harry Lucas continues:

At 03:02, shortly after daybreak, I went forward with Ted Healey to recce a route forward and attempt to contact Commando HQ. We met many walking wounded, including Captain Mike Long and Lieutenants Martin Ferrey and 'Ally' Wilson – the latter with a gaping eyesocket and a battered face – as well as stretcher parties carrying more serious cases. Having rounded the east shoulder of Ornito and entered the long valley leading north-west towards the lower slopes of Faito, we could see many dead, especially on the hillside flanking this valley. We remained in that area for perhaps twenty minutes without seeing or, apparently, being observed by either our own troops or the enemy, from which I concluded that either our troops were in possession of Faito, or at least that the enemy were not.

Returning to 3 Troop, I found an order to report to the Brigadier, who ordered me to take 3 Troop forward to the forward slopes of Ornito, to which what was left of 9 Commando had been withdrawn, and where a counter-attack was expected. On the Brigadier's instructions, I first went to see if I could get any volunteers from among the walking wounded who were hanging around the RAP. I walked among them, saying I was going forward with 3 Troop and that every man was needed to hold the ground they had won at such cost. Corporal Walsh of my old Troop, 4 Troop, whom I knew to be a first-rate soldier and a brave man who later won the MM, was the senior NCO present. He said, 'Ye cannae ask these men to go back there the day, Captain Lucas, sir – in the morn maybe, but no the day.' I believed him and went to rejoin my troop.

It must be said for these men, that every one rejoined the unit within a day or so, and that before the end of the month they were again fighting gallantly in the Anzio beachhead. They were the bravest of the brave but, for the moment, they were numbed with the shock of the bombardment I had witnessed. I went on ahead with my recce group, including Lieutenant David Balls, to make contact with Commando HQ and select defensive positions for the MMGs and the remaining three-inch mortar leaving the Troop Sergeant Major to bring up the rest of the troop, manhandling the heavy weapons and as much ammunition as they could carry. Morale was high for we were, at last, going to get our chance. Occasional light shelling merely served to get the adrenalin going. One shell, however, had an unfortunate effect.

It fell more or less in the middle of the recce group, badly wounding me so I departed Italy on a stretcher, on my way to Blighty, three months in hospital and eighteen months in Holding Operational Commando. Luckily no one else was hit, and 3 Troop went on under the command of Lieutenant Balls. Their subsequent fortunes must be told by other witnesses but they performed gallantly until the end of the war. David Balls was killed at Anzio, and one of his successors at Lake Comacchio.

My experience after I was hit may be of interest. I received immediate attention from the Troop medical orderly, who dressed my wounds. David gave me a morphine injection and wished me luck. I was a bit depressed, because I had no sensation below the hip level, and believed (rightly as it turned out) that I had been hit in the spine. A troop stretcher party carried me to the RAP near Brigade HQ where the doc, John D'Arcy, gave me thirty sulphathiazola tablets, redressed the entry wound, packed it with drugs to prevent gas gangrene and turned his attention to more promising cases.

I was then carried by four German POWs, who did not seem at all depressed by their present fortunes, to an area just behind the crest where a long line of wounded were lying on stretchers under the dubious shelter of a drystone dyke, waiting to be collected by one or other of the Field

Ambulance stretcher parties which had been allocated to the Brigade for this operation. I was lying on my face, so I could not see much of what was going on. Shells still fell from time to time, some quite near, some in the distance. I wondered how David and 3 Troop were getting on. A padre (it may have been ours) came along at one point and offered to say a prayer with me.

Perhaps in answer to my prayer, Sergeant Miller of 2 Troop, whose mother lived next to my aunt in Bournemouth, came along and asked if I would like a drink. 'The CO is two stretchers away from you,' he said. 'His flask is sticking out of his pocket and he's fast asleep. I'll borrow it.' . . . and he did. I asked him the time and he said, 'About 16:00 hours.' I had been hit at about 13:00 hours – it was clearly going to be a long job. Happily, I was only conscious for half the time and I was strangely relaxed about the whole business. I was certain by now that I was not going to make it, and it didn't seem to be my problem any more.

My bearers struggled, slipped, fell, swore, dropped me, picked me up again, carrying me with my head sometimes above and sometimes below my heels. One party were very jolly Gurkhas, who never stopped laughing, and who, whenever shelling came close to the track, put me down and lay on top of me. I was luckier, however, than some of my comrades who were carried on stretchers strapped to our old friends, the mules. All this time, units of the Hampshire Regiment were struggling past us up the narrow track, on their way to relieve our Brigade. One of them was my cousin, but at the moment he actually passed me, I was asleep or unconscious.

At last we came to our original Advanced Assembly Point, where the Admin Officer, Andrew Cochrane, bent over me. 'Who's this? Ah, Harry, my poor fellow. I am sorry to see you like this. Well, you'll not be needing your G1098 kit any more so I'll just have your boots, helmet, compass, revolver and field-glasses.' I persuaded him that the glasses were my own, but he had the rest. A most

143

efficient Admin Officer, our Drew.

One more stretcher party down to the road, a short ride with my stretcher strapped on a jeep, over the pontoon bridge, thence by ambulance (a converted three-tonner) to the Casualty Clearing Station. By this time I was pretty wide awake, and I was very conscious that Sergeant Albert Cruickshank of 4 Troop (whose leg had been shattered some 24 hours earlier and whose stretcher was just above mine) was having a haemorrhage. Fortunately Albert survived, and only died in 1987. I was operated on immediately, and successfully, by Major Robb, MC, RAMC, and his surgical team, to whom I am eternally grateful. He removed some shell splinters and a handful of bits of map and mapcase, flowers and Italian real estate from my abdominal cavity, but told me he had had to leave one splinter embedded between two of my lumbar vertebrae, but that I was a lucky chap, and I would make a very good recovery. He was right on both counts.

During this Ornito operation, 2 SS Brigade had been joined by the doughty admiral, Sir Walter Cowan. After his capture in North Africa, where he was last observed attacking a tank while armed only with a .38 pistol, he had been released by his Italian captors as 'being at 71, too old to take any further part in the war', and promptly made his way back to the Commandos. While at Ornito he assisted the wounded Colonel Tod to make his way from the battlefield. No. 9 Commando lost a quarter of its strength at Ornito, including fifty per cent of the officers, but its part in the Anzio fighting was not over.

On 29 February, Nos 9 and 40 Commando found themselves en route for Anzio again, where the situation had deteriorated sharply in the previous three weeks. No. 40 joined 169 Infantry Brigade ten miles north of Anzio town, while on the same day No. 9 Commando took up position in the 167 Brigade area, a region of deep gullies or wadis which seamed the central plain, west of Anzio town. Lieutenant-Colonel Tod, now recovered from wounds received at Ornito, returned to the command and in the first eight days at Anzio, apart from holding its share of the line, No. 9 sent out eleven fighting patrols, killing or capturing 62 of the enemy, losing nineteen men itself, killed or wounded.

On 10 March, Colonel Tod was ordered to mount an attack, codenamed Operation X, to clear three wadis, only 500 yards from the beachhead perimeter, in which the enemy were forming up. The three wadis were codenamed Haydon, Laycock and Charles, and in the centre of these stood a small hill called Beechers.

Corporal Clifford Searle begins the story:

We had gained the impression that if there was an unusual task on hand, Captain Callf was sent for and patrols of 5 Troop were sent up to a wadi where a company had recently disappeared, to investigate and test the enemy strength there.

At the approaches to the wadi and near the forward troops I found a young lad, deeply distressed, in a dugout. He told me he was sixteen years old and had only arrived in Italy that day having been immediately sent to the front. All I could say to him was that he had little to worry about – especially while we were around – and as soon as possible he should disclose his correct age to his superiors. Shortly afterwards we found the ration-dump of the missing company. As usual, the Mortar Section covered the rear of the formation as we moved into the wadi – we were fired upon from the high ground to our right. Automatic fire hit Tommy Bostock's hand and we went to ground. I called upon the mortar man to range a few rounds on to the high ground and Captain Callf quickly reorganised us for an attack. We attacked up the side of the wadi and over the top with bayonets fixed, yelling and shouting as we moved in extended formation.

Captain Leslie Callf, MC, takes up the story:

My most thrilling and proudest moment of the war was in leading my troop in an attack against a superior force of paratroopers at Anzio. 5 Troop was about half-strength, mustering one officer and twenty-eight ORs. We arrived at first light and contacted the officer-in-charge for information as to the enemy's whereabouts. The only information was a vague wave of his hand down the wadi with the words, 'There . . . somewhere down there . . . I've just been promoted Major!' With these words the officer disappeared down his dugout and left us to it. The assault team under Corporal Bostock pushed ahead with covering from the Bren-gun team on the highest part of the wadi. We usually did our raiding and fighting patrols in the dark but this was special and urgent and we had to find them quickly, which we did, rather too quickly, in broad daylight. The enemy were well dug in on high ground overlooking the wadi and they opened fire with automatic weapons, slicing Corporal Bostock's trigger finger off as he returned fire.

The only way was a good old-fashioned bayonet charge. We left the wadi and spread out in the dead ground below the enemy positions, with Brens on the flanks giving covering fire. Fusilier Storey, who was lying just behind me, was killed as we were getting into position. Every man always carried two No. 77 smoke grenades, so that a smoke screen could be created for about two throws of about forty yards. They knew the drill; throw and run like hell through the smoke. This was the moment, and one I shall never forget. In broad daylight we had to cover about sixty yards of open ground against German paratroopers, well dug in. I looked to the right of me and the left and to CSM Walsh next to me, and gave the order, 'Throw!' and as the smoke formed, 'Charge!' and in we went, hard.

I think we must have looked a fearsome body as we came through the smoke on to them. Many of them were killed and others put their hands up. We suffered three killed and nine injured. I'm not sure of the German casualties, but the official report gave 25 killed and 23 POWs, which was approximately twice the strength of No. 5 Troop on that day.

Corporal Hankinson took part in Operation X:

We came under sporadic fire throughout the night, making several sorties and attempting to improve our position, and at dawn, together with my section, I found myself on the front edge of the wadi. We beat off with rifle fire and grenades an immediate attack, and as the sun rose it became apparent that the enemy was holding a position in some broken ground under a few broken and stunted trees, and in what had probably been their reserve line, some thirty or forty yards to our front.

All through that day we came under heavy mortar, shell and small arms fire, and although we were exposed and suffered repeated casualties, it was impossible to drop back further into the wadi without losing our field of fire. We were in an uncomfortable situation; it became a very long day! I could visualise no successful end to our predicament but, as I later discovered, after dark it was intended for a barrage to be laid down around our position, under which the unit would attempt a withdrawal. Before this plan could be put into effect, at dusk and under a smoke screen, we received a frontal assault from the enemy and the situation became very confused.

I remember hearing enemy cries of 'Hands up,' and of firing at figures seen dimly, but only a few yards away. Somewhere behind me in the wadi the bagpipes were playing. I sensed, heard, felt or whatever, something land on the ground next to where I was lying, and as I turned I saw a stick-grenade. Without consciously thinking, I put out a hand to throw the thing further away, but it exploded. Although I felt at first no more than a blow on my arm, I soon discovered I had been wounded in the right upper arm and hand, and slightly, no more than scratches, on the ear and face.

Eventually, under cover of the creeping barrage which had by then been started, I was able to regain the comparative safety of our own lines, and at last, by jeep ambulance, was taken to the tented hospital at the rear. On that day the

Commando, with a strength of little over 200 all-told, sustained casualties of 23 killed and 50 wounded. Of the dead, three were from my own section and included the then Troop Commander, Captain David Balls.

At 10:00 hours, twelve stretcher casualties were evacuated under a Red Cross flag, but this procedure meant that 24 men had to be away for some time and this depleted the Commando's strength considerably. The enemy respected the Red Cross flag and allowed the party to cross the open ground, but once the party had disappeared behind cover, they were subjected to a heavy artillery concentration.

Mike Allen, MC who later commanded No. 9 Commando, gives his version of events:

The operation involved a series of attacks for the occupation of three wadis, from which the enemy were in the habit of launching counterattacks. After the principal wadi was taken and held, it became evident that we had disturbed a wasp's nest, which the enemy had no intention of vacating, and repeated counter-attacks, interspersed with deadly accurate artillery fire at what was no more than a large hole in the ground, meant that the Commando would have been annihilated unless reinforced or withdrawn.

As the operation plan had made no provision for back-up support or relief, Ronnie Tod, our CO, suggested to 5th Division, to whom we had been attached for the operation, that 2 Commando Brigade would be displeased if 9 Commando was left to be expended as the Division's protection against counter-attacks. We accordingly received orders for disengagement and withdrawal to the start line, at which point wireless contact with Divisional Headquarters broke down. As second-in-command, I was consequently dispatched back to warn the front line, through which the Commando had advanced, of our impending return, to arrange defensive artillery fire during the withdrawal and to marshal and guide the Commando in as it reached our own start line. We took particular pride in the fact that, apart from those killed or known to have gone missing through direct hits, the Commando brought back all its wounded, through both enemy and friendly wire and minefields.

At about 18:00 hours the enemy fire increased considerably, and at last light, which was about 19:00 hours, smoke was put down along the whole length of the wadi. A strong enemy attack developed on to 3 Troop's position in the centre of the wadi and directly opposite the Commando Headquarters. At the same time two weaker attacks, each about a platoon strong, were made on the left and right flanks. The attacks on the flanks were quickly driven off and the enemy contented itself with establishing small groups three or four hundred yards away on each flank and firing into our positions. In the centre, meanwhile, the attack was pushed home with determination. A wave of the enemy assaulted over the crest throwing grenades and firing their weapons as they came. This first wave was followed by a second, armed mainly with automatic weapons, which tried to overrun 3 Troop's positions. A third wave came in behind the second, apparently to consolidate the positions won by the first two waves.

The first wave achieved some success and drove a wedge into 3 Troop's and HQ's positions. All the wireless sets at HQ were put out of action by grenades, and half the HQ became fully engaged in the battle. The second wave, however, was unable to take advantage of this initial success as it was mostly broken up by concerted fire from the whole of the Commando. The remainder of Commando Headquarters and 4 Troop moved forward to take part in the battle while 3 Troop's line was stabilised. With bagpipes playing and all weapons firing, 3 Troop and HQ, with the help of tanks, recaptured their positions and drove the enemy attackers back again.

Lieutenant-Colonel Tod ordered all the riflemen in the Commando to withdraw first, carrying the wounded on improvised stretchers made from rifles and groundsheets or greatcoats. Once the wounded were safely away, the machine guns of all troops were withdrawn. No opposition was encountered during the withdrawal, which was completed in the nick of time and followed closely by our own artillery fire. The start line area was again heavily mortared and shelled and some casualties were inflicted on the Commando as it passed through the area. 9 Commando was withdrawn within the next few days to Anzio town where it joined 40 (Royal Marine) Commando, and re-embarked for Naples.

Operation 'X' cost No. 9 Commando two officers and seventeen other ranks killed, two officers and 48 other ranks wounded, and four other ranks missing, of whom two were believed killed. Careful enquiry from prisoners estimated the number of casualties inflicted on the enemy at over 105. The Commando had therefore inflicted considerably more casualties than it had received. It had maintained its initial successes against heavy counter-attacks and had extricated itself from a difficult position without undue casualties; Anzio, Comacchio and Monte Ornito were No. 9 Commando's greatest battles and Captain Harry Lucas remembers the men who fought them:

I am sure you will have heard about that legendary, heroic and original character 'Mad Jack' Churchill of 2 Commando, but less perhaps about his brother Tom, who was our Brigadier in Italy. He too was a regular officer, but of a more conventional kind. He was undoubtedly a very fine soldier and when he got his Brigade, he was recognised as an outstanding Commander, in whom we had complete trust, and the Brigade had a brilliant record under his command. I have always felt that Commandos, by their very nature, needed a sobering hand at the top. At that stage in the war, and perhaps especially in the Mediterranean theatre, we were in some danger of being used in field operations for which we were well qualified, but ill-equipped, having no administrative 'tail' or transport to speak of. This had cost other Commandos dear – like No. 6, for example, in North Africa. We certainly believed that Brigadier Churchill, while eager to see us play our full part in defeating the Germans, would do his best to ensure we were properly employed.

Like all Commando leaders, he was a front-line Brigadier, and much liked and respected for that. He is always associated in my mind with Brigadier Haydon, the very first Commando Brigadier, who also had that cool, professional approach, and who, no less than 'Brigadier Tom', greatly cared for his men. Others will have told you of MT Sergeant Coupe, mortally wounded at Anzio, singing 'Here's to the next man to die' – or of the Cook Sergeant, manning a Bren with the CO, Ronnie Tod as his No. 2, in the same battle; of Lieutenant 'Ally' Wilson of 5 Troop at Ornito, who fought on after his eye had been knocked out, until he was ordered to fall out; and of Troop Sergeant Major George Drury and 'Piper' Ross of 4 Troop going out, on the morning after Ornito, almost up to the German positions, in broad daylight, to bring in Sergeant Albert Cruickshank, who had been lying there all night with a smashed leg . . . and many others, whom I never knew about. They were fine people.

Captain Mike Long, MC, takes up the story after No. 9 Commando returned to base:

After our casualties at Ornito and Anzio, the Commando moved across to the east side of Italy, to Molfetta. Colonel Tod called up all the officers for a conference and said that our casualties were similar to those suffered by 2 Commando at Salerno. He told us that they were shortly made up by intakes from home, but it had taken three to four months to get back the true 2 Commando *esprit de corps* which was very high before Salerno. Colonel Tod said this was not going to happen to 9 Commando. On no account were the men to start feeling sorry for themselves because their friends had been badly wounded or killed. To prevent that, he ordered two daily drill parades, one in the morning, one in the afternoon. In ten days the standard of drill

151

was so high – it was organised by Captain Davies, MC, ex-Coldstream Guards – that the Colonel said if there was a good drill in the morning the men could have the afternoon off.

When the new intake arrived, they drilled morning and afternoon, the old No. 9 mornings only. When the new intake were up to our standard, and only then, they were allowed to put up the 9 Commando black hackle. This created a pride and self-esteem in 9 Commando which continued until the end of the war, and even continues to this day.

Captain Long's 4 Troop was then sent on two operations along the coast of Italy, to bring out escaped prisoners of war:

We were first based in tents near Bari, and it was fairly hot, so every day I took the men to the sea and we had swimming lessons. At the time, only about half the troop could swim, but we soon had everyone swimming at least fifty yards. We then went to Manfredonia and embarked in an LSI (Landing Ship Infantry) and sailed to rescue 150 escaped POWs from a beach near the mouth of the River Tena, near Ancona. On our first expedition we brought off 132 men, having some difficulty getting the fully loaded craft off the beach.

On 14 June 1944 we sailed again for the same beach on an LCT (Landing Craft Tank). On board were six or eight heavily armed jeeps, two machine guns in the front, another two in the back. These belonged to 'Popski's Private Army,' who were to go ashore and raid from the Tena area while we returned with the prisoners. Anyway, I thought we were going in very fast and we hit the beach so hard that we got firmly aground and couldn't get off again, even though the Navy put out kedge anchors and did all they could. We had been escorted by an armed motor patrol vessel, which now came in until it struck a sandbank. It then withdrew to 200 yards offshore, and Major Popski, abandoning the operation, ordered us all to swim for it. His people stripped off, but all of us from No. 9

swam with our weapons and ammunition.

After our swimming lessons and wearing Mae Wests, they were all confident, but on the way out one soldier turned to Troop Sergeant Major Scott and said, 'Sar'nt Major . . . I'm going to drown . . . tell my mother I was thinking of her before I died.' 'Steady on, lad,' said Scott. 'Keep going, it's not far.' 'No . . . I'm going to die now,' said the soldier – and then stood up – in three feet of water! They had arrived over the sandbar. Major Popski was furious that the 9 Commando men had brought their weapons to the heavily loaded launch, but Colonel Tod insisted that whenever we crossed a river, we swam or crossed with our arms, and we would much rather have faced the wrath of Popski than an RTU from Colonel Tod.

We must now leave No. 9 Commando for a while, resting after its exploits in Italy, and follow Jack Churchill's No. 2 Commando across the sea to fight with Tito's Partisans against the German garrisons occupying the Yugoslav islands of the Adriatic.

10

YUGOSLAVIA,
1943–5

*'I see wars, horrible wars, and the Tiber foaming with
much blood.'*

Virgil

When the German Army entered Yugoslavia in April 1941, it
found a country apparently ripe for conquest. The former
Yugoslavia – now dissolved – was never a homogenous
nation, with Croats, Serbs, Slovenes, Montenegrins and
Macedonians among her ethnic communities . . . and these
components did not always see eye to eye. In 1941 such differences were compounded by faction fighting between two
political groups, the royalist Cetniks under Draia
Mihailovitch and the Communists under Josip Broz, a man
who later became known as Marshal Tito. United only in
their opposition to the Germans, both parties took to the hills,
and began a ruthless guerrilla war against the invader – and,
in what time they had to spare, each other.

In the months following the German invasion, the two parties
worked together, but their basic differences soon drove them
apart. The Cetniks began enlisting German help against Tito,
while the Communist Partisans struggled on virtually alone
against the German Army. In the beginning, the British supported Mihailovitch, but as his German connections became
clearer, the British switched their aid to Tito. In spite of this

assistance, the Germans tightened their hold on the country and by mid-1943 had driven Tito's Partisan army from all but a few mountain strongholds on the Yugoslav mainland and a handful of islands in the Adriatic, Vis, Hvar and Brac.

In 1942, the British sent a military mission to the Partisans, commanded by Brigadier Fitzroy Maclean, and in December 1943, Maclean sent the request that military assistance be sent at once to reinforce the Partisan garrison on Vis, and help them to raid – and if possible retake – the other islands off the Dalmatian coast and forestall further German expansion. On 16 February 1944, therefore, men of No. 2 Commando, commanded by Lieutenant-Colonel Jack Churchill, began to arrive on Vis. Ted Kelly was among the first arrivals:

We travelled by Partisan schooner and were carefully schooled in how to answer a Partisan challenge in Serbo-Croat. At the time it seemed to be a bit unnecessary, but when we came to know and work with these dedicated, trigger-happy people, we saw the point. The British sense of humour, particularly that of the licentious soldiery, does not travel well and soon created problems.

The Partisans rejoiced in singing patriotic and political songs which they took very seriously indeed. The British soldier who finds a good tune likes to set his own irreverent and obscene words to it, and our hosts took great offence at our version of one of their most cherished songs. I am not sure that they were any less offended when we taught them to sing what we said was one of our most patriotic songs: 'Please don't burn our shithouse down, Mother has promised to pay.' We drank a lot of wine with them, admired them and, in an odd sort of way, loved them, but we never really understood them. The world of the Partisans was very strange to us; it had an almost theatrical quality. The walls of buildings were daubed with slogans and Communist symbols, women soldiers carrying guns were a novelty, and the Serbo-Croat language, with unpronounceable consonants like 'crvna' was totally incomprehensible.

From our point of view, their love of Communism was a difficulty, not only because it was foreign to our thinking but because of their total commitment towards it. Their intense patriotism, constantly expressed, seemed to us overdone, boring, and not in the best of taste considering we were on their side too. The British habit of understatement was deeply ingrained in us and demonstrations of patriotic emotion embarrassed us while the Partisans' attitude towards us was not unlike our attitude to the Americans. They welcomed our help, both in manpower and in *matériel*, but they didn't actually like us. They regarded us as pampered, with our fancy equipment and uniforms and our food tastes, and as soldiers lacking in commitment to defeating the Fascists: 'Overpaid, oversexed and over here' probably summed us up to them.

Nevertheless, we drank coarse red wine with them in dimly lit bars and learned to sing their songs. They had some stirring tunes and we learned the words phonetically. In the mixed Partisan army, sex was strictly taboo and transgressions were punished by death. There were many good-looking girl soldiers and we did not take kindly to being forbidden even to chat them up, but who would risk the life of a Yugoslav girl to satisfy his own ego?

We also found their treatment of prisoners barbaric. The German prisoners we took were terrified that they would be handed over to the Partisans, and much friction was caused by disputes with the Partisans over who captured them. Our prisoners were shipped back to Italy as quickly as possible as we could not condone the Yugoslav illtreatment and summary execution of prisoners . . . but we understood it. Although many of the stories which we heard may have been exaggerated, we had no doubt that their people had suffered the most appalling atrocities under the Germans and especially from their own hated Ustachi, the Yugoslav Fascists.

The war in Yugoslavia was never a gentle affair. Neither side was very interested in taking prisoners, and the Yugoslav

Partisans tended to shoot any Germans they captured out of hand, and were equally harsh with their own people. 'I can sum it up best with one story,' says Bishop Ross Hook, MC, then padre with No. 43 (Royal Marine) Commando:

> When I visited a field hospital and found it full of wounded children, many with feet blown off and terrible injuries to their legs. Some of these children were no more than ten years old. It transpired that the Germans were laying *Schu* mines – small anti-personnel mines – in front of their defences.
>
> So, before an assault, the Partisans sent waves of children running across these minefields, to set off the mines and create gaps. I was shocked at this. I told our interpreter I thought it *barbaric* to send young children into battle, but he was quite unrepentant. 'It saves the lives of our soldiers,' he said, 'and we have plenty of children.'
>
> The Partisans were fiercely disciplined, shooting people for quite minor infringements. Since their armies contained women, sexual irregularities were not tolerated. Some months after arriving on Vis, some men of No. 2 Commando had to watch while the Partisans shot three women before their eyes for the crime of pregnancy.

Colonel Jack Churchill's much depleted No. 2 Commando was still not up to full strength after Salerno, and the force sent to Vis included a mixed bag of troops: Americans, many of Greek or Yugoslav stock, or speaking at least one of the many Slavonic languages, the Yugoslav troop of No. 10 (IA) Commando, and some Royal Engineers and Royal Artillery, plus naval MTBs. This force landed at Komiza, on the island of Vis, on 16 January 1944. 'Beauty was everywhere,' records Brigadier Tom Churchill. 'Grey stones set against the blue sea, red earth and green vines climbing up the terraced hillsides, and flowers everywhere, pink cyclamen, blue gentian, purple orchids, all standing out clearly in that rich, clear air.'

Operations began at once. The Germans were determined

to recapture all the Dalmatian Islands and reinforce their scattered garrisons, and diverted a division of mountain troops, the 118th Jaeger Division, from the mainland for this task. Colonel Jack believed that only by constant activity and raiding could the Allies' slender hold on Vis remain secure, so ten days after landing he led the Americans and three troops of No. 2 Commando to Hvar, a large island just off the Yugoslav coast, attacked a garrison near the port of Milna, and returned with four very frightened prisoners. Hvar was raided again, twice in swift succession, and in early February No. 2 Commando expanded its operations to the island of Brac, where Second Lieutenant Barton stayed ashore with a small party for several days before shooting and killing the German Commandant.

On 27 February the American Operations Group returned to Hvar to fight a gun battle with a German patrol, and on the same day the redoubtable Second Lieutenant Barton took another patrol back to Brac and killed a number of the garrison with grenades before returning to Vis with many prisoners. For these two actions Barton received the DSO, a rare award for a junior officer. He also went on the German death list, 'to be shot if captured', and was therefore transferred back to Italy.

After these successful beginnings, the Commando contingent on Vis began to expand. No. 43 (Royal Marine) Commando under Lieutenant-Colonel R. W. B. Simmonds arrived on 20 February. On 5 March, Brigadier Tom Churchill and Brigade HQ arrived, taking over command of both Commando units. On 17 March two troops of No. 2, plus some Americans and the Heavy Weapon Troop of No. 43, attacked the island of Solta. The enemy garrisons were now alert to the possibility of Commando raids and the defending Germans engaged the raiders with rifle fire as they scrambled up the terraced hillsides around the town of Grohote. Kittyhawk dive-bombers pounded Grohote at dawn before the attack went in, the two fighting troops of No. 2 Commando supported by 43's mortars and MMGs.

Ted Kelly was there:

We were briefed from photographs as usual. The plan was to surround Grohote in a horseshoe formation, the open end leading to an open space to be used as the killing area. It was understood that the German forces on the island were due to be relieved on the day after the raid. Our objective was to present the relieving force with an island totally empty of Germans. We landed on the night of 17/18 March on to a rocky beach, making a ridiculous amount of noise. Every dog on the island barked to warn their masters of the intrusion and we expected trouble. The Partisan guides who met us included a shepherd who had brought his flock of sheep with him. Their bells tinkled and apparently convinced listeners that the dogs had been disturbed by the flock. We tiptoed along behind our guides and arrived at our prearranged positions without incident.

We waited in as near silence as we could manage, dying for a cigarette – until first light when 'Mad Jack' had a German-speaking member of the Commando announce our arrival over a loudhailer and invite the Germans to surrender. Sporadic small arms fire was the response. The announcement indicated that failure to surrender would result in Grohote being bombed and at the appointed second, the Kittyhawk fighter bombers arrived and gave a demonstration of bombing and strafing which had us virtually throwing our hats into the air. Immediately the last bomb dropped we went into the village to take our prisoners and do a house-to-house clearing operation. From captured documents a roll call was taken of the German garrison and every man was accounted for.

The dead were buried, the wounded treated and all German survivors, numbering over 100, accompanied us back to the embarkation point. Most military operations include an element of shambles, sometimes on a truly grand scale but Solta was as near perfect a combined operation as possible. To take the whole of the German garrison off an island hours before they were due to be relieved was a masterstroke of intelligence, planning and execution. The reprisal attack on Komiza with Stuka dive-bombers showed that the Germans agreed.

One of the available volunteer duties was to go on operational with the MGBs and MTBs which patrolled the Adriatic. Our role was that of boarding party and a number of prizes were taken, including a schooner loaded with butter which enhanced our diet for some time. There was never a shortage of volunteers. This had nothing whatever to do with bravado. It was simply that the food on board Navy vessels, especially the freshly baked white bread, was so good. After six eventful months with the Partisans we were relieved and returned to Italy, minus our beloved 'Mad Jack' who had been taken prisoner on Brac.

Six days after Solta, the Commandos went back yet again to Hvar to attack the garrison of Jelsa, the island's port. This was a considerable landing, with Lieutenant-Colonel Simmonds taking all of No. 43 Commando, plus a 3,000-strong Partisan brigade. In spite of communication problems, and the fact that the Partisans were a law unto themselves, attacking only when and where they wished, the raid went off as planned. A German counter-attack was beaten off, the garrison lost about 50 men killed, and 100 more were taken prisoner before the Commandos and the Partisans withdrew. The Commandos then experienced considerable problems keeping their prisoners alive, for the Partisans demanded that they be handed over to them for interrogation – an interrogation that inevitably led to execution.

During this period, life on Vis, if never orderly, became much more organised. An airstrip had been built by the Royal Engineers, and when not on operations the men lived in small tents set in the hills around the airfield, where reinforcements came in every night from Italy. There was a squadron of Spitfires on the island now and a squadron of MTBs and MGBs in the harbour. There was even an island newspaper, *Vis a Vis*. Vis was now rightly named 'The Malta of the Adriatic', and considered able to resist even all-out attacks . . . and meanwhile the raids continued.

Patrols from No. 2 Commando went with Partisan brigades

to raid Korcula, Mijet and many other small islands, while Commando sections, notably from No. 2, took up patrolling with the Royal Navy, boarding the small caiques and German coastal craft on passage between the islands. The Royal Navy craft would lie close inshore, hidden in the dark by the loom of the land, until an enemy supply ship or schooner convoy came by. Then they would roar out of the dark, guns blazing, swoop alongside a ship, the Commando boarding party would leap over the rail with pistols and grenades and swiftly overcome the crew. All in all, it was an exciting, piratical life.

In May the island received further reinforcements when the veteran Royal Marine Commando, No. 40, arrived from Italy, still commanded by Lieutenant-Colonel 'Pops' Manners – an officer who, in spite of his nickname, was in his thirties. On the 23rd, Nos 2 and 43 Commando sent a party, including the indefatigable Admiral Sir Walter Cowan, to Mijet, which was said to have a garrison of 150 German troops. In spite of an extensive and exhausting search, the Commandos failed to find the enemy, lost a number of men to snipers and heat exhaustion and withdrew, disappointed.

Dudley Cooper again:

Vis was transformed during our stay. A light ack-ack battery was next to us, to cover the area around the harbour at Komiza. They received a sudden and unexpected visit from several Ju 88 bombers, which came in low over a small hill and clearly knew the gun positions. All four guns were bombed and received casualties and damage. One lost its crew, and the gun at the canning factory received a direct hit, destroying both gun and crew. Our strength continued to grow; an airstrip was built and fighters arrived and we saw more Americans, including some Rangers, but then we suffered a lot of losses on a raid against the garrison of Brac.

In May 1943, the Germans mounted a major offensive on the Yugoslav mainland, aiming to capture or kill Marshal Tito and disperse his forces. This attack forced the marshal to flee and to deter the Germans from switching more troops to the mainland, it was decided to mount a major operation against Brac. A large force, consisting of two full Partisan brigades and both Commandos, Nos 2 and 40, went on this operation and encountered fierce resistance in which 'Pops' Manners was killed and Colonel 'Mad Jack' Churchill was captured; total Commando casualties on this raid amounted to over 100 men and eleven officers, killed or wounded.

Fortunately, the Brac raid succeeded in its overall objective. The Germans kept their garrisons on the islands and even reinforced them, with no troops crossing to the mainland or mounting any major attacks against Vis. Dudley Cooper again: 'When the news reached No. 2 that Colonel Jack was a prisoner, volunteers went to Brac to try and get him back, but we landed on Brac only to hear that Colonel Jack had already been moved to the mainland.'

Brigadier Tom Churchill returned to Vis on 12 June, and when Marshal Tito arrived from the mainland on 23 June, he inspected No. 2 Commando, and thanked the British forces for their efforts on the islands. This was very gratifying and well-deserved, but relations between the Partisans and the British gradually deteriorated as the Russian Army advanced into the Balkans and support from the West became less important.

At the end of June, No. 43 Commando attacked Hvar, killing eighteen out of a twenty-strong German patrol, while No. 40 Commando concentrated on making life wretched for the Germans on Mijet. At the end of the summer, the Germans began to withdraw from the islands, first from Brac and then from Solta, but while No. 43 Commando stayed on Vis to harass the departing enemy, Nos 2 and 40 Commando had returned to Italy in May 1944 to meet up again with No. 9 Commando. In October 1944, the last Commando unit in Yugoslavia, No. 43, returned from Vis and rejoined the 2nd Special Service (Commando) Brigade in Italy. In ten months of operations it had raided almost at will around the Dalmatian Islands and tied down three German divisions, while inflicting steady losses on the island garrisons.

These exploits were not without loss and some bad feeling. When British and American help was needed, the Communists were all smiles; now that the Russians were on hand, the Partisans became sullen, unhelpful, even hostile to the soldiers of the Western Allies. 'Although,' says the Rev. Ross Hook wryly, 'their faith in the Russians took a sharp knock when the advancing Red Army raped and pillaged its way through Belgrade.'

Whatever their ideological differences at the time, since the war the old Commando soldiers have returned to the islands many times, privately or in organised groups from the Commando Association, and built up warm friendships with the former Partisans. At the time though, the British Commandos were glad to leave and turn their attention to fighting the German forces in Albania and Greece.

On the night of 28/29 July 1944, Lieutenant-Colonel Fynn, the new CO of No. 2 Commando, landed at Spilje in Albania at the head of a considerable force totalling, with his own 250-strong Commando plus attached ranks from No. 9 Commando and the Highland Light Infantry, some 700 men. For once they outnumbered the Germans, but when they attacked four German positions they found them well prepared and stubbornly defended. The German garrison beat off the attack, inflicting about 60 casualties on the attackers, before the Commandos returned to their ships. Spilje fell two days later to a full Partisan brigade which overran the German positions and took very few prisoners.

Two months after this reverse at Spilje, No. 2 Commando was sent to attack the town of Sarande on the coast of Albania opposite the island of Corfu. The Germans were now withdrawing from the Balkans, urged on by local partisans and No. 2 Commando landed in a cove, codenamed Sugar Beach, six miles north of Sarande; on the night of 22 September. The landing rapidly halted when it became apparent that the Germans were prepared to defend Sarande at all costs, and had over twenty artillery pieces ranged on the only road the Commando force could follow from the beach towards the town.

The information coming from the Intelligence people had

also been faulty, for the total enemy forces at Sarande amounted to nearly 2,000 men, not the anticipated 200–300, and the terrain was extremely rugged. Brigadier Churchill therefore moved his men into a defensive position close to the beach and sent for reinforcements; No. 40 Commando, now commanded by Lieutenant-Colonel R. W. Sankey, accompanied by some field artillery, arrived from Otranto on the 24th.

Meanwhile it rained . . . and rained . . . and rained. The Commando troops who were out on the hills around Sarande remember the next week well, mostly because of the terrible weather, and the units suffered over 200 cases of exposure before the weather improved on 4 October. By now the guns were ashore and, with artillery able to fire on Sarande, the attack went in on 9 October. Nos 2 and 40 Commando were supported by artillery and had the help of the Royal Air Force Parachute Levies, who mounted a diversionary attack on the outlying German positions. The town fell after a stiff fight on the afternoon of 9 October.

Eric Groves of No. 2 Commando recalls the Sarande operation:

During the afternoon of 22 September, in bright sunshine, we boarded three LCIs just south of the town of Bari in Italy. By the early evening the sky had clouded over, a strong wind was blowing and the sea was looking unfriendly. Soon we were into one of those notorious Adriatic storms, the *bora*, which come up without warning. Within half an hour we had a monstrous sea, spume, rain and tearing winds, hurling us about, and LCIs – Landing Craft, Infantry – are not very stable at the best of times.

We quickly lost sight of the other vessels as our own craft pitched, rolled and corkscrewed through troughs and peaks of water. My companions on the troop deck were all looking the worse for wear and most, including me, had already parted with their recent meal. At this point I decided it might be more comfortable on deck. No luck there, with waves dashing about, so I tried the engine room which was certainly warmer, but the engineer was stretched out alongside his thumping GMC diesels, looking green. Eventually the storm abated and we were still on course for our landing point, a sandy cove about five miles north of Sarande.

The time was now after midnight and the moon had come out. Having recovered, we prepared our weapons and the run-in commenced with the ramp partly dropped. At this point we hit a sandbank in the middle of the lagoon and stopped. Keeping our fingers crossed that no enemy artillery was in the vicinity, we backed off and had another go. Better luck this time, straight on to the beach and off at the run through soft sand to take up defensive positions among scrub and stunted trees.

Captain Parsons, who had signalled us in, told us that a mobile 88mm gun had been positioned at the head of the valley earlier in the evening, but had fortunately moved off before our arrival. Supplies of ammunition and other items were unloaded and some mules were taken off. These had been brought over to carry ammunition up the valley and across the volcanic hills to our proposed attack 'start-line', about five miles away. These animals proved useless and, pending the purchase of small, sturdy, local animals, the men were employed carrying bombs and ammunition to the top of the cliffs, an exhausting operation.

Captain Bob Bavister also remembers the mules:

Seventy-five mules were landed, some belonging to the Raiding Support Regiment, which was a new formation offering us gunfire support. We had to learn to handle the mules after landing, so the RSR were there to teach us what they were like. The beach party was responsible for loading them and leading them into the hills, but when some mules were killed, the other mules would not go past the spot where it happened. They were much fussier than horses about water, and if they decided the path was too difficult, they would just lie down and have to be unloaded, so most of the kit was man-packed to the destination.

Eric Groves again:

The local mule purchase was an interesting affair. This involved an officer seated behind some piled-up ammunition boxes, on the top of which lay a bag of Mint-fresh 'Victorian' sovereigns while a Tommy-gunner stood by, with a suitably ferocious expression. In front stood the villainous-looking Albanian, proclaiming the outstanding virtues of the bag of skin and bone held at the end of a length of grass rope that masqueraded as a mule and apparently the only payment these people would accept was in Victorian gold sovereigns which, I understood later, were still being minted in England for such purposes. These local mules looked terrible but much to our surprise these seedy-looking animals performed very well.

Active patrolling towards Sarande across volcanic rock became a daily activity, which quickly destroyed the boots we had been issued with for what was supposed to be a forty-eight-hour operation. With a deterioration in the weather and useless boots, men started going down with trench feet. The problem of water also became acute for those of us in the forward area. First thing in the morning, water could be found in small depressions in the rocks, perhaps half-a-cup at a time – but the problem was getting it out. The Sarande operation was pretty hard, pouring rain, rough terrain, short of food and water, even without the enemy putting up a tough fight, overrunning our forward position on one occasion.

Eventually 2 Troop came steaming back, having heard the firing and found the forward position empty. The men manning it had either been taken prisoner or evaded the enemy. In the excitement the Bren gun had jammed so they were all captured and were only freed after we took Sarande. We learned later that 40 Commando had seen an enemy fighting patrol of about 100 men leave Sarande and move towards our position, staying out of sight until it got behind a rocky outcrop about 100 yards in front. The Marines tried to signal us but their signals were not seen, but after overrunning our position, the enemy decided not to advance further and immediately retired to Sarande, leaving us to spend a terrible night in the open, while the rain pelted down.

With the full dawn came the sun and our clothes started steaming and we were told that a good breakfast awaited us on the beach, plus a supply of new boots which had just arrived – and were just as welcome as hot food at that time. This was a great day, one of real recuperation. We swam in the clear waters of the bay, lay in the sun, dried our clothes and kit and watched the landing craft unloading stores. All the earlier misery was forgotten, we had clean socks and – most important of all – well-shod feet. We learned that the supporting 25-pounders had been landed further along the coast, and that night we moved forward again across the rocks to our start line some 400 yards short of the enemy positions where they had 2-pounders and 20mm cannon. Just before dawn our artillery laid down a short barrage and we advanced.

Just short of our objectives, the fire became heavier, mostly coming from the Albanian Partisans who had decided to join in the fight and were shooting dangerously low over our heads from far too great a distance. The problem eventually became so serious that Colonel Fynn threatened to arrest the Partisans' leader unless he called them off and allowed us to get on with the job. We were into mid-morning now, and Captain Parsons, moving at the head of the Troop, took the 20mm cannon position. We were now into the main enemy position and the Germans were finally surrendering.

The successful operations on the Albanian coast following the fall of Sarande led to the fall of Corfu, just across the straits, where Nos 2 and 40 landed in mid-November. The brigade then suffered the loss of its popular brigadier, Tom Churchill. With No. 40 Commando detached to Corfu, the

167

RAF Parachute Levies removed from his command, No. 9 Commando now in Greece and No. 43 Commando still in Yugoslavia – and with no transport – Tom Churchill was ordered to pursue the Germans across Albania with his much-depleted No. 2 Commando. He replied to this order with a one word signal: 'How?' There was a short dispute with Middle East Headquarters and the command of what was now No. 2 Commando Brigade went to Brigadier Ronnie Tod, formerly of No. 9 Commando, which had recently been operating in Greece, trying to prevent civil war breaking out between the government and the Communist Greeks of ELAS, a far from easy task. This did not last long and in the spring of 1945 the much-travelled units of No. 2 Commando Brigade finally came together again at Ravenna in Italy.

11

COMACCHIO and ARGENTA, 1945

'Let there be no battle on a ground of dissolution but on bad ground the only thing to do is keep going.'

Sun Tzu
The Art of War

In mid-March of 1945, in the dying weeks of the European War, Brigadier Tod was ordered to lead his brigade against the German positions astride Lake Comacchio, a great inland sea a few miles north of Ravenna, a natural obstacle which barred the northward advance of the Eighth Army towards Venice. The fighting that followed is largely told in the words of the men who were there, in a battle where the terrain was as much of an obstacle as the mortars and shellfire of the enemy.

Lake Comacchio is a very shallow lake, separated from the Adriatic Sea by a narrow spit of land and fed from the south by the River Reno. Brigadier Tod's plan was for No. 2 Commando to cross the lake in small boats, land a third of the way up the spit and seize two bridges which carried the only road across some drainage ditches. No. 9 Commando would then cross the lake and clear the western half of the spit, while No. 43, now under Lieutenant-Colonel Ian Riches, RM, attacked up the spit from the south.

This plan called for three Commandos to clear the spit,

while the last, No. 40, was first to hold the south bank of the Reno, and then cross the river to the north bank, after which the whole force would advance up the spit, clearing German positions and opening a way round the lake for the advancing British divisions. All the German positions were given biblical codenames; Acts, Joshua, Ezra, Leviticus, and so on, and were garrisoned by German and Turkoman troops well-equipped with machine guns and field artillery.

Commando units were small and No. 9 Commando, now totalling 368 all ranks, moved from Ravenna at 16:00 hours on Easter Sunday, 1 April 1945, when the war in Europe had just over five weeks to run. For its part in the operation, No. 9 Commando was allotted six 'Fantails' small assault boats, one Weasel and 26 stormboats, plus six large assault boats. The loaded Fantails bogged down in the shallow water and mud and soon had to be abandoned, the Commando going on in the stormboats and Goatley boats, the men often having to get over the side and push. The Commando had been organised into two Troop 'squadrons' for this attack, 'A' Squadron consisting of 1 and 2 Troops, and 'B' Squadron comprising 5 and 6 Troops, under Major L. S. Callf, MC:

When this attack, Operation Roast, began there was some confusion at the stormboat area prior to wading off, and no blue guiding light was visible to mark the start line as we had been told – indeed, no clear order given for setting off at all. However, the word was passed down to 'Follow your Serial' so the Squadron moved off, the men pushing their boats and keeping within voice range. There was still no blue light visible to head for, the light which was to mark the Forming-Up Position (FUP) for the attack, and it appeared that 'the blind were leading the blind' but we kept on wading. Various degrees of difficulty were experienced by the boat crews, owing to the different loads each craft carried, and we soon became very spread out.

6 Troop appeared to keep together, and went out in to deep water where they could ride in their boats, while 5 Troop's lighter boats kept in-shore. My own boat got

halfway and became stuck in the mud on three different occasions and fell slightly behind. Information from a fol-boat canoe manned by SBS resulted in us pushing and wading into deeper water, where it was possible to paddle. The coxns, had orders not to start their engines before reaching the blue light, but upon receiving the word from HQ we made several attempts to start ours while still half a mile or more from the light. By putting most of the weight in the bows, we managed to gain sufficient clearance for the propeller and soon made the FUP, where Major Porter was waiting in a folboat, together with three boat-loads of 6 Troop and several sections of 2 Commando. Eventually, the remaining boats were complete and tied together in convoy, and we set off.

4 Troop went westwards, wide of the small islands en route, and 5 Troop, going between the islands, therefore took the lead. The mist became thicker near the coast, and we strayed slightly to the north, becoming stuck in the mud, and had to untie all four boats, and push and paddle and allow each boat to find its own way in. Meantime, the pre-attack phase had started. The smoke screen was perfect and the phosphorus smoke bombs lit up the house opposite our landing beach. Mud within 300 yards of the shore was especially sticky and the last wade-in was very tiring. On shore we found that 4 Troop had organised the beachhead, and we quickly formed up near the road, ready to move when all the 'Squadron' had reported in. Time of landing was approximately 05:30 hours. I reported on wireless about 05:45 hours – first light – that the Squadron was ready to move, and that we already had three prisoners.

HQ told us that there was a company of the enemy with three machine guns covering the beaches and approaches. I gave orders to proceed and B Squadron moved on in extended order. In 5 Troop, 9 Section led and put down smoke opposite the house and overran it, leaving 10 Section to search the garden and the surrounding area in detail. No prisoners were taken here. A very heavy mist came down at this time and I decided that we could take advantage of it to cover our advance and endeavour to overrun the 'Leviticus' position where the bulk of the enemy seemed to be. Two 38 radio sets were already 'di owing to immersion in the water so I could not get in contact with 6 Troop, so I had to hope they would push on in the same manner.

10 Section and Troop HQ came through 9 Section and still in thick mist, the whole Troop pushed to the gun lines with Sergeants Searle and Stephens pushing round the flank to engage and silence the Spandau firing on the beach. One 75mm gun was blown up just before we reached it, and another was captured intact though it had a demolition charge strapped to it, ready to be ignited and the German about to blow the charge was killed.

Controlling the attack in the mist was very difficult and it was impossible to go on without reorganising the Squadron. We were now mixed up, and had picked up about ten prisoners. The mist was just lifting, and I gave the order to consolidate and reform the line. I could now see that two sub-sections had pushed ahead on the right flank, nearest the beach, and had stopped the Spandaus firing on the boats which were still coming in. Troop HQ had pushed ahead of the remainder of 9 Section, and were in the middle of the dunes, between the road and the beach 10 Section were slightly behind, finishing the mopping-up process and prisoners were being pushed up to Troop HQ and were coming back from the forward subsections. The enemy, in ones and twos, were being pulled out from dugouts near the guns.

Thinking that an obstinate enemy still remained in a dugout, CSM Walsh MM, rushed up and used his flame-thrower, setting alight the camouflage netting which raised a column of smoke and at exactly this moment, the area was subjected to a mortar stonk of disastrous accuracy, followed by two or three more in quick succession.

The fire came from both south and north, the northerly fire mainly covering the outer edge of the dunes overlooking the beaches. Troop HQ was situated in a large shell crater and two direct hits killed four men here, Sergeant Dickinson, Sergeant Porter, Private Drummond and Private Urquhart, together with one prisoner. It also put the wireless out of commission and wounded all Troop HQ except Private Lancaster. The passage of time from overrunning the forward positions of the enemy to the stonking was very short, five minutes or even less.

Realising we were in range of an enemy DF (defensive fire) task, I ordered the remaining men to advance to the next ridge and consolidate and reorganise. An extremely trying period ensued, with us under Spandau fire from the front and left flank, while wounded were accounted for and our Brens got into action. All wireless communication, together with walkie-talkie, was dead, and I had no knowledge of 6 Troop's whereabouts. Two runners were sent off to 6 Troop to give them our position and situation report. 10 Section was ordered to advance to the next ridge, where they engaged targets to the front. My runner returned with Captain Kennedy's runner and I decided to visit 6 Troop and make further plans over his wireless.

Meanwhile, I detailed Lieutenant Long to organise all prisoners and walking wounded to help the badly wounded back to HQ, give our situation and try and send up a wireless set – not having any communications was very difficult, and meanwhile a sniper was pushed forward to engage and observe. At approximately 08:00 hours I contacted Captain Kennedy and learned that he had also been subjected to mortar fire. After sending through our casualty return, I arranged an artillery shoot of HE and smoke on Smarlacca House for five minutes. 6 Troop would then advance to the line of the house under our covering fire, followed by 5 Troop advancing past Smarlacca, which would mark our second bound up the road.

I then returned to 5 Troop and withdrew the forward section about 100 yards as a safety area for our own artillery support, which went down at 08:45 hours. The smoke quickly billowed up into the air and was thickened by two-inch mortar smoke from 6 Troop, who then advanced but came under an immediate and accurate mortar stonking, which killed Lieutenant Morris and wounded eight other ranks. I advanced 5 Troop forward again to their old positions on a ridge about 200 yards north of Smarlacca House, and at the same time another stonk fell on our lately occupied positions. I sent two more runners to find out what had happened to 6 Troop, and meanwhile dug in on our new position with two weak sub-sections on the right flank, and one in the middle with Troop HQ, under Lieutenant Robinson being on the right flank.

It was impossible for my Troop to move until I could again establish contact with 6 Troop. Without command or knowledge of events, I decided to wait where I was. Two Spandau positions, one to our front, in the vicinity of a pillbox by the house, and the other on a knoll east of the road, were engaged by our fire. Our mortar was employed without success, and each time a further stonk was returned by the enemy, from somewhere behind our positions in the vicinity of our previous line. A further four prisoners were taken on our right flank as they were trying to crawl through our lines. My runner returned with information of 6 Troop positions, which were again approximately opposite, but further east and hidden in dead ground.

The 'cab rank' of fighter bomber aircraft overhead was now being employed by us, but their bombs were dropping behind and nearer to us than to the enemy and very close to 6 Troop positions. The mortar operator must have again spotted our position and two stonks were put down within twenty-five feet of us. Captain Bassett-Wilson, MC, had now come up between mortaring and informed me he was liaising between 6 and 5 Troops, and had sent a Forward Observation artillery officer to 6 Troop. We were both digging deeper positions as we discussed a plan for moving forward, when a direct hit landed by the side of Captain Bassett-Wilson, badly wounding him and injuring another man.

A second direct hit immediately afterwards killed Captain Bassett-Wilson and Lance Corporal Lody, and I decided to withdraw the line. Meanwhile, Lance Sergeant Stephens and Private Sherwood had been hit by automatic fire while endeavouring to bring more fire power on to the right flank. They had both been evacuated prior to the last stonk, assisted by five prisoners and Lance Corporal King. 5 Troop withdrew in small groups and although mortared, did not suffer further casualties. One sub-section remained isolated on the right flank. Our next line was taken up on the edge of the vines, 400–500 yards south of our last position. As we were digging in, two bursts of fire came down through the vines and wounded a number of men.

This fire swept the whole of the vine area and was fired in an indirect role, guarding the gun lines which we had attacked in the mist at the start. Our remaining prisoners helped the last of the wounded back after this Spandau fire had ceased. We now dug in again as I was quite sure that we would be unable to advance in daylight while those mortars were in operation. It was obvious that the whole of the area of Leviticus was easily controlled by the enemy's knowledge of the ground. About half an hour later, the artillery support came down for 'A' Squadron (1 and 2 Troops, you will recall), and later still the welcome sound of bagpipes heralded the appearance of 1 Troop. It was learned later that two enemy mortar observers were hiding, watching 1 and 2 Troops advance, but were captured by 6 Troop, when they tried to crawl through our lines. One of the Spandau gunners also ran off, and managed to evade capture . . . and that was about it.

Lieutenant Don Long, MC, of No. 9 Commando, recalls his experiences at Comacchio:

I remember walking to the lorries with George Robinson, who said, 'The one thing I could do with before the war ends is an MC' – a Military Cross. We were all quite sure the war would be over shortly, so I said, 'Don't be bloody silly, just hope you don't get one of those white crosses the Pioneers make.' Well, we landed at Comacchio, and as you will have gathered, it was an awful nonsense. The 'fantails' got stuck, the stormboats wouldn't float, the mist was as thick as it could get. We were worried about the *schu* mines, which could take your foot off, and as I went over to one of the sergeants I was blown into the air. I came down with the most awful bump, but was delighted to see I still had both my legs, although I was now pretty useless. It turned out later to have been a stick grenade which was a 'blind' (undetonated) until I kicked it, whereupon it went off.

Dudley Cooper of No. 2 Commando won the Military Medal at Comacchio:

We were on the start line where, according to the briefing we would board the collapsible Goatley boats and be towed by the outboard up the lake. We would then carry them over a dyke and go ashore on the east bank, after a barrage had been laid down at dawn.

Some sappers joined us for mine-clearing duties. They had not been briefed by their officer and were in clean fatigues and had no weapons. They were soon given rifles and ammunition and told they would have to look after themselves in an assault landing. We got in the boats and the mosquitoes rose off the lake in millions. The driver of the outboard started the engine and put it in the water, where it immediately stopped.

None of the engines would work. Eventually we all got in the water and found mud up to the thigh, and water to the lower chest. We pushed and pulled the boats up that lake for hours until the water became deep enough to put the engine on. We all climbed in and away we went, only to stop in five or ten minutes at the dyke. We could have walked the collapsibles up there instead of the heavy outboard. We lay on the dyke and awaited the barrage which was on time. Our officer did not wait for the ceasing of the barrage and we were soon too close for comfort to the shelling. I stopped paddling and the officer told me to keep going.

At that moment a large piece of shrapnel passed our

heads, and it was a panic back-pedal until the barrage ceased. The officer and my Number Two and I moved forward with the PIAT and saw the Germans regrouping for a counter-attack. I ranged the PIAT and sent all the bombs into the woodland where they were sheltering. We were out in front of our own lines with only small arms to defend ourselves, and no one knew where we were. I told the others I would cover them as they retired, as there was a machine gun firing on our position. I used my .45 Colt to keep the machine-gun owner busy, but once I had emptied the gun, the machine gun kept me from moving or reloading. After a hit on the shoulder-piece of my PIAT and holes in my battledress blouse and trousers, I decided to play dead as the slightest move drew fire.

After what seemed hours but was probably only half an hour, Willy Neil came up behind, calling my name. I said to him, 'If you can get out here, we can get back . . . so run!' . . . and we ran back to our lines. My Number Two had been unfortunate. He was in a shell hole with German prisoners and others when a mortar bomb burst in the hole, killing them all. The engineers were set to work and found mines on the bridge and on the river bank on both sides. The tanks came up, drawing gunfire down on us and also a large number of foreign soldiers, Turkomans, came from the German lines with their hands up. They stated that they had shot their German sergeant and his aides. A lot of men were lost, but the objective was finally taken.

It took No. 2 Commando Brigade – the 'SS' Brigade title was finally abandoned at the end of 1944 – until 4 April 1945, to fight its way up and across Comacchio, sustaining heavy casualties. Following Operation Roast, the brigade came under the command of 56 Division for their next operation, around the Argenta Gap, where Lieutenant Peter Bolton of No. 9 Commando takes up the tale:

We only had a couple of days' respite after Comacchio until we were off again on Operation Impact Royal with

24th Guards Brigade. The plan was to cross the south-west of Comacchio in 'fantails', land and advance up the west side of the lake to secure a crossing point on the Fosse Marina Canal, which would open the way northwards towards to the Argenta Gap.

We landed as planned with no opposition but as we deployed on the lakeside we came under mortar fire. Luckily we had dug in fast on arrival, so there were no casualties this time. A bomb exploded very close to the slit trench occupied by my batman, Private Woodcock. As I stuck my head up after the bang to see what had happened, I saw Woodcock rising like an angel out of a cloud of smoke, and go thundering off towards a nearby house. 'Come back, Woodcock,' I shouted, but he was obviously in a daze and disappeared into the wood. A further stonk precluded immediate investigation, but some ten minutes later he came staggering back, asking what had happened. My rucksack, which was on the edge of my slit trench, was peppered with shrapnel, and an emergency ration tin of black chocolate in the top had been completely pulverised. Woodcock was pretty deaf, and had to be left with the MO.

It was getting dark as we slogged on and we must have been pretty tired as one of my lance corporals walked off the side of the track and fell into an old slit trench. Unfortunately, he had a tin of detonators in his trouser pocket and as he fell they were crushed and went off. He was pretty severely peppered in the groin. Another casualty, and we hadn't even begun the operation! My first objective was a group of farm buildings dominating the bridge over the canal. When secure we were to signal our arrival there by playing the Troop tune on the bagpipes (we had the piper with us) and then press on to the second objective, a bridge. It was dark as we approached the farm and when we were some 300 yards away, we got down off the raised roadway and made our way along the base, hidden, we hoped, by the bank.

We had just started to move again when there was a shout, a grenade went off and there was a burst of fire.

Next, two prisoners were hustled back and it appeared that my leading scout had fallen into an enemy advance post in a trench. He thought they must have been asleep, but one of them had been quick enough to throw a grenade at him. No casualties at this stage, but our silent approach gambit was completely blown.

I shouted at the Troop to spread out in line across the field to our left and charge the buildings ahead. This we did and I must admit it was exhilarating . . . real 'over the top' stuff. We had bayonets fixed and whooped in, screaming like Dervishes. Someone appeared at an upstairs window and fired several bursts at us as we ran. I replied on the run with my .45 pistol and fired three shots – all of which went miles wide – and then I caught my foot in a hole, went over in a clash, and the .45 spun out of my hand. I did not have a lanyard on it (they get terribly in the way) so I lost it. This was not the time or place to hang about looking for it, so I scuttled after my chaps and ran into the farmyard. As I entered the yard there was what I can only describe as a God Almighty bang . . . and I lost consciousness in a great blast of air. As I dropped to the ground there was another great flash and bang, and to my horror I saw the barrel of what looked to me a most enormous gun just in front of me.

I also saw Corporal Daniels of 4 Troop moving towards it. I then heard the characteristic whine of an engine that wouldn't fire. I immediately thought, 'That was an enemy tank' and on the third flash-bang I saw Corporal Daniels astride the turret, Tommy-gun in hand, shouting '*Hande hoch – Raus, Raus*' to the crew . . . and out they came.

It was not in a tank but a self-propelled gun which, as we ran in, tried to get clear – and to put us off until they got it started, they fired at point blank range across the farmyard. We hustled the prisoners inside the building and I raced out again to see if we had in fact secured our objective.

I ran round the buildings with Gunner Riddall, and as we approached an adjacent building, a figure appeared and fired a long burst of Schmeisser in our direction. I felt a terrific bang on the head, fell down and thought 'What a ridiculous time to die, right at the end of the war.' I felt with my fingers for the hole I was sure was in my forehead, and then Riddall was shouting, 'Are you all right, sir? Your helmet's on fire!' I took it off and found that a bullet had struck the front rim, splitting the front of the helmet, and the spark had ignited the scrim and the camouflage netting.

Riddall had taken a shot at the guy, but we didn't proceed with that approach and returned, collected a few more chaps and assaulted the building from the opposite side. I happily gave the order to play the pipe tune, signalling our success, and I must add proudly that 4 Troop's piper was the first one to play. As the night wore on, one by one, the other Troops were heard playing their 'on objective' tune. It was most heart-warming. We seemed to be a bit thin on the ground and I found that we had three chaps wounded in the initial charge up to the farm.

We pressed on into phase two of the operation, to seize the bridge. George Bisset, our own RE chap, went forward to recce the area for booby traps, and to see if it was wired up to be blown by the enemy. As we ran towards the bridge we came under pretty heavy fire, and suddenly there was a flash just beside me, and to my horror I saw Private Young on fire. A bullet, or maybe a bit of shrapnel – we were under mortar fire at the time too – had hit a 75 phosphorus grenade in his belt pouch. We tore his equipment and denison smock off and pushed him down in the mud to try to put it all out. We didn't really succeed, and as he was in great pain I gave him a shot of morphine – all officers had a pack of five of these – and was just about to leave and carry on, when he gasped, 'Is it all right if I have a fag, sir?' It didn't really matter, as his face was alight anyway. As I left him, I'd taken only about three paces when the whole earth erupted and I was blown flat on my back. The bridge had been blown and had I not delayed those few minutes with Young, we would all have been on it.

As I tried to make my way back, I had to crawl across an area under fixed line fire. It was pretty frightening as they were using tracer bullets. As I crawled and stumbled past a small building, a helping hand drew me in, saying, 'Wait a minute, laddie – what's going on?' It was Angus Ferguson, and he told me that Harry Kither had just been killed at that place. Anyway, we withdrew to the safe(?) side of the roadway and awaited events. My Troop was now at about half strength and as in most battles, I didn't know where everybody was.

Gradually, as dawn came, we realised what was happening and it was decided that we would dig in and assault the canal that night so we holed up all day and tried to sleep. I was told that some REs would be bringing up assault boats with which we would cross the canal but unfortunately the assault boats had to be carried up and over the road and as the road was under almost continual fire, this posed problems.

Each boat needed at least four men, better still six, to manhandle it, and the REs who delivered the boats to us evaporated before I could press them into helping. What was left of 4 Troop tried and we got two or three boats across the road but took casualties and really did not have an effective Troop left to do anything with: one of my stalwarts, Corporal Tanner, an ex-City of London policeman, was killed, and we had several chaps pretty badly wounded. And at the height of all this, in pitch dark, lit only by tracer bullets, I was in a hole when I saw a tall figure standing over me with a large map case at the ready.

'I say,' said the figure, 'are you an officer?' 'Yes,' I snarled, 'who the hell are you?' 'Oh, I'm the IO of 2nd Scots Guards,' he said, 'and we're going to take over from you tomorrow. I was just having a look around first.'

'For God's sake get down before you get your head blown off,' I said. 'Oh dear,' was the reply. 'Is it really as bad as that?' I tried my best to enlighten him but it was difficult. At the time I had a sergeant from another Troop on a stretcher awaiting evacuation, and another of my chaps so badly wounded that the only place I could give him a shot of morphine was in the belly. I must say I was greatly impressed by the bearing of the Guardsman. His inability to recognise an officer was probably genuine. We did not wear pips on an operation like this. Section Commanders wore a piece of greenish rope on each epaulette and Troop Commanders wore two pieces. I think the CO and God wore three, but I never saw either of them close-to at the time.

My next memory is of lying on a canal bank with Major Leslie Callf and Captain Mat Kennedy, awaiting the return of Lieutenant Mark Cloake of 4 Troop, who was sent to see what the chances were of getting across the canal without the boats. When he came back he was literally bubbling mud and ooze. 'Mud,' he said. 'Mud, right up to here,' indicating his chest. I had the remnants of 4 Troop with me on the bank, waiting to lead the way across, then let other Troops, less decimated perhaps, come through. However, it was not to be. A decision was taken to stay where we were until dawn, then reassess the situation. As we lay there a rum ration came up and CSM Scott of 4 Troop enthusiastically dispensed the tots.

As dawn lightened the sky it was obvious that our present position was untenable so we decided to withdraw to a wood about 200 yards to our rear. Out of my section of twenty-four men I had seventeen casualties. Not all were killed or seriously wounded, but seventeen were sent back, one way or another. Our padre, John Birkbeck, was a tower of strength during this operation. His jeep, with its two stretchers for our dead and wounded used the open road, and his presence was a great assistance. Later, back we went to Marina de Ravenna, and that was the end of our war in Italy.

12

D-DAY and NORMANDY, 1944

'It is lawful for all Christian men, at the command of the magistrates, to carry arms and serve in the Wars.'

Articles of the Church of England

Having finished with the war in Italy, it is now necessary to go back a little in time and distance, to Britain in the summer of 1944, and rejoin the 1st Commando Brigade for the Normandy landings – D-Day. No. 3 Commando, 280 strong, which had returned to England on 4 January 1944 to join the Allied armies preparing in Britain for the D-Day landings, found that things had changed a great deal in Combined Operations while the unit had been in Italy, and that the Commando organisation had expanded considerably.

By mid-1943, three Brigade Headquarters had been established, one in the UK, the second in the Middle East and a third, No. 3 Commando Brigade, about to form in India, for operations on the Arakan coast of Burma. Another was needed in the UK. Therefore, when Brigadier Laycock became Chief of Combined Operations in 1944, one of his first tasks was to reorganise the entire Commando set-up, replacing the old ad hoc arrangements with a more formal though flexible structure.

By 1944 there were four Commando (or Special Service) Brigades: No. 1, preparing for D-Day in the UK; No. 2, as already described, in the Mediterranean; No. 3 in or en route for the Far East, and No. 4, also forming in the UK for D-Day and consisting entirely of newly raised Royal Marine units from the old Royal Marine Division. These new Royal Marine units caused some heart-searching among the Army Commandos.

The root cause of this concern was that Royal Marine Commandos were not all-volunteer units. The original Royal Marine Commando – No. 40 – had been entirely composed of volunteers and the two Royal Marine units which followed, Nos 41 and 43, had taken their full share of the fighting in Italy and Yugoslavia and had been quickly accepted in the pressure of battle by their Army Commando comrades. The units now training in England, Nos 42, 45, 46, 47 and (from March 1944) 48 (Royal Marine) Commando, were a slightly different proposition. Brigadier Durnford Slater, for one, was dead set against them.

Now Deputy Commander of Commando Group which, under General Robert Sturges, controlled all four Special Service Brigades and the supporting establishments, Durnford Slater felt that 'units of conscripted Marines could not be expected to maintain the high standards achieved by volunteers'. His feelings were widely shared by other ranks of No. 3 Commando, who barred Marines from the pubs they frequented in Worthing, an act which led to a number of brawls.

John Kruthoffer of No. 40 Commando and No. 30 Assault Unit (No. 30 Commando) found the Army/Marine conflict little to worry about:

Most of the instructors I met in Scotland were Army types and absolutely first-class. They could not have been more helpful or encouraging to the RM Commando – the 'A' Commando as it then was – in 1942. I can say the same about other units or Army individuals met in training or elsewhere. There was always cheerful banter but a lot of mutual respect. I suspect this was because we all suffered the same niggling criticism from our regular units, who did not like the idea of Commando units anyway.

Durnford Slater soon found that his most important task was to promote co-operation between the old Army and the new Royal Marine units, who had got rid of their unwilling recruits at Achnacarry, or during early training, and were now eager to play their part on D-Day. From his Mediterranean experience, Durnford Slater also knew that the best way to promote comradeship among front line units was to brigade the units together. So No. 45 (Royal Marine) Commando was sent to Brigadier Lord Lovat's 1 SS Brigade, which came to include Nos 3, 4, 6 and 45 (Royal Marine) Commando, plus the French Troops of No. 10 (IA) Commando, under Commandant Philippe Keiffer, attached to No. 4.

Lieutenant-Colonel Peter Young also found few problems with inter-unit relations:

> No. 1 Commando Brigade – 1 SS Brigade, as it was then – was under Brigadier Lord Lovat. 45 (Royal Marine) Commando was under Charles Ries, a good man and a good friend of mine. Ries also had a very good Second in Nicol Gray, a very strong-minded soldier, who later commanded the Palestine Police. A very good feeling soon existed between all units of 1 Brigade, later brilliantly led by Derek Mills-Roberts, a wonderful soldier.

The second D-Day brigade, No. 4 (Special Service) Brigade, was under a Royal Marine Brigadier, 'Jumbo' Leicester, and consisted of Nos 41, 46, 47 and 48 (Royal Marine) Commando.

For D-Day, the tasks facing the two Commando brigades were very different and since this book is primarily concerned with the Army Commandos, the tasks and actions of No. 4 (SS) Brigade can be dealt with swiftly. There was a difference between the two brigades' tasks. No. 1 (SS) Brigade had to land on Sword Beach, break through the German lines and link up with 6th Airborne Division six miles inland, across and astride the River Orne and the Caen Canal at Benouville, coming under the command of 6th Airborne for the subsequent battles in the bridgehead.

The units of No. 4 (SS) Brigade were employed separately

to extend and link up the flanks of the British and Canadian divisions landing on Gold and Juno Beaches, west of Ouistreham around the Bay of the Seine and up to the junction with the Americans landing on Omaha, west of Port-en-Bessin, a fishing port at the junction of the two Allied armies

Since many people think that Commandos always specialised in assault and went ashore first, ahead of the main landing, it is worthwhile pointing out that on D-Day all the Commando units were in the follow-up waves and landed *behind* the assault divisions when, in an ideal world, the beaches would already have been secured. On D-Day itself, matters worked out rather differently. To begin with, all the assault units in every wave suffered during the crossing from the weather. No. 6 Commando embarked at Spithead on 5 June and sailed for France at 20:00 hours on a starry evening, with a good sea running, as Philip Pritchard recalls:

As the craft cleared the Isle of Wight, the Channel gale began to do its worst among the troops, many of whom were soon desperately seasick. 1 (Special Service) Brigade were led ashore on 6 June by No. 4 Commando, followed by Brigade HQ, 6 Commando and the two remaining units, 3 and 45 Commando. No. 4 Commando with the French troops, veered to the east to attack Ouistreham, while the other units made all speed for the bridges of Benouville, six miles inland across the Orne and the Caen Canal.

No. 4 Commando, now commanded by Lieutenant-Colonel R. W. P. Dawson, landed from LCAs at La Brèche, a mile west of Ouistreham at 08:20 hours on 6 June, advancing across beaches where the East Yorks Regiment of the 8th Infantry Brigade were still pinned behind the sea wall by rifle, mortar and machine-gun fire. Private Farnborough recalls D-Day with No. 4 Commando:

We sailed during the night of 5/6 June, and from the deck of *Princess Astrid* I saw a destroyer blow up and sink soon after dawn. Soon after this, we embarked in the LCA, were told to keep quiet, and headed for the shore. Suddenly all hell broke loose, as we sailed close to a ship firing hundreds of rockets. The noise was terrific. We were crouched in our landing craft when a voice suddenly said, 'A bloody racket out there and we've all got to keep quiet!' This made everybody laugh and the tension eased. As we beached, the front went down and out we poured.

I had my left arm smashed by bullets before reaching the top of the beach; I found myself lying in front of a big gun emplacement. The gun was still firing when up the beach trundled a tank and put a shell through the aperture, knocking it out. I was between the pair of them and remember hoping that the chap in the tank was a good driver, otherwise I had had it. He couldn't see me, of course, but luckily he veered off to the right of the emplacement, missing me by about four feet. I must say I didn't realise how big a tank was. While recovering in hospital, I read that the tank commander received the MC for this action.

Colonel Dawson was wounded by mortar fire, and forty more of his men were lost crossing the beach before Colonel Dawson was hit again, this time in the head, and the command passed to Major Menday. With the two French troops of No. 10 (IA) Commando under Philippe Keiffer leading the way, No. 4 advanced towards Ouistreham, clearing sniper and machine-gun posts as it advanced, overrunning a German strongpoint in the casino before moving on towards the 6th Airborne perimeter on the eastern side of the Caen Canal. Meanwhile Brigade Headquarters came ashore, landing at 08:40 hours with No. 6 Commando, followed by Nos 3 and 45 Commando, all heading for Benouville and Pegasus Bridge which a glider force under Major John Howard of the Ox and Bucks Light Infantry had taken during the night.

Peter Young, now CO of No. 3 Commando, recalls the landing:

Three of the landing craft were hit on the way in and a shell hit 6 Troop's supply of mortar bombs, which detonated, killing the Troop Sergeant Major and a number of others. The first man ashore from No. 3 was the Unit Administrative Officer, Slinger Martin, who had served in France during the Great War.

Sidney Dann of No. 6 Commando gives his account of D-Day:

The crossing was very rough and I was very seasick. I took a blanket up on deck and crawled under a lifeboat and lapsed into a stupor. I awoke to a very big bang, which I realised was a shell exploding. A destroyer was burning furiously only a short distance away, and soon we were running into the beach. The troops were coming up on deck for the landing and my equipment was still below, but I made it in time.

We were on the starboard ramp and Colonel Mills-Roberts and half of HQ Section were on the port ramp. The beach was covered in smoke with mortar bombs and 88mm shells dropping in. From a concrete blockhouse an MG 34 was spraying the area and bullets were zipping past. Burning tanks, flails, bulldozers and other weird armoured vehicles lay at all angles over and across the beach. The East Yorks (8th Infantry Brigade) were still at the water's edge and digging in behind the derelict vehicles.

Most of us had never seen a dead body before, so it was a shock to see bodies floating in the water and others, minus head, limbs, etc. lying on the beach. We pushed through, formed up in order-of-advance, and with 3 Troop leading, headed inland to join the Airborne at the River Orne bridge, and then on to the high ground which overlooked the landing area at Breville and Amfreville.

Ken Phillott was in the Intelligence Section of No. 4 Commando on D-Day:

Having crossed the beach, we then had to cross a dyke full of green, stinking, muddy water. A Marine Commando ahead of me was climbing the far bank, another chap was in the middle of the water, and I was sliding down the near bank when a mortar bomb landed in the middle of us. The Marine had ammunition in his pouches and this was hit, yet he sustained only a slight body wound. I suffered no injury, but the one in the middle was leaking blood from shrapnel wounds all over his body. We had to leave him to the medics and thought that was the last of him. To our astonishment, some months later we learnt that he had survived and was in a hospital in England.

Sidney Dann of 6 Commando again:

We had our first casualty some 200 yards inland – a lad called Adams, who had only joined us the day before we sailed, was shot in the head by a sniper. We were being strafed by a *Nebelwerfer*, a battery of six mortars firing thermite bombs. We then met three pillboxes, which were defended. My section's pillbox was soon cleared. We gave covering fire to Jimmy Templeton, who carried our flame-thrower; he gave a couple of quick spurts through the slit and no more Germans.

Major Coade, our second-in-command, joined in the attack on the other two positions. He was hit in the face by a potato-masher grenade, and the CO's batman, Corporal Smith, was shot through the arm. He took the Major back to the beach. We cleared the pillboxes and took two prisoners, our first sight of Germans close up.

Peter Young again:

The Germans seemed very keen to defend Ouistreham, but our job was to get across the Caen Canal and the Orne and on to the Ranville heights – near where the cemetery is now. We reached the bridges just a couple of minutes late and had a friendly reception from the Airborne, who were very glad to see us. I had been detailed for Cabourg but Lovat sent us to the Bas de Ranville and told us to defend it as a German armoured division would be along later. I wasn't too pleased as I had no weapons to hold off armour and, even worse, the inhabitants of Ranville had built their village in a rather *alfresco* style, making it ill-designed for defence by infantry sections.

Sidney Dann continues:

We reached Benouville but found a small-scale battle going on there with Germans holed up in the church. We by-passed that as we were supposed to be at the bridge by midday. As we came out on to the road, about 200 yards from the bridge, we could see a small group of men. There was a short pause while we tried to decide whose side they were on, and then a long cheer and much waving of Union Jacks – the agreed signal. Our OC of 3 Troop, Captain Pyman, apologised for being two and a half minutes late to Brigadier Poett (5 Para) and Lieutenant-Colonel Pine-Coffin (7th Para). Several versions of that historical meeting have been written but 3 Troop were first there and we carried straight on, over both bridges and on to the Ranville heights.

As we crossed the canal bridge, in extended order, we were fired on from the roof of a hospital downstream towards Caen. So it was heads down and run like hell. We passed Ranville, from which came the noises of battle for the Airborne and the Germans were slogging it out. On up the hill to Le Plein and to our position, a large house on the crossroads of the Benouville to Bavent road. We had been told in our briefing that Benouville was undefended. This was not quite so. Two hundred yards from our position was a troop of four German 105mm howitzers and a 20mm dual purpose gun. We were mortared and shelled for three hours and lost 22 of our 65 men and our Troop OC, Captain Pyman, was killed by a sniper while trying to attack the gun position.

As all the Troops of No. 6 Commando had suffered casualties, instead of holding the whole ridge as originally intended we pulled back and dug in at Saulnier's Farm at Le Plein. We brought back our walking wounded – the dead were left behind – and the more seriously wounded were left with villagers. We did a two-Troop attack next day and recovered wounded and dead, destroyed the four 105mm guns and towed back the 20mm dual purpose.

Peter Young:

The Brigade established itself east of the Orne on the high ground from which the Germans could have aimed artillery fire on to the beaches and the offshore shipping especially off Sword Beach. We then had to edge down to the sea and retake the Merville Battery which 9 Para had taken on the night of D-Day but which the Germans had since reoccupied. 45 Commando had a go at that and the No. 3 had a go and we lost John Pooley there.

Philip Pritchard of No. 6 Commando:

Before the landings No. 3 Troop was located in Hove, Sussex. We went on several warm-up exercises which consisted of leaving Newhaven by LCIs and landing (always wet) at a point between Lancing and Worthing. We got to know the LCI crews very well. In our crew was a three-badge AB, a fine seaman of the best type. We always referred to him as 'Sergeant' because of his three red stripes (long service badges) and this made him mad at us as he had explained the difference on every voyage. From here we went in at speed to the River Arun, as it passed through Arundel. We always chose a spot away from the bridge, and used rubber boats brought up by (I believe) No. 1 Troop (using bicycles) to cross the river in the dark. We then marched on for a further distance and dug in to await the dawn. Thereafter we returned to our billets. We did this on several occasions, each time carrying heavier loads over the distance, which was about twelve miles. This was supposed to equate to the type of ground; and distance we would have to traverse on D-Day. During one exercise, a rubber boat overturned and Private White was drowned, his body being recovered several days later at the river's mouth.

Our packs were of the Bergen type, with iron frames. As our supply lines were uncertain, we had been issued with the rucksack type so that we could carry a greater load than normal infantry. This was intended to give us a measure of self-sufficiency until our supplies caught up. My Bergen, which I weighed on a railway station weighing machine, together with my belt and Bren pouches, came to 96 lbs. In addition, I carried a rifle – Lee-Enfield Mk 4 (303 in) and bayonet which would put the average weight carried by any Commando soldier in 1st SS Brigade at well over 100 lbs which, I imagine, would make us the most heavily laden foot soldiers of the war (possibly of any war!) We marched in a bent-over position, it being impossible to remain upright for long, and often had to assist one another to put on the packs.

On the late afternoon of 4 June we made a final check of our kit and were issued with our combat rations. Each soldier received two 24-hour ration packs which had been specially formulated for the invasion. The pack consisted of dehydrated meat with boiled sweets, chewing gum and blocks of sweetened oatmeal, together with a ration of 'compo' tea (tea, sugar and powdered milk mixed together). Included was a round paper cylinder of eight hexamine (solid fuel) tablets and a small stove, the first I had ever seen. In addition to the two ration packs was the usual 'iron ration', which as always consisted of a brass-coloured tin about the size of a flat tobacco tin with a thick bar of plain vitaminised chocolate. Embossed on the lid of the tin was a warning: 'This ration only to be opened on the order an officer.' I should mention that none of us carried the useless entrenching tool, and in lieu we carried the general service shovel with one man in three carrying the general service pick (as I was!)

In the early evening we paraded in full kit and went by

TCV to Warsash, where we waited in a field near where the LCIs were moored in pairs alongside each other. We kicked a football about and some of us caught a horse that was in the field and attempted to ride it. About 20:00 hours we got back on the TCV and returned to camp where we were informed that the invasion was postponed for twenty-four hours. We thereafter saw a film called *Going My Way*, starring Bing Crosby and Barry Fitzgerald, which we were told had not yet been generally released in the UK, and that we were the first to view it. It was, I recall, a suitable film to take our minds off the coming assault. Not, I must admit, that I noticed anyone who was obviously nervous.

Personally, I was looking forward to the great adventure, having seen very little real action up to that date. We were volunteers and our morale was always of a high order, and we were extremely proud to be Commandos, come what may. We came from every corps in the army and had no intention of letting either our regiment, corps, or No. 6 Commando down.

On the next evening we boarded the LCIs. After a squeamish night due to a combination of the rough weather, rich fruit pudding and engine fumes, we were ordered on deck for the run-in. I noticed many ships, including large rafts with vehicles on them. One was sinking and a small naval vessel like a corvette was alongside it, taking off survivors. I could not help noticing an LST with banks of rockets on the upper deck which was broadside on to the beach and which had just let go a salvo with a great flash of flame. Once up on deck we fell into two parallel lines from bow to stern. As I was No. 2 on the two-inch mortar (Private Wally Hutton [Green Howards] was No. 1) and was, in addition to the load previously mentioned, also carrying eighteen 2-inch mortar bombs (twelve HE and six smoke) at an approximate weight of 2 lbs each, I was considered to have a heavy load and I was ordered, together with the No. 1, to the bow of the vessel (starboard side) so that we would be among the first off.

The ramps were dropped and down we went into waist-deep water, about thirty yards from the beach. I can remember getting out of the water beside a DD (amphibious) tank and pausing behind it. In the rather grey and overcast weather I noticed sparks appear on the turret of the tank, caused, I imagine, by bullet strikes. I then went up the beach to the remains of some houses which had been demolished leaving only open cellars lined with concrete. Here I bound up a slight hand wound on Trooper Tim Corrigan, who was our sniper.

No. 3 Troop was not the leading troop, and we moved across a road with a tramline alongside it. We then moved over about 500 yards of open marshland intersected with several dykes which had evil-smelling muddy banks, and which we had to wade through or jump, until we reached a three-strand cattle-wire fence. We noticed little yellow pennants with black skull and crossbones hanging from this fence and learnt later that this indicated a minefield. As nobody, to my knowledge, was injured during the crossing I imagine this may have been one of those phoney minefields intended to deceive us.

We assembled in a small wooded copse for an attack on some concrete pillboxes. I was in a ditch which lined the edge of a cornfield, firing at the pillboxes, and from here I was ordered forward through the corn after dumping my heavy Bergen rucksack, not before I had accidentally fired my rifle in the air. I seemed to spend most of this attack crawling through the waist-high corn until a light tank appeared and we were ordered back to our assembly area in the copse.

Here we picked up our kit and moved on through a small village where some of the local people came out into the street. I was handed a bottle by a middle-aged Frenchman and found it to be a strong, rawish spirit, which I later discovered was Calvados. We went through this village into open country, until we came to the canal bridges, which we doubled across as best we could with our heavy loads.

As I ran across one of the bridges, I stopped near a dead

British officer who had a Colt automatic .45 pistol attached to his neck with a lanyard. I broke the lanyard by putting my boots on it and secured the pistol in an inner pocket of my BD blouse. The pistol came in very handy later on. This officer was one of the glider party that had landed during the night and did such good work in capturing the bridges intact.

We moved very rapidly, and by about 14:00 hours were in Bréville. Here we dug in and I, with several others – Gunners Puttick and 'Ginger' Smith were two I can remember – looked through the house, set in its own grounds of about an acre enclosed by a high brick wall. In one room we found a German Army leather pistol holster (empty) on a bedside table, and in a wardrobe in the same room a uniform coat. The evidence seemed to point to a hasty departure. In a chest we found a couple of pairs of neatly rolled socks made of some heather-coloured coarse mixture; I believe Gunner Smith put a pair on in exchange for his own.

We had started to dig in when my subsection was ordered to accompany Captain Pyman, our troop leader, together with Lieutenant Colquhoun on a recce to find the enemy. We moved out from the rear of the house, and went into the garden of another quite large house nearby. Captain Pyman was lying on the other side of a hedge with Lieutenant Colquhoun, and the rest of us were lying in the garden behind the hedge. I was actually behind a large manure heap with marrows growing on it, next to Private 'Lofty' Layton and Sapper Ron Pealing. Captain Pyman said, 'I can see someone waving a yellow air identification slip. I will wave back with one of ours: who has one?' This was a fluorescent yellow cloth with loops sewn on and one was passed to Captain Pyman who put it on the barrel of his rifle, stood up and waved it. There was a burst of machine-gun fire, followed by a pause, when Lieutenant Colquhoun said, 'Captain Pyman has been hit.' Another pause. 'Captain Pyman is dead.'

The enemy then fired mortar bombs into the garden, wounding several of us, including Private Layton. As things were getting hot we moved to the front of the house. I managed to carry Private Layton plus his weapon and mine. I stopped in a lane and laid Private Layton on the ground. An old French couple came out of a house adjoining the lane. They became very concerned about Layton, and asked us to put him into the house, which we did. His face was grey and his eyes appeared to roll up into his head. The enemy started to press us and we moved back to the main house as quickly as we could, firing Brens to slow them down. Once there we started to dig in again. Several shells then hit the house, causing many casualties, including my chum Gunner Puttick who was very badly wounded.

About 19:00 hours a jeep arrived and took some wounded away, and we moved back to Le Plein where the main Commando was, carrying the remainder. I helped to carry Gunner Puttick. He must have been in great pain as a shell had exploded virtually alongside him, shattering his right leg and arm. He made light of these injuries and cracked jokes when he could. We were forced to keep in the open and under constant enemy fire. Corporal 'Taffy' John or Trooper 'Pluto' Friend fired a few 2-inch mortar smoke bombs to cover the worst area, which was just after we left the house. On our way through Bréville back to the main Commando in Amfreville-Le Plein, during one of many halts, some French people came out and gave a drink to Gunner Puttick. He made a joke about 'Lips that touch liquor will never touch mine,' which caused us all to grin.

I cannot speak too highly of the attitude of the local people, who gave us all the help they could. On arrival at Amfreville we put the wounded into the RAP, located in a large cider press which was part of a fine farm called, I think, La Grande Ferme. By this time we had lost 22 killed and wounded out of the 64 present at the landing. I know this because I wrote it in the back of an address book I carried with me and which I still have. The survivors of 3 Troop, now under the command of Lieutenant Colquhoun, were ordered to dig in on the left flank of

No. 6 Commando position in an orchard about seventy yards back from a crest.

While we were digging, we heard aircraft engines and we saw hundreds of gliders, mainly Horsas, coming in to land between us and Caen. Flak was bursting among the aircraft and I saw one catch fire, dive steeply and then level off about 300 feet from the ground.

We were soon dug in and a standing patrol was placed on the crest by the orchard, where there was a cornfield stretching about 150 yards to the enemy positions on the edge of a wood in Bréville. In this wood was a German four-gun battery of 105mm guns which had fired on us in Bréville and which was attacked the next day by two Troops from 6 Commando. The wood was captured and my troop was sent in to assist with the removal of the guns. Lying about the gun area were many German dead and several horse wagons loaded with supplies. These consisted of 105mm ammo in wickerwork containers and some rations. I checked the ration wagon and found several sacks of sugar, and had filled a pack about half-full when I saw German infantry forming up for a counter-attack. I called out a warning to my section officer, Lieutenant Leaphard, and to another friend of mine Private S. J. Dann who was looking through another wagon. As we hadn't been spotted, we prudently moved back to our main position, leaving one gun (less striker) as the others had been removed.

Apart from the half pack of sugar, which went to the RAP, we had gained an MG 34 Spandau, complete with a beautifully made tripod, which we set up in our trench line. Later I heard that my friend, Gunner Puttick, had died of his wounds some two hours after we brought him in; I remember him as a fine friend. We continued to occupy the position in the orchard, and were shelled and mortared day and night from then on.

After landing on Sword Beach, just west of Ouistreham, and with 3 Troop of Derek Mills-Roberts's No. 6 Commando in the lead, 1 (Special Service) Brigade had marched hard across country towards Pegasus Bridge, with individual troops peeling off to attack enemy pillboxes, artillery emplacements and strongpoints encountered on the way. Once across, the canal and the River Orne, No. 6 Commando linked up with 9 Para to clear the village of Le Plein, while No. 3 occupied Le Bas de Ranville, and No. 45 moved towards Franceville Plage and Merville. No. 4 Commando came in to the brigade perimeter later, after clearing the Germans out of Ouistreham.

By mid-afternoon the Brigade was on to the heights around Ranville, with No. 6 Commando dug in around Le Plein. The rest of the Brigade was established, in a line between Merville in the north, near Franceville Plage, and Bréville in the south, anticipating the enemy counter-attack. They were very relieved when the glider troops of Sixth Airborne came in to land, bringing heavy weapons, including more anti-tank-guns. Many of the gliders landed in or around No. 3 Commando's positions, and on the morning of 7 June, two troops of No. 3 Commando were directed to retake the Merville Battery, which had been overrun by British paratroops on the night of 5/6 June but reoccupied by the Germans later when the parachute soldiers had to withdraw.

Major John Pooley, a veteran No. 3 Commando soldier, was killed in the assault, and among many other founder members of the unit Lieutenant George Herbert. He and many other soldiers of 1 (Special Service) Brigade who were killed in the D-Day fighting now lie buried in the Ranville Military Cemetery.

S. J. Dann again:

We had been briefed to expect the German counter-attack four days after the landing, as it was anticipated it would take the Germans in reserve that long to reach us. However, three days after the landing, late in the afternoon, we heard – with some consternation – a number of tanks moving in our direction. These were reported as twelve Tiger tanks each with an 88mm gun. Fortunately we had a capital ship – I believe it was the HMS *Rodney* – offshore and 16-inch guns are heavy. We plugged our ears and got down in our slit trenches as her shells came over, sounding like railway trains and shaking the earth even at two miles. This was followed by an RAF Typhoon strike with rockets and the Tigers were no longer a threat.

During that night, 9/10 June, we could hear a lot of movement from the enemy as there was only a cornfield separating us. We could hear tracked vehicles – mobile 88mm guns, we assumed. The night passed quietly and at dawn, after 'Stand-to' I was shaving when Derek Mills-Roberts came along and gave us his 'Not a step back. 6 Commando will fight to the last man and last drop of blood' routine. It looked like being a lousy day. He told us that the Germans were expected to attack at various points and exploit any weakness in defence. Our orchard was an expected target. At 08:00 hours all was still and quiet, and then all hell broke loose – mortars, shells and machine guns – but all this fire fell on the leading edge of the orchard. We held our fire and waited until we saw the glint of the sun on the helmets of the German infantry as they advanced through the corn.

They came at a steady pace through the hedge and penetrated several yards into the orchard, where they stopped and looked about. By all the rules we should have been defending the leading edge and looking down a forward slope to their positions. Instead the CO, Mills-Roberts, had us dig in at the back of the orchard and only have standing patrols along the front. Very crafty.

On the given word, we opened up with everything. My own subsection (I was a lance-corporal by now) had a Bren, a Vickers 'K' gun, a Browning and the captured German MG 34. The Germans were lifted off the ground by the weight of the fire. Some tried to crawl back and the second wave beat a hasty retreat. A period of quiet and then the next attack came in from our right flank, which was clever of the Germans as several of the troops had no field of fire there. However, this attack was a weak affair and soon died out. Then, at approximately 11:00 hours it was our turn again, with a barrage of mortar and shells. This time their shelling was accurate and casualties mounted. Their infantry crawled through the corn and fired from the hedgerow, and when the enemy thought we were softened up enough, they charged.

Of the whole day's activity, this was the crucial moment. They made half the distance between us before faltering and then retreating. Their next attack came from the right flank and there was a danger of a complete breakthrough. Our TSM came dashing along, saying, 'Take one man from each slit trench and get across to 4 Troop. They are in trouble.' To get to 4 Troop we had to go round a pond. This took us out into an open area. A stick of mortar bombs fell and the man behind me was killed and three others wounded. I dived into the first slit trench but got out a lot quicker. The two occupants had both been hit: one was dead, and the other had a serious back wound. I was to meet him again, 35 years later, still paralysed from the waist down, at the Commando reunion.

The attack died down but within minutes German troops had infiltrated through houses to our right, where a self-propelled 88mm gun was moving up the road from Ranville, and I could see Captain Powell with a section going after the SP gun on our left. We were confronted with approximately ten Germans running towards us, using the gardens and walls of the houses as cover. We let them get halfway and opened up. Our aim was poor but two fell with leg wounds and the others dived over a low wall.

Then came one of my lasting memories of the war. I go back to Normandy each year for the D-Day Pilgrimage, and I relive these few minutes each time I walk down that road. We could not move out, and we were down to our last magazine for the Bren and could only keep the Germans' heads down with single shots. They were behind a low wall and could only pop up for a quick burst with rifle or Schmeisser. Then one stood up, jumped over the wall and charged up the road towards us, firing from the hip; he had fifty yards to go and stood no chance. A short burst stitched his chest and, arms flailing, he fell. There was no support from his comrades, so we moved down cautiously and I turned him over. He was a tall, blond, pure German type, wearing an Iron Cross 2nd Class, the Afrika Korps ribbon and several campaign ribbons. I thought what a terrible waste, what a way to finish his career and life.

About 18:00 hours the Germans had had enough and withdrew and peace reigned over our little corner of Normandy. We had been engaged by three battalions, we were now about 350 in number, but I think we did a good job – about one-third of the unit were casualties.

Peter Young recalls the counter-attack:

They hit us with some division they'd brought over from Le Havre and some of their infantry got to within five yards of my HQ . . . very nice of them! Anyway, we beat them off and took 45 prisoners. Then we went to the Bois de Bavent and on Operation Paddle, the advance to the Seine. Lord Lovat had gone, hit by shellfire at Le Plein and Derek Mills-Roberts was the new Brigadier.

I gathered that I was Derek Mills-Roberts's favourite CO, so he kept putting us in first; a fine way to treat a friend. Anyway, we didn't get lost on the move out to the Seine, which was the main thing. 45 Commando put a sharp volley into our rear as we moved off, but I don't hold that against them.

Kenneth Phillott remembers one incident from this period:

One of my tasks was to go down from Brigade HQ to the forward observation posts of the different Commando units and bring back the latest information. One day I passed a 6 Commando OP, which had two Commandos manning it, but after that point I saw no one, felt uneasy and decided to turn back. When I got to the OP I stopped, and one of the soldiers there asked me where I had been going. I replied, 'The forward OP. Why?' They told me that one of their jeeps had gone down that road earlier but had not returned. At a reunion after the war, I was talking to Cliff Bryen and he told me he was in that jeep with some of his men, got ambushed by the Germans and finished the war in a POW camp. A lucky escape for me though.

C. L. Bryen, the RSM of No. 6 Commando on D-Day, takes up the story:

I have no evidence which would implicate any German in obeying Hitler's order to eliminate Commando prisoners and I feel well qualified to discuss this. I was wearing a green beret and Commando flashes and the Combined Ops badge on each sleeve when we were taken prisoner. These caused a little comment by the German Intelligence Officer who interrogated me at their Army HQ, but brought no ill-treatment to me or the other Army and Marine Commandos captured in Normandy.

Indeed, when I came to Stalag IVB in Germany, where some 9,000 British troops were imprisoned, I was the only Commando still in possession of flashes and green beret. The rest had had theirs removed by the Germans as souvenirs. My appearance provoked no comment from our guards or the SS with whom the camp was well supplied, though a green beret was still a novelty. Shortly before D-Day, I heard that the Germans had opened a special camp for Commando prisoners and I got accounts of it by hearsay, but never encountered it myself. Whether this was because the Germans knew they were losing and wished to whitewash themselves, I don't know. Personally, I doubt it, as they continued to shoot Russian prisoners on the slightest provocation.

The time after D-Day was full of incident. No. 45 Commando had retaken Franceville Plage on the 7th but was driven out by a fierce mortar and infantry attack. On 10 June a troop of No. 4 Commando lost all its officers in one attack but stayed in position, commanded by a sergeant. On 12 June Lord Lovat was wounded by a shell splinter, and

Lieutenant-Colonel Derek Mills-Roberts took over command of 1 (SS) Brigade. No. 6 Commando launched an attack on the village of Bréville, which it captured, taking several prisoners, while infantry attacks came in almost daily on Nos 3 and 4 Commando positions. All four Commando units suffered steady losses from mortaring, sniping and infiltration during the days after D-Day. On the 12th, 1 (SS) Brigade, supported by 12 Para Battalion, counter-attacked Bréville and took it, although No. 6 Commando suffered very heavy casualties from artillery fire.

The Brigade then settled into defensive positions around Salenelles, a small village overlooking the coastal marshes, where the men were plagued by mosquitoes and snipers, but kept the enemy occupied with fighting patrols while the armoured divisions fought over the plain around Caen to the southwest, striving for a breakout from the D-Day bridgehead. Philip Pritchard takes up the story:

Some two days after D-Day, we were briefed for an attack on the village of Bavent. We were reserve troop and once the attack had gone in we moved up and crouched in a ditch on the outskirts of the village. Here we met RSM Woodcock (South Staffs) who was a well-known figure to us all. He directed us forward and as my subsection passed him, he yelled out to Private Doug Underhill, who was carrying the Bren and about twenty full magazines: 'Get that top button done up, Underhill!' which caused all of us but Doug to grin. We were not needed in this attack but were used almost immediately on reaching the objective to attack a small hamlet called Robehomme where we started to dig in. We could see across a large flooded valley (Dives Valley) to some heights. We had grown used to digging in by now and had developed a pattern. Each slit trench was occupied by two men. We were given a location which we tested by checking on the field of fire from ground level, and once this was established we dug a trench, five-feet deep, generally 'L' shaped. We then put overhead cover on either end, leaving the middle open for fighting. The cover was either doors from houses or (if we could get them) 4.2-inch mortar ammo boxes, which were made of steel and which could be filled with earth. This afforded a modicum of protection from a direct hit by 81mm mortar. I fancy a shell would be a different matter.

At Robehomme we used the doors from abandoned houses on a 'first-in-best-dressed' basis. After a quiet day and night we were told that we were to move out that evening. A jeep and trailer arrived and as many as possible climbed on board. We had something like twenty fully equipped men in one lift, and very soon all of 3 Troop was ferried down to the edge of the flooded area. We moved over this area via the remains of broken bridges, occasionally wading in the flood-water, until we arrived at a small hamlet, where 3 Troop were put into a large barn with huge cider vats full of rough cider.

We were told to get what sleep we could and about midnight we were roused and moved out along an old railway track until we moved off to the left and up the ridge. We heard some firing ahead and then took the lead. As we were going up a country lane, a thundering of hooves was heard, and down the lane towards us came a German Army horse-drawn wagon towing a 20mm cannon with two horses in the shafts and two men on the seat. A burst of Bren from Corporal 'Taffy' John brought it to an abrupt halt. I did not have time to check the wagon but I understand it was full of ammo and women's clothes and shoes. We pushed on to the top of the ridge and all we saw was a field telephone in a ditch, still connected. One of our number cranked the handle and got an answer from the German at the other end, much to their mutual surprise.

By this time it was quite light and we moved forward along the top of the ridge for a few hundred yards. 3 Troop were detailed to hold an area to the left of the road, while 6 Troop (Major Leaphard) held the right half. I was with my subsection on the road which formed the boundary between the troops. By virtue of my exalted rank, I had acquired a Thompson sub-machine gun, which was one of the original models with the claw-shaped foregrip. With half my section I was ordered to move further up the road to some buildings, where we found a line of German packs in a neat row but no Germans.

Not long afterwards we were heavily shelled. Fortunately for us the aim was too high and the shells exploded in 6 Troop area. I can remember seeing one poor devil blown up into a tree. In fact, I could actually see the German guns, with the gunners loading the rounds from those wickerwork baskets. Our artillery were soon on the job and the enemy guns were silenced. In the meantime quite an attack developed on our right flank, mainly against 4 Troop. Doug Underhill, who had the Bren, moved out of his trench with Gunner 'Mog' Morris, his No. 2, to a position where he was able to enfilade the enemy, and he caused havoc in their ranks by firing along their exposed flank. They pulled out, leaving many dead behind.

The Commando units around Salenelles quickly settled into a routine, standing-to at dusk and dawn, sending out snipers and patrols to harass the enemy in the Bois de Bavent, digging their trenches a little deeper each day as the mortaring continued, getting what sleep they could between turns on sentry-go. This constant bickering with the enemy caused a steady stream of casualties. By D-Day plus four No. 3 Commando had lost 125 men, including nine officers, and while the Holding Operational Commando at Wrexham was sending reinforcements out from the UK as soon as they became available, all the units needed men. By the time No. 3 Commando received a much needed draft of 52 men, it had lost another 62 soldiers, but it continued to harass the enemy.

'A policy of "Live and let Live" is no good when you are fighting the Germans,' wrote Peter Young. 'If you leave them in peace, the next thing you know they will start beating up your own quarters so you have to keep after them.' On 1 August, No. 3 Commando left Amfreville and arrived at new positions in the Bois de Bavent, where it was greeted by a hail of mortar bombs. Heavy mortaring became a feature of its stay in this part of the line and on 6 August, no less than 120 mortar bombs of varying calibre fell on its front-line positions. Keeping to his personal philosophy, Peter Young promptly borrowed the mortars of No. 4 Commando on his right flank, and with eight mortars at his disposal, gave the enemy as good as he got in the shape of a tremendous mortar barrage.

By now the Commando units of the 1st SS Brigade had been two months in the line, which was not a role they were designed for. The declared intention, prior to D-Day, was that they would be withdrawn after the bridgehead had been consolidated but, here as elsewhere, the need for well-trained infantry kept them in the forefront of the battle.

From time to time small parties would go to the rear or back to the beach to clean up or have a full night's rest but patrols went out every night to dominate the No-Man's-Land between the two armies. However, fighting and casualties continued until the break-out from the beachhead began on 18 August when the Commandos were in the van.

On 17 August, 1st SS Brigade was ordered to attack across the Dives. The enemy was believed to be pulling out units along their front and the Brigade were ordered to take the high ground to the east, far across the Dives. This was a night attack across open ground overlooked by the enemy, and began at 23:00 hours with the Brigade advancing in single file, led by No. 4 Commando, followed by Nos 6, 3 and 45. In this formation, the Brigade infiltrated through the enemy lines without detection and the opening shot of the battle was fired when Lieutenant Pollock of No. 4 Commando killed a sentry outside a German HQ. By dawn No. 3 Commando had taken the village of Varaville and 1st SS Brigade was established on the heights behind the Dives, where it dug in to resist counter-attacks, beating off four determined assaults during the day.

This was its last action in the Normandy campaign. In early September 1944, the Brigade returned to the UK, where it began to prepare for a move to the Far East. At the end of

September, No. 4 Commando was detached from No. 1 Brigade and returned to the Continent to replace the much-reduced No. 46 RM Commando in 4 (SS) Brigade. This brigade was now preparing for the next great Commando operation of the war – the assault on the island fortress of Walcheren.

13

WALCHEREN TO THE MAAS, 1944–5

'It is imperative to contest every point for complete victory, so the profit can be total.'

Sun Tzu
The Art of War

To continue their advance across Belgium and into Germany during the autumn and winter of 1944, the Allied armies needed a working port much closer to the front line than those they had already captured during their advance up the Channel coast of France. By September 1944 the armies were grinding to a halt, mainly through a shortage of fuel, and as more and more troops landed, so the fuel shortage grew more serious. The answer to this logistical problem was a new port, close to the front line, which now lay in northern Belgium and far to the east of Paris.

The ideal port was Antwerp, the second largest port in Western Europe, and the only one fully capable of supplying food, ammunition and reinforcements in adequate quantities to the advancing Allied armies, which now numbered over two million men. The British 11th Armoured Division entered the port of Antwerp on 4 September and found it had been thoroughly wrecked by the Germans. Work began at once on restoring it to full efficiency, and within days it was possible to unload small ships at some of the quays, but as usual with military affairs there was a snag.

Antwerp lies forty miles from the sea, at the inner end of the Scheldt estuary, which widens out below Antwerp, and divides into two parts, the East and West Scheldt, which are separated by a long peninsula, South Beveland, and two islands, North Beveland and Walcheren. These three features had been fortified and were strongly defended by the Wehrmacht. Until they could be captured and the enemy cleared from the Scheldt, the port of Antwerp was useless.

The task of clearing the Germans away was entrusted to the 52nd (British) Division, the 2nd (Canadian) Infantry Division and No. 4 (SS) Brigade, which was specifically charged with capturing the island of Walcheren.

Walcheren had been very strongly fortified by the German Fifteenth Army, who had prepared an interlinking series of minefields, machine-gun posts and heavy-calibre coastal batteries set in concrete blockhouses. The island itself is triangular and largely below sea-level, the shores protected by dykes and sand dunes. The RAF bombed Walcheren thoroughly before the assault, doing little damage to the blockhouses but breaching the dykes and letting in the sea, which flooded the centre of the island, so that the guns and defences were occupying a position rather like the rim of a saucer.

For the assault on Walcheren, Operation Infatuate, 4 (SS) Brigade, still commanded by Brigadier 'Jumbo' Leicester, consisted of Nos 41, 47 and 48 (Royal Marine) Commando and No. 4 Commando, the latter once again commanded by Lieutenant-Colonel Dawson recently recovered from his D-Day wounds. This force, with tanks, engineers and supporting units, amounted to about 8,000 men. To get them ashore and provide gunfire support, the Royal Navy provided 'Force T', a squadron of craft which included the battleship *Warspite* and two 15-inch gun monitors, HMS *Erebus* and *Roberts,* plus a host of support craft, rocket ships and Landing Craft Guns (LCGs) which would help to quell the coastal batteries.

Brigadier Leicester sent his three Royal Marine Commando units to capture the strongpoints at Westkapelle along the rim of the saucer and No. 4 Commando to attack and capture the town of Flushing, the island's principal port. The attack took place on the afternoon of 1 November 1944, and as this book is devoted to the story of the Army Commandos, our tale will follow the fortunes of this last unit.

No. 4 Commando was to land on Uncle Beach at the south end of the island, take Flushing and then advance along the dyke to join the Royal Marines advancing along the coast from Westkapelle. Artillery support would come from Force T's ships and field artillery firing from the southern shore of the estuary. While the three Marine Commandos were battering their way ashore at Westkapelle, No. 4, accompanied by their two French troops and part of the Dutch troop of No. 10 (IA) Commando, landed on Uncle Beach in three waves, starting at 05:45 hours, covered by a fierce bombardment from the Allied ships and artillery.

The first wave did not have an easy landing; one craft became impaled on an underwater obstacle but the troops scrambled up on to the 'Orange Mole' and were soon appearing among the enemy positions. With the first wave established, the second wave came in, landing at the same point, following the leading troops through the wire and into 'Orange Street', making at once for the German barracks and an arsenal. On the way they overran a 50mm gun, turned it round and used it for fire support, clearing pillbox after pillbox as they advanced. By 09:00 hours the second wave of No. 4 were on their objectives in the town.

Meanwhile, the third wave had come ashore, meeting an alert and aggressive defence along the dyke which greeted them with machine-gun and cannon fire. With all the unit ashore, work now began on winkling the enemy out of Flushing. This meant street fighting, house-clearing, street by street, and the steady reduction of the many concrete pillboxes. Each man carried a special explosive charge and much of their progress through the town was made through the walls blasting their way from house to house and passing through, rather than moving down the fire-swept open streets. Any strongpoint that proved too stubborn was reduced by rocket-firing Typhoon fighters called down from a 'cab-rank' in the sky. The bulk of the town was safely in No. 4 Commando's hands by nightfall, and that night it was joined by elements of the King's Own Scottish Borderers, who secured the port and began to dig in.

On the following day, No. 4 linked up with No. 47 Commando which had advanced along the dyke from Westkapelle, and the next two days were spent mopping up pockets of resistance and removing 3,000 prisoners to the mainland. The last resistance on Walcheren ended on 8 November and with the island taken, supply ships began to move upstream to Antwerp, led by minesweepers.

After Walcheren, No. 4 (SS) Brigade which, like all the other Special Service Brigades, became a 'Commando' Brigade on 6 December, returned to Ostend to rest and prepare for the advance into Germany; but increased German activity and the Ardennes 'Battle of the Bulge' from mid-December until January 1945 soon saw it back in the line along the River Maas. The enemy were very active here during the Ardennes counter-offensive, putting great pressure on the Allies.

During the winter of 1944–5 all the Commando units of 4 Brigade made raids across the Maas. In mid-January half of No. 4 Commando raided German positions on the island of Schouwen, north of Walcheren, landing undetected, taking nine prisoners and killing sentries before withdrawing under fire. The No. 4 Commando Brigade mounted forty separate operations against the enemy between 1 December 1944 and the end of the war in Europe on 8 May 1945.

No. 1 Commando Brigade had left France in September and spent the autumn in England, absorbing new recruits and training for operations in the Far East. Lieutenant-Colonel Peter Young was detached from his beloved No. 3 Commando, which passed to Arthur Komrower, and was sent to the Arakan as Deputy Commander of No. 3 Commando Brigade under Brigadier Campbell Hardy. In January 1945, No. 1 Commando Brigade, under Brigadier Derek Mills-Roberts, DSO, MC, of the Irish Guards ('and a soldier if ever there was one', says

Brigadier Peter Young, (DSO, MC and two bars – no mean soldier himself) was ordered to return to the fighting on the Continent.

Mills-Roberts insisted on high standards of training and discipline, and professional soldiering at all levels throughout his Brigade. 'If a morning exercise went well, the Brigadier might give us the afternoon off,' records one officer. 'If it didn't go well, then we did it again and again until we got it right. "Just good enough" wasn't good enough for the Brigadier.' A fighting soldier, who led from the front, Mills-Roberts had the experienced units of his brigade at peak efficiency when he led them back to the war.

Bill Sadler of No. 6 Commando continues the story:

The Brigade had only recently returned to Europe to commence a second tour of operations, having previously been in action continuously for some three months after landing on the beaches of Normandy on D-Day. The Commando replacements and other troops travelled overnight from Tilbury to Ostend before being entrained for Brussels, a journey of some sixty miles, which took exactly twelve hours to complete, allowing ample time for some troops to flog their blankets from the carriage windows to the local villagers. An occasional stop at a wayside station allowed everyone plenty of time to descend and explore, so very little of the currency gained actually left the area.

After arriving in Brussels we spent two or three days at a staging camp awaiting transport to Brigade. Our enjoyment of the facilities for well-heeled soldiery was confined to the bistros. We eventually arrived at HQ 6 Commando and were given billets for the night in a partly-destroyed barn containing straw, but of course we had no blankets. Next morning Jim South received the full blast of RSM Woodcock's extreme displeasure, and later that of the CO, Lieutenant-Colonel Lewis. Due to the intense frost overnight, Jim had slept in his trousers and battledress jacket, which did not improve his appearance on CO's

Orders. The proximity of the enemy would allow no diminishing of the general standard of turnout in the unit where a good soldier also meant a smart soldier.

Arriving in the line on the River Maas, No. 1 Commando Brigade split up. No. 46 Commando was detached to guard Antwerp, No. 3 Commando went to Maeseyck, while No. 45 (Royal Marine) Commando and No. 6 Commando went into action along the Maas. On 23 January, No. 45 Commando attacked St Joostburg and with No. 6 Commando, which had crossed the frozen Juliana Canal on the ice, occupied Maasbracht. Both units were soon engaged in the fighting round the Montfortbeek, where Lance Corporal Harden, RAMC, a medical orderly attached to No. 45 Commando, gained a posthumous VC for treating the wounded under fire.

Bill Sadler again:

The final crossing of the Maas was the first operation after our arrival, a previous attempt to cross the ice-covered river having resulted in failure. I doubt if the success of this second operation was due to our recent arrival. As far as I can recall, 2 Troop occupied its position against little or no opposition.

Each Commando was allocated a sector beforehand and each troop within the Commando given its respective task within that area, each troop being required to capture and hold its sector while the remaining troops passed through their position to extend the operation – a method of investiture and occupation which resulted in those initially at the rear becoming the foremost during action. If a troop experienced little or no opposition, it still occupied its own sector, leaving the continuation of the advance and expansion of the operation to the column moving up from behind. This proved highly effective and we kept moving along and pushing the enemy back.

Philip Pritchard of No. 6 Commando tells his story of the fighting on the Maas and his experience of being wounded:

My Troop was detailed to go forward and take over the advance from a Troop of 45 (RM) Commando. We were in a sunken road which was being shelled with large-calibre shells from gun positions in the Siegfried Line, one of the frontier defences of Germany, which was not far away. We peered out of the sunken road and could see the shells exploding on either side of us. The fire was not accurate and we understood that this was because there was no German forward observer and the guns were firing off the map. At the head of the road, where it came out into the open, we could see several hay and corn stacks burning and behind one was a British tank firing its main armament.

We got what cover we could near some houses, when we were ordered back down the sunken road into the town again. Here we got a meal and moved into a house. This house had a small, narrow cellar with a stove in it. Straw was on the floor and we used this to sleep on, only to find subsequently that there was a teller-mine in the stove. As no one had attempted to light the stove or close the door – it had been wired in the open position – we were lucky! That evening we were again briefed that we were to attack where 45 (RM) Commando had been held up the previous afternoon.

Early next morning we were given a cup of compo tea, two pieces of cold Spam and four biscuits each, prior to moving into some old German trenches built World War One fashion, opposite a creek with a windmill on the far bank. The creek, which was lined with leafless trees, was about 300 yards away. Somehow my section had acquired an issue water bottle, full of rum, which we passed along the trench. It had just reached me when we got the signal to go. We swept forward to the creek which was frozen over. After a short while in the creek bed we were ordered to take some buildings over to our right. These proved to be the remains of a condensed-milk factory with a large cellar, in which many Dutch people were sheltering.

We took over some existing enemy positions which had

been dug by the Herman Goering Parachute Division. Some of their dead were lying around, well clad in snow-suits, which was more than we were. We were still wearing brown and green camouflaged parachute smocks and brown leather jerkins, which stood out clearly in the snow-covered countryside. There was a railway line nearby, and very soon I was ordered, together with the section, to go down this line and prevent some Germans from unloading a wagon.

In the section at that time were Private 'Inky' Penn, Sapper Hedges, Sapper 'Big Bill' Scott, Gunner 'Mog' Morris and Private Ernie Crouch to mention a few. Sapper Hedges had the Bren and we opened fire from the railway track at 700 yards on some German infantry, only to notice that we were having no effect on them. We then left the railway and ran over an open field some 150 yards to the road. This road led down to a cluster of houses and we did a rapid search when suddenly we noticed a considerable number of Germans, a hundred yards or so away, converging on the houses.

We started a lively fire (Bren and rifle) from the windows of the houses. In one such action Bill Scott fired his rifle through a window while 'Inky' Penn played a one-finger version of 'In the Mood' on a piano that happened to be there. Subsequently this was reported in one of the Northumberland papers as 'Fishburn man fights to music', Fishburn being the home of Sapper Scott. Sapper Hedges was hit in the calf and I took over the Bren and kept it firing until we all got back to the factory area. Upon our return it was noticed that Private Crouch was missing. He was a great pal of 'Inky' Penn, and they were both Londoners. They went through the depot at Achnacarry together and were in the same billet. So far we had had nothing to eat since our sparse breakfast, and I was told that a meal was on its way.

During our absence someone had discovered a Kitchener type of fuel stove with an oven attached. It had been lit using brickettes of brown coal which were plentiful. I opened the oven door, sat down on a box and put my feet in the oven to dry my boots. While I was thus occupied, I heard the familiar sound of an enemy gun firing but decided that as I was under the lea of the factory, the shell would either hit the other side, or go well over the top.

Unfortunately the enemy shell came through the roof, much lower than I calculated, and landed immediately behind me; I felt a sharp bang on my left elbow and dived for the dug-out. There were several in the shelter and when I said I thought I was wounded there was a chorus of 'You lucky bastard'. Once the shelling had died down, I went over to the factory and down into the cellar, where our medic, Gunner 'Darkey' Williams – half West Indian from South Shields and a thorough gentleman – took off my jerkin and smock and proceeded to cut along my left sleeve seam.

Blood was pouring down my arm. I thought I had been hit in the elbow, only to find that I had been hit in the armpit. 'Darkey' put a shell dressing on it. Meanwhile the Dutch people were busy praying in front of a large crucifix and I assumed they were praying for me, which I appreciated. I then made a dash for the RAP which was in a cellar beneath a barn some 200 yards to our rear. Here I descended a ladder into the straw-filled cellar, where there were many wounded. The cellar was lit by a Tilly lamp and our MO (Captain Keat, AC) checked my wound, replaced the dressing and wrote out the waxed envelope which he attached to my BD blouse pocket buttonhole. One of the medical orderlies (Corporal Taffy Eyles) who had been checking the dead said that he could identify all but one. This man had no apparent ID and the only positive thing was a silver ring with 'Armentieres' written on it. I knew at once he was Private Thomson who was one of my section. The ring had belonged to his father who, I believe, was killed in the First War.

It was dark by now and I was taken outside and put on a stretcher, which was strapped to the top of a jeep which then took off back down the road to Maasbracht. As the German guns from the Siegfried Line were still shelling the road, the driver had to judge when the shells were likely to come, so he waited until a salvo fell and then, during the lull, went at full speed over the icy road, swinging and swerving all over the place.

As a casualty, lying on an open stretcher on the top of the jeep, with one arm useless, you can imagine my feelings. As my companion on the other stretcher was in a bad way, I had to try and hold him on as well as keep myself on. I was very relieved when we came to the Casualty Clearing Station where I was taken into a school room. The desks had been piled in one corner and the floor space covered with wounded. The long master's bench was being used as an operating table and I was placed on it under a portable light. The doctor told me that he had been going since 06:00 hours and that there had been such a great influx of wounded that he had run out of anaesthetic and apologised that he had only 'local' left. He then injected my left shoulder, and once it had gone numb proceeded to remove sundry bits of shrapnel. I was then given a penicillin injection, to be repeated every three hours. Somebody had given me a blanket, which I was beginning to need as my left arm was completely bare.

So far I had had no food or drink except water since breakfast, well before first light, and I was really hungry. I did not receive any food or hot drink at the CCS, and a couple of hours after my operation I was put into a proper ambulance with three other casualties – one of whom was in a bad way and who kept crying out at intervals – and sent further down the line to an 'Advance Dressing Station', where, at last, I was handed a small enamel bowl full of hot sweet tea. The bowl had no handle, which made it rather hard to hold, but I managed to drink most of that 'Nectar of the Gods', or so it tasted to me.

The Dressing Station was in another public building, and I was laid in a corridor with several others, mostly from the Brigade. Next to me was a soldier from No. 3 Commando who had a badly fractured knee. He was part of a section which had been trapped in a house in a narrow

217

street by German tanks at either end. There was no way out except by the door. They had only two-inch mortar smoke left, and he had fired the mortar by placing the baseplate just above his knee. This was the only way he could fire it so as to hit the wall of the house opposite but the recoil broke his leg. I seem to remember him saying that he fired at least two bombs. This enabled the section to blind the tanks and get away. It said much for his courage that he did this, and despite his injuries, he got away.

Eventually I left in an ambulance, which took me to an ambulance train. This train, after many stops, finally arrived at Brussels and here we were met by ladies of the Red Cross, who checked with each of us if we had any immediate requirements. We were then driven to a large hospital in the centre of Brussels, the Hospital Militaire Belgique, which had been taken over by the 110th British General Hospital. I was taken up a flight of stairs and placed in a bed. It was nearly dark and I could see out of a window a dark object, somewhat like a fighter plane, with an orange flame coming from its rear. I was told that it was a flying bomb (V1 rocket), one of many that flew over that area and which generally exploded at, or near, the site of Waterloo. As nobody seemed very much concerned by this, I decided that I would not be worried either, and anyway I had other things to worry about.

The ward was full of amputees, which did not bode well for me as my arm had become very stiff and an acid-yellow colour. I was looked at by several surgeons, one of whom was a woman. She asked permission to try a penicillin drip on me, together with a blood drip. This was carried out immediately and I was held captive in bed for two days or so. The Sister fixing the drip took several small pieces of shrapnel out of my left hand and fingers which had been overlooked at the CCS. After I had been taken off the drips, I used to go down each day to a room where my dressings were changed by a very nice-looking VAD.

Later I had an interview with the CO and persuaded him that I could find my unit if he would release me from the depot. I suppose he liked the look of me, as he immediately gave me permission. The next morning I picked up the necessary documentation and thumbed a lift on a truck that was going towards the front line, which took me nearly to Maasbracht. It was just getting dark when I was dropped off at 6 Commando HQ. I was told that 3 Troop was in a small town on the banks of the River Maas called Wells, and that a jeep was going that way. I found the Troop spread out in the town with Troop HQ in a fine house, obviously owned by a Dutch bishop. The house was in ruins and the HQ occupied what remained of the ground floor. My section was in a small cottage at the entrance to the town. We had a Bren post on the road. I was told that the enemy was in the habit of infiltrating over the river and appearing in the town, and the fact that we were in a rear area should not be regarded as a sinecure.

Nos 45 and 6 Commando, joined by No. 3, had beaten off repeated counter-attacks in freezing weather, and continued to advance from the Maas against aggressive German forces which now contained Parachute Troops, SS and Luftwaffe units, until the Brigade reached the Montfortbeek Canal near the town of Linne. No. 3 Commando tried to coax the enemy out of Linne with feint flanking attacks, but when this failed, Nos 1 and 6 Troops stormed the town, roaring across the flat open ground on the back of Sherman tanks, and the enemy wisely withdrew.

Beyond Linne, the Brigade faced a strongly defended part of the Siegfried Line, and began to reduce it with fighting patrols which went raiding across the Maas, and with tank-supported sweeps along the front – all cold work in freezing winter weather. The fighting took a steady toll and the Brigade lost over 100 men in the next few weeks before a sudden thaw in February turned the ground into a quagmire, bringing the tanks to a halt and reducing offensive activity to infantry patrols. On 6 March the Brigade withdrew to Venray on the Maas, and began to train for its next major operation, the crossing of the Rhine into Germany.

14

INTO GERMANY, 1945

'There must be the beginning of any good matter but the continuing to the end, yieldeth the true glory.'

Sir Francis Walsingham
to Francis Drake, 1587

The objective of No. 1 Commando Brigade during the Rhine crossing was Wesel, a large industrial town on the east bank of the Rhine. At this point the Rhine, a fast-flowing river, especially after the spring thaw, was some 300 metres wide and contained by high banks known as *bunds*, which varied in height from fifteen to twenty feet.

Brigadier Mills-Roberts's plan required No. 46 Commando to lead the assault in Buffaloes – amphibious half tracks, accompanied by Brigade HQ, and secure a bridgehead on the Grav Insel, a flat area a mile west of Wesel. They would be followed by No. 6 Commando and No. 45 Commando in stormboats, with the veteran No. 3 Commando bringing up the rear, also in Buffaloes. Once across, the Brigade would wait until the covering air bombardment was over and then advance swiftly into the stricken town. No. 46 was to fight its way into the town centre, with No. 6 Commando following to mark a cleared route, and then the whole Brigade, in single file as during the Normandy breakout, would enter the town.

No. 46 would clear the town centre, No. 6 Commando would

put in a flanking attack on the north-west suburbs, while No. 45 Commando would seize a large factory which overlooked the northern limits of the town, and No. 3 Commando would clear the surrounding area. If all went well, they would soon have a wide bridgehead through which infantry from the Cheshire Regiment, ferried across in Buffaloes, could reinforce them. Finally the US 17th Airborne Division and the British 6th Airborne Division, alongside which the Commandos had fought in Normandy, would drop north of Wesel and move south to link up with the Brigade. During the parachute drop no artillery support was possible, so the Brigade must hold Wesel for half a day without any gunfire support

After a four-hour bombardment by artillery and RAF Lancaster bombers, the assault began at 21:30 hours on 23 March 1945. No. 46 Commando's Buffaloes set off across the Rhine for the Grav Insel, and reached the far side in four minutes. B Troop of No. 46 Commando were the first British troops to set foot in Nazi Germany. No. 6 Commando crossed under heavy fire in its stormboats, and a number of men were hit or drowned when their boats were sunk. A number of other boats were swept away downstream when their outboard engines failed, but most of No. 6 Commando got on to the Grav Insel, and followed No. 46 in the advance to the now-burning city, marking a route with white tape through the dark rubble-filled streets.

By midnight, two hours after landing on the east bank, Nos 3 and 46 Commando were in the town, No. 45 had captured the factory and No. 6 was in the northern suburbs, with No. 3 filling in the gap between Nos 45 and 46. Enemy mortar and sniping began at dawn but the damage wreaked in the rubble-choked streets by the RAF prevented a counter-attack developing and by mid-morning the American Airborne and the 1st Battalion Cheshire Regiment were arriving to expand the Commando perimeter. The troops gave themselves over to patrolling and sniping, in which 4 Troop of No. 3 Commando did particularly well, ambushing several German patrols, and dealing with snipers by drawing fire and then concentrating several Brens on the snipers' positions. By the evening of 25 March, the whole town was in Allied hand and, apart from several hundred dead, some 800 Germa prisoners were being ferried back across the river. Profes sional soldiering also saves lives. The Rhine crossing and th capture of Wesel by No. 1 Commando Brigade was achieve at a cost of eleven men killed, sixty-eight wounded an seventeen missing.

Bill Sadler again:

A general who has a clear idea of what he intends t achieve can dictate his requirements in detail to his Staf before the battle, in full knowledge that the success or fail ure of his efforts will be analysed later with all the advan tage of hindsight. But an individual in battle has only tim to cope with what is at hand according to the extent of hi responsibilities, so I have been obliged to add some detail to my account gained from other sources. I have alway been intrigued by accounts which state, quite clearly and ir great detail, who shot who, when and how often. I was always more concerned that no one shot me.

The Brigade used one of the estuaries of the Maas to perfect its movements and formations during and after the Rhine crossing, and continued to train daily until the Brigadier expressed himself satisfied with the standard achieved. The Rhine crossing was scheduled for the evening of 23 March. During the morning of the 23rd, all Commandos taking part in the crossing received a final briefing, being then issued with a toggle rope and a Mae West to add to the miscellany of kit already carried. As the positions to be taken up after the crossing were directly among those already occupied by the enemy, there could be no direct means of supply, and all rucksack and equipment pouches were therefore loaded to capacity.

My personal extras included, among other things, a field telephone, a reel of telephone wire and HT batteries. I was fortunate in not possessing a rifle, being armed with a .45 automatic slung at the hip, but the overall weight, when fully loaded, prevented me standing erect. On entering the boats later, I released the buckle of the webbing belt to which were attached the equipment pouches – each of which also contained a packet of Army biscuits, an item quite capable of stopping a bullet – and unfastened the epaulettes of the camouflaged jumping jacket, which kept in place the carrying straps of the other items carried. This would allow me to instantly discard all the items carried if suddenly projected into the river during the crossing. I was a good swimmer, but not while still attached to a full and heavy rucksack, battle equipment, a 38 patrol set, a reel of telephone wire and a field telephone. I re-fastened the belt buckle and epaulettes only on stepping ashore on the far side.

The morning programme prior to the crossing included the final briefing and an inspection requiring a full depot standard of turnout in both weapons and dress, all equipment being blancoed to perfection for the last time until after the war, when it would be scrubbed white. Highly polished brass would be dulled later for the crossing. We then enjoyed the last meal not out of a tin until the end of hostilities – half a chicken to each man – after which we were dismissed to rest in preparation for the night operation.

Towards 17:30 hours, however, at the time of the expected first raid on Wesel by 100 RAF Lancasters, we proceeded to high ground to witness the event, the town of Wesel being visible in the distance. Exactly on time, 100 Lancasters, flying line astern, approached from the rear. Veering slightly, and passing overhead they flew directly towards Wesel, each plane on arrival dropping its ten-ton blockbuster bomb on the town before veering away and heading for home. The ack-ack fire was negligible, their positions having been heavily bombed on a previous occasion.

Exactly at the moment the last plane dropped its bomb and headed for home, every gun for miles around opened fire, to begin a pattern of continuous firing which extended to the following day. The ground literally shook as every gun fired simultaneously. The cattle and horses in the nearby fields became crazed with fear, neighing and bellowing as they stamped and galloped around in a vain attempt to escape the noise.

At 19:30 hours, 6 Commando formed up in Indian file to join the column commencing its march to the river, the projected time for the commencement of the Crossing being 21:30 with the entry into Wesel timed for 22:00 hours. 46 (Royal Marine) Commando and Brigade HQ embarked in Buffaloes to head the assault, closely followed by 6 Commando whose task on reaching the opposite bank was to lead the Brigade column to the outskirts of Wesel by laying a continuous white tape to indicate the route taken. Here they would await a second 100-Lancaster attack before leading the Brigade's entry into the town. En route to the river, the column passed through a number of heavily engaged artillery positions, and from then on the march was to the accompaniment of the crash-and-thunder of the guns and the sound of shells continually passing overhead, while the constant flashes of the guns assisted the groups of searchlights playing their beams on to the clouds, often obscuring the almost full moon to create their own artificial moonlight.

After some miles of marching, the packs and equipment began to assume twice their original proportions and weight, but shortly before reaching the river a halt was called to supply the column with some unexpected and welcome refreshment, the packs and equipment being left in a position to move off again, while each man collected his issue of tea, rum and sandwiches – the last bread we would see until after the war.

Normally, when occupying the hole you had dug in the ground for the night, the RSM came round with the rum ration, each man receiving one dessert-spoonful of the life-giving fluid. But on this occasion we were told to take as much as we wished from the large dixies of tea and rum standing at the roadside, with RSM Woodcock advising, 'It will kill some of the noise later.' Apparently we had so far only experienced the overture to later events, when we would be in close proximity to the ten-ton blockbuster bombs being dropped on to the town.

I took a mug of half-and-half, and on return to the packs and equipment, picked them up and placed them on my shoulders with surprising ease but I believe no one took enough of the refreshment to interfere with the efficient performance of his duty that night.

On arriving at the riverbank, 6 Commando began to enter the small boats, operated by Royal Marines, which had been under fire since appearing from their places of concealment further up the river. 2 Troop, commanded by Captain Peter Cruden, initially consisted of three officers and forty-eight other ranks, but this number became somewhat depleted when the boats were hit during the crossing. The second-in-command, Lieutenant Hume-Spry, drowned with other members of the Troop, although some were picked up, to return to the Troop on later operations. The boat I was in completed the crossing successfully, but on arrival we discovered we had landed on an island so another short embarkation and landing was required, again without loss.

2 Troop HQ's intended position was at a road junction close to a railway embankment or at least that was what was on the map. Now it was an area of complete destruction, pitted by large bomb craters and surrounded by shattered ruins. 6 Commando took up their positions, and 3 Commando and 45 (Royal Marine) Commando passed through to extend the operation. 46 (Royal Marine) Commando, who had made the original crossing with Brigade HQ, now came up from the rear to complete the area of occupation, which had to be held against all opposition until mid-morning the following day, when the 17th US Airborne Division were scheduled to arrive. It was quite a spectacular and colourful sight when they did.

Operations throughout the night and the following day took care of a considerable number of the enemy, including the Wesel garrison commander, Major General Deutsche, who was shot dead for refusing to surrender to a patrol led by RSM Woodcock. The RSM was reputed to have had three boats shot from under him during the crossing. An attempted counter-attack by the enemy next morning was effectively broken up by directed shellfire, but another contact with the enemy made by 2 Troop resulted in the wounding of Lieutenant Barnes, which left Captain Cruden in sole charge of the twenty-five men remaining in 2 Troop. One patrol reported that when a number of the enemy had approached them in apparent surrender, one of them had dropped down on his hands and knees with an LMG strapped to his back. The patrol were the ones to return, so they must have reacted swiftly.

Although wireless silence was in force throughout the operation, a twenty-four-hour listening watch was maintained. Telephone communication had been established to the rear from Brigade HQ but such communication was hardly possible between the positions now held among the enemy. I never saw the field telephone and reel of wire I had brought across again, for which I was extremely grateful. Due to this wireless silence and lack of direct telephonic communications, I was at one time required to convey a message to Brigade. After checking the route on the map, I proceeded through the rubble and destruction to deliver the message.

On return I halted momentarily to check my bearings. Most houses look alike after being knocked about by bombing and shellfire, but I soon discerned the route for my return, and also observed one which I thought would prove quicker. As I stepped off in the new direction, a bullet passed through the spot where I had just been standing, followed by the crack-thump of a rifle. Another bullet passing behind me caused me to make an instant decision. He could shoot a lot further than I could and would probably shoot first. He could also see what he was aiming at. Deciding that known ways were best, I returned to HQ by the previous route. Circumstances don't make a man a hero or a coward. They simply reveal what he already is; I was just being careful.

Philip Pritchard picks up a point from this story:

In a garden in Wesel, we found a lance corporal digging a grave. This seemed strange to us and we asked him why. It appears that he was one of a party searching through the cellars when he was confronted by a German officer. The lance corporal immediately said, 'Hands up!' whereupon the German replied, 'I am General Von Deutsch and I only surrender to an officer of equal rank.' This was well on in the war and we had no time for all that nonsense and the lance corporal is supposed to have said, 'Well, this will equalise you,' and fired his Thompson gun at the General, with fatal results. The story goes that Brigadier Mills-Roberts was furious and ordered the lance corporal to bury the General as a punishment. Anyway, this was the gist of the story and the unfortunate lance corporal said, 'That's the last time I kill a General!'

On 3 April, once again under the command of its old D-Day friends in 6th Airborne, No. 1 Commando Brigade was on the move again, heading for Osnabruck, which was seized by No. 3 Commando in a night attack supported by No. 45 Commando. The town was in their hands by dawn and the Brigade took over 400 prisoners.

Bill Sadler again:

The Brigade entered the outskirts of Osnabruck during the very early hours of a Sunday morning, a tactic that would be repeated on later operations. The route laid down for the column required it to cross thirty or forty yards of open concrete into a tram or bus depot, which led to a number of casualties from machine-gun fire. This resulted in the immediate Commando reaction 'Bash on regardless' – the possibility of the column being halted could not be accepted.

The attack had to be continued, immediately, and was carried out by groups of four, five or six men, running straight across the open space at irregular intervals, directed by an officer crouched at an intersection, who selected a group from the column as it edged forward under cover, then ordering 'Go!' The group took off at a speed guaranteeing instant selection for the next Olympic Games. The Spandau concerned was silenced by a well-placed PIAT bomb from 2 Troop, the depositor later receiving one of the Military Medals awarded for the action.

Halfway across the open space, when one of my boots actually made contact with the concrete beneath, I heard a metallic clatter as the German entrenching tool I carried on my belt fell to the ground. I considered the advisability of its retrieval at a speed that would have given a modern microchip an inferiority complex, and before the other foot touched the ground I said, 'B**** you – stay there!' and continued.

The column continued into Osnabruck and completed the capture of the town by 10:00 hours, except for one or two isolated pockets of resistance, taking 400 prisoners, including a number of Hungarians. The local Gestapo chief was shot dead in his office by the Brigade field security officer, Major Viscomte de Jonghe. 6 Commando occupied its allotted positions in town and 2 Troop established Troop HQ and its signal station in the library of one of the larger houses, which also contained an extensive collection of classical, dance and military band records, together with recordings of German rally songs, including 'We march against England'. Some of these accompanied us further into Germany together with an excellent portable gramophone carried for us by the troop jeep, which always arrived after a position had been taken. The jeep driver was also the cook, so his arrival was always welcome.

The discovery of a garage showroom resulted in some of the cars being commandeered by those who had the rank to do it, but their possession ended with the Occupation. However, I believe the 1000cc BMW motorcycle commandeered for Brigade use ultimately accompanied the Brigade back to the UK.

228

Arriving at the next obstacle, the River Weser, the Brigade found that the town of Leese on the far bank was in the hands of a depleted battalion of the Rifle Brigade, closely engaged with the enemy. No. 45 Commando was hastily ferried across to reinforce them, crossing in assault boats under heavy fire from SS troops of the 12th Training Battalion, who gave the Commandos and the riflemen a very testing time for the next twenty-four hours, until the rest of the Brigade could get across about midnight on 7/8 April. To do this the Brigade once again formed into its single-file, infiltration formation, encircled Leese and attacked the SS positions from the rear, while 2 Troop of No. 6 Commando stormed a gun position and captured four 20mm cannons, and No. 3 Commando seized a factory manufacturing V2 rockets on the northern side of the town.

Bill Sadler again:

Some months previously, on D-Day, I had been safe in Southampton docks. I would now be among the first half-dozen or so heading the advance of the entire British Army into Germany. I can recall no regrets. As the crossing was to be made some distance down river from the town, the boats to be used were carried to the chosen spot on the shoulders of 2 Troop during the hours of darkness. What that distance eventually was I have no idea, but no halt was made to change shoulders. I came to the conclusion during the march that either I was the tallest man on my side, or had got the heaviest part. It's quite likely that everyone else thought the same, as the boat was in addition to the battle equipment, ammunition and weapons we already carried.

The crossing was carried out undetected, in complete silence, and within minutes of arriving on the opposite bank, 2 Troop formed up to lead 6 Commando and the remainder of the Brigade on the all-night march, with the responsibility of leading the column in the right direction, at the correct speed, to arrive at the correct place at the right time, being that of Captain Cruden who would use map and compass to negotiate unfamiliar territory. The march began an hour or so before midnight, and was timed to end with an attack from the crossroads at the rear of the town around 07:00 the following morning.

During the march, the column encountered ditches, hedgerows, woods, ploughed fields and marshland, returning to a metalled road shortly after crossing a railway embankment, its first success being a rush through the darkness to capture a surprised 20mm gun crew, who were interrogated and handed over to field security. We were not immune to surprise ourselves, Captain Cruden later confessing to a few moments' unease when he had to resort to the use of a torch in a barn to check his position on the map.

Normally, however, the strict silence maintained throughout the march, with all conversation reduced to a whisper and smoking forbidden, combined with the use of the silent Commando boot and the practice of approaching from the direction least expected, in Indian file during the hours of darkness, usually made the approach of the column difficult to detect until too late.

Throughout the night march the artillery maintained sporadic periods of fire on the surrounding countryside, directed by the 'Forward Observation Officer' (FOO) accompanying the column, so that the Brigade continually traversed around and eventually moved ahead of its own shells. 2 Troop led the column towards the crossroad selected for the commencement of the Brigade's attack, keeping close to the hedgerow on one side of the country road.

While still approaching the crossroad a sentry appeared from behind the houses on the right, whereupon the column stood stock still. The sentry wandered out into the centre of the crossroad and looked down towards the town, where another shell had just fallen. He then turned and looked in our direction. Whether the camouflaged jackets and green berets against the hedgerow background were sufficient to conceal us is hard to believe, but he apparently failed to see us and turned back towards the town. It was then the realisation of what he had seen suddenly hit him and he stiffened, to turn back with his arms slowly rising. On being made prisoner, the half-empty bottle of Advocaat in his right hand revealed the real reason for his slowness of recognition. He had not been shot on sight as that would have raised the alarm. In his present condition he might not have cared.

Having led the all-night march, 2 Troop was now in the front position for first entry into the town. The Brigadier's ruse had apparently succeeded, the enemy still being contained at the riverside, convinced that this was the area that would be attacked. 2 Troop was thus able to occupy its own positions against little or no opposition; the remainder of the Brigade then passed through to successfully engage the riverside and other positions from the rear and 3 Commando captured a V2 rocket factory, complete with its staff of scientists.

The Brigade was then transferred to the 11th Armoured Division and moved on again towards the Aller, crossing the river on the half-blown spans of a railway bridge to take the town of Essel by assault, No. 6 Commando charging the enemy position to the sound of hunting horns. Covered by fire from the support Troop MMGs, No. 6 Commando cleared the enemy out of Essel at the point of the bayonet, advancing over a quarter of a mile at the trot and killing everyone who stood in its path.

Bill Sadler continues:

The crossing of the River Aller involved the only road bridge for miles in either direction, a post defended by the 2nd Battalion of Marine Fusiliers (Kriegmarines). A direct assault would undoubtedly result in its immediate destruction, but a mile or so north a railway bridge, now a mass of twisted rails and girders, also spanned the river. Shortly after dark, the leading troop of 3 Commando crossed this bridge in stockinged feet and captured its defenders and the demolition party preparing its final destruction, at a cost of five men wounded.

The Brigadier then decided that where these few could go the rest of the column could follow so, headed by 3 Commando, we all crossed in Indian file, to move around and behind the enemy positions in complete silence, until 3 Commando and Brigade HQ engaged the enemy in close-quarter fighting in the woods later in the morning, an action which resulted in temporary stalemate as far as the objective was concerned. It was then decided that the position had to be taken by storm by 6 Commando, at the point of the bayonet.

6 Commando were withdrawn from the positions they had dug during the night, in which they had only recently experienced some searching mortar fire, and were entrenched in line along the long dry ditch immediately facing the open area they had to cover to reach the enemy's position; Vickers machine guns from Heavy Weapons Troop also extended along the line, then opened fire for a pre-determined period, completely lacerating the enemy positions. The moment they stopped firing, each man knew what he had to do.

Lying there with bayonets fixed, nine rounds in the magazine and one up the spout, safety catches off, there was no time for the philosophical introspection beloved by Hemingway and other authors when describing such moments. The Commandos just waited for the bullets to stop. The moment they did so, 6 Commando rose to its feet as one man, and with the second-in-command sounding a 'Tally ho!' on his hunting horn, charged forward. This was carried out at an all-out run, firing from the hip whenever an opportunity presented itself. It made more sense to kill a man at a distance than to get close enough to use the bayonet. Doing it at the run shortened the time he had available to shoot you.

The enemy finally broke and ran, for which they couldn't be blamed, but not before they had left their battalion commander, two company commanders and the

RSM among the many dead. On reaching the enemy position, my immediate opponent, who I had spotted as we ran in, was already dead. I thought it was as well for me that he was. He was well over six feet and around sixteen stone. He was lying on his back, stone dead, smiling serenely, as if enjoying a private joke, or having just solved a problem whose solution had previously eluded him.

The bridge position was taken after a 400-yard charge across open ground and into the wood but the enemy soon proved his mettle by staging an almost immediate counter-attack, shouting 'Cease firing!' as they came back through the wood. We didn't and neither did anyone else, and the position held after another brief fight. We were then rewarded by the one concession made by the Brigadier throughout the entire campaign: 'No one need shave for the time being.'

On the following day, Nos 45 and 46 Commando expanded the Brigade bridgehead across the Aller, but met heavy resistance from fresh German troops. On 13 April they tried again, No. 45 achieving its objective and No. 46 Commando seizing the town of Hadensdorf after a very stiff fight in which its 'Y' Troop lost all its officers and continued to advance under the command of Sergeant S. Cooper, MM, who led the troop until the town fell.

D. Blackburn of No. 6 Commando, tells of an incident that happened about this time:

I have told this story several times but I am sure many people do not believe it and think it's just a good 'Old Soldier's Yarn'. You will recall that when we withdrew from the Battle of Green Hill in North Africa we had to leave many wounded behind in the care of our section stretcher bearer, who volunteered to remain with the wounded and be taken prisoner. Well, after D-Day and various other campaigns, we returned to Germany for further action, and one of the tasks included clearing the enemy from a vast area of forest, thick woods, shrubs and poor

233

roads or dirt tracks where large forest fires broke out from the continual shelling.

We were lying up in the wooded areas, awaiting orders, when the look-out shouted, 'Movement to immediate front!' and we saw two figures. One was in RAF uniform and the other wore khaki dress of some sort. We were very cautious, as on previous occasions the Germans had played tricks on units to expose their positions, with dire results. It was full sunlight and we lay very low as the two figures unsuspectingly approached, straight in line with our position. When they were within shouting distance, we hailed them. 'Halt, who goes there!' The reply came, 'British prisoners of war.' We replied, 'Advance slowly,' and as they came towards me I couldn't believe my eyes. 'Good God. It's Garth!' The stretcher bearer who had stayed behind two years ago on a hilltop in Africa had walked straight into his own section in the middle of Germany. Out of, I suppose, possibly one million British, American, French and Canadian troops, he walked into his own unit – incredible! His comrade was an RAF prisoner of war, and he couldn't believe it either.

Philip Pritchard continues the story of No. 6 Commando in Germany:

The enemy were in Leese where a small bridgehead across the river had been created by British troops. We were briefed for a crossing further up the river and were due to go over in Folding Boat Engineers (FBEs). These were canvas-sided collapsible pontoons capable of holding an infantry section (ten men). There were eight paddles and therefore eight rowers with one man each at the bow and stern. They were excellent for silent crossing of small rivers and were highly portable.

While having our evening meal we were joined by a number of Russian prisoners. One of them had several bottles of what he called vodka, but said by those who had tried it to be more like methylated spirits. One Russian was pointed out as being a colonel. He didn't look any different from the others and appeared rather young for his rank, apparently in his late twenties. At nightfall we all paraded in an assembly area, where we picked up our boats. These were carried to the river's edge and then in successive waves we crossed the river and moved along the opposite bank away from the town for some distance until we all moved over the bank and into a very wet and swampy area where we made our way in a wide sweep round the town to enter the opposite end to the small British bridgehead.

At one point we crossed a road upon which was the black outline of a tank. This proved to be a British Cromwell, apparently knocked out and abandoned. They must have got out of it in a big hurry because I could see through the open driver's hatch the red glow of the master switch light. Having passed the tank we were all halted. We could see, not far away over to our left on the outskirts of the town, a German gun firing, with a long flash of flame coming from its barrel. I can remember seeing one of its crew actually remove a shell from the wickerwork container. One of our Troops made a surprise capture of this gun. The attack on the town no doubt came as a complete surprise to the Germans and they had no idea that we were behind them.

It was operations such as this that gave us such confidence in our Brigade Commander. To me he was a thinking soldier and during any action he was always well forward, generally with the leading Commando, and on occasions with the leading troop. We were never surprised to see him where the bullets were flying. In fact, if my troop was leading, we could be sure that he wasn't far behind. He was thirty-six years old and had come from being a Lieutenant in the Irish Guards Reserve of officers in 1939 to a Brigadier in 1944. A fine effort indeed and in my book he was a true professional soldier and represented all that was best in the British Army.

Once into Leese we started to get long-range machine-gun and shellfire from the railway embankment which had a few wagons still on the line and the enemy was firing from behind these and even at that range managed to kill one of the Forward Observation Officers who was with us. One of our Troops came in from a flank along the railway line and soon put paid to the Germans. We did not tarry long in the town, just long enough, however, for the RSM to have his teeth checked and as we didn't have a dental officer he enquired if there was a civilian (German) dentist available. One was produced and the RSM is alleged to have sat in the chair with his .45 Colt automatic pointing at the dentist – the treatment was successful, no doubt much to the relief of the dentist.

On 19 April 1st Commando Brigade reached Lauenberg, passing the terrible concentration camp at Belsen, coming under the command of the 15 (Scottish) Division, before preparing for what turned out to be its last operation, Operation Enterprise, the crossing of the River Elbe.

Bill Sadler takes up the story:

Nos 3 and 6 Commando had been directly concerned with the capture and occupation of the bridge position, and remained there for some time afterwards during which time 45 and 46 Royal Marine Commando moved out to extend the bridgehead to the north and east, where they met another Kriegmarine Fusilier Battalion approaching to reinforce the German position. The war was clearly ending but they were still willing to fight though an immediate all-out charge by the Marine Commandos caused these to eventually turn and run. One of their officers shot himself where he stood when he failed to stop them. The capture of the bridge resulted in the discovery of Belsen concentration camp later that morning.

On returning from a visit to the camp, the padre attempted to give an account of what he had seen, but no one at that time could fully appreciate what he was attempting to describe. 6 Commando were ordered to proceed to Belsen to assist in the general clearing up, each man being thoroughly impregnated with anti-typhus powder. At the same moment as the trucks arrived to take us to Belsen, a message also arrived with instructions to accompany the armoured advance in the direction of the Elbe.

We accordingly sped along an *autobahn* towards the Elbe without calling in at Belsen. After an hour or two of progress along the *autobahn*, a counter-order was received, halting the Division in its present position, possibly because an immediate crossing of the Elbe was no longer considered feasible. Armour extended along the *autobahn* in both directions as our trucks were guided on to the wide grass verge, where we halted to receive further instructions. On being told to jump down and stretch our legs, my oppo and I strolled over to the nearest tank, only a few yards away, where one of the crew was brewing up a couple of petrol tins. Eventually, after consolidating at the top, 6 Commando moved out to capture the bridge over the Elbe canal.

1st Brigade's task was to cross on the right flank of 15th (Scottish) Division to seize Lauenberg and the bridge across the canal. The assault began at 02:00 hours on 29 April when the war in Europe had just nine days left to run. No. 6 Commando again led the way, crossing under fire in Buffaloes, two miles downstream from Lauenberg. The enemy had dug in on top of a 150-foot cliff and engaged the Commandos with rifle and machine-gun fire and by tossing down potato-masher grenades, but the advance went on.

Spreading out to the flank and covered by fire from across the river, No. 6 Commando swarmed up the cliff and beat the enemy back from the rim. Then Nos 46, 3 and 45 Commando came up, and having seized the high ground, the Brigade advanced to take Lauenberg where an advance patrol from No. 6 Commando reached the bridge just in time to stop a demolition party firing the charges.

It was near here that Field Marshal Milch surrendered his baton to Derek Mills-Roberts, who, disgusted with the sights the Brigade had uncovered at Belsen and elsewhere, broke the baton over the Field Marshal's head.

Bill Sadler again:

> The Brigade continued north unopposed, to enter Lubeck and Neustadt, where we found the bodies of some 300 men, women and children, all clad in pyjama-type prison clothing, lying at the edge of the sea. All had been shot or drowned though the circumstances were never made clear. The Brigadier ordered the burgomaster to provide a burial party from the most elderly citizens, and the dead were buried in one mass grave. Some years later I read in an international paper that a mass grave had been discovered in the area of Neustadt but apparently no one in the town had any knowledge of its existence or origin . . . a remarkable case of German mass amnesia.

Still advancing, 1st Commando Brigade reached Neustadt in early May and the capture of that town brought its war in Europe to a close.

15

BURMA,
1944–5

'Good rest to all, that keep the Jungle Law.'

Rudyard Kipling

Peter Young was commanding No. 3 Commando in the Bois de Bavant when General Robert Stuges arrived at his headquarters and offered him promotion to full colonel and the post of Deputy Commander of No. 3 Commando Brigade which was operating in South-East Asia. 'No one has less objection to promotion than I have,' says Peter Young, 'but I asked the General to defer my transfer at least until the end of the Normandy campaign and I finally arrived in Ceylon in the middle of October 1944.'

No. 3 Commando Brigade, under the command of Brigadier W. I. Nonweiler, had been dispatched to South-East Asia at the end of 1943. This brigade, the 3rd (Special Service) Brigade, which became No. 3 Commando Brigade in December 1944, consisted of two Army Commandos, Nos 1 and 5, and two Royal Marine Commandos, Nos 42 and 44, plus the Dutch Troop of No. 10 (IA). Both Army units had already seen service, No. 1 in cross-Channel raids and in North Africa, No. 5 in the landings at Madagascar, but the two Royal Marine units were new formations raised from the battalions of the Royal Marine Division.

On the voyage to India the Brigade suffered a severe

setback when the ship carrying No. 1 and No. 42 was bombed in the Mediterranean, and had to put in at Alexandria for repairs, but Brigade HQ, No. 5 Commando and No. 44 (Royal Marine) Commando arrived in India in January 1944. No. 1 and No. 42 did not rejoin the Brigade until September, by which time the other two units had seen some action and were back in Ceylon – today Sri Lanka – training and preparing to return to the Arakan front in Burma.

Peter Young again:

3 Commando Brigade had some brilliant people in it and a very good Staff. Douglas Drysdale from the Royal Marines was Brigade Major, and there was Tony Piggot, a very good officer . . . it was a damned good Brigade. Of the units, I'd rate 42 Commando for steadiness and No. 5 for dash. 42 had a very good CO in David Fellowes, a good friend of mine. I rate him and Campbell Hardy very highly. However, I have to say that No. 1 Commando was probably the best of them, a thoroughly good infantry unit, one which deserves to be mentioned in the same breath as 3 and 6 . . . and 2.

Even with half his Brigade missing, Brigadier Nonweiler had had the two units under his command committed to battle. Their field was the Arakan, the coastal strip of Burma between the central mountains and the Bay of Bengal, a vast region of swamp and jungle, seamed with rivers, of which the largest is the Irrawaddy. The Arakan was the territory of the 15th Indian Corps, and No. 44 (Royal Marine) Commando made the first landing behind the Japanese lines on the coast near Alethangyaw on 11 March 1944, going ashore in three waves from old, leaky landing craft. The Marines took Alethangyaw, enduring much harassment from Japanese snipers tied into trees, and after fighting their way through the village put two fighting troops across the *chaung* (river) behind the village and sent out fighting patrols to bicker with Japanese outposts, until the unit re-embarked after two days ashore to relieve No. 5 Commando which had carried out a similar landing at Maungdaw further north, closer to the main battle area.

Frank Atter of No. 5 Commando takes up the story:

Alethangyaw was an operation where both Commandos went into action very much on their own without close support from either the Navy or the Air Force. The object was to take the strain off the main corps battle on the Maungdaw–Buthidaung road, and attract attention so as to divert Japanese troops who might have been used there. My opinion is that we did that efficiently enough. Alethangyaw was under very accurate Jap mortar fire the whole time. We patrolled out quite a bit, but the village was our base, and we took quite a few casualties there.

Then our CO, Colonel Shaw, decided we should attack the Jap mortars overlooking our positions. The exact sites of the mortars were not known, so he sent 3 Troop out across open paddy fields to draw their fire. As I was in one of the leading subsections I can assure you this move did succeed. We went forward steadily, running forward and dropping when the bombs fell. Curiously, we took few casualties while we were moving as the soft paddy absorbed the bomb fragments. We reached a village across our path and were told to halt on the forward edge. We were a bit cramped, and my subsection commander agreed that I should move my Bren group to a depression on our right where there was a better field of fire. Having no sense of smell, I was not aware this was the village lavatory.

As my group were complaining bitterly about the smell, a bomb hit the trees to our left and caused casualties, including one dead, so the complaints stopped immediately. It became quite obvious that without artillery or air support we could not continue. The largest mortar we had was a two-inch, so we were at a great disadvantage, and later we withdrew into a 'box' (a defensive square) at Alethangyaw. That night we sent out a fighting patrol which clashed with a Japanese patrol on its way to attack the box. At the time we did not know what was happening;

bullets and firebombs whistled over our heads, and only when our patrol had seen off the Japs and rejoined us did the picture become clear.

We had the best of it; I think we lost about ten killed, and we had several wounded but the Japs made no further attempts on the box apart from continual mortaring. They realised we were there to stay, and would only leave when our task was complete and Alethangyaw taught us valuable lessons. We had taken our Vickers guns instead of our three-inch mortars. We never did this again, and our Heavy Weapon Troop soon became really expert in the use of mortars in close country, which is a tricky business.

Corporal John Wall of No. 5 Commando remembers an incident at Maungdaw:

We made a landing in the Alethangyaw area south of Maungdaw, where some fierce fighting was taking place. We made a box from which to make forays on the Japanese communication lines. One night my troop was warned to prepare for a sortie and at sunset we left the box in a 'T' formation. 'Titch' Shoreman was at the extreme right of the leading line, when something brought the whole formation to a standstill. At that moment a figure appeared in front of Titch and it was obviously a Jap.

Perhaps the Jap thought Titch a comrade as he was short and stocky . . . but quick-thinking Titch was in a quandary as he was the grenade rifleman and the discharger was fixed to his rifle, which was only loaded with a cartridge. What should he do, as there was a long bayonet at the end of the foe's rifle? At that moment the Jap, obviously confused, jabbered at Titch, whose answer was an equally incomprehensible jabber. At the same time Titch waggled his left thumb to indicate that the Jap should proceed a few steps more to the left and a convenient British bayonet. As the Jap walked to the left, the next man to Titch also waggled his thumb, thinking that Titch was OC the patrol. This thumb-wagging went on until the Jap reached the centre of

242

the line, where he was conveniently shot. Titch was there-after famous in 5 as the only man in the Commando who had carried on a conversation with a Japanese soldier.

As soon as the Jap was shot all hell broke loose; we had run into a large party of Japanese, dug in, with well-sited machine guns. Our response had been to form a box with our Brens sited at the corners so that they could enfilade each side if they came out. However, we did not get away lightly as our Bren magazines were loaded with one-in-three tracer and automatically became the target for almost every enemy gun in the area. At the distances involved, grenades were largely ineffective, and the two-inch mortar had to be brought into action to silence the Japs. From this action we quickly learned how the Japs would shout in English something they had heard. One of our chaps, very badly wounded, was calling for his Troop Commander and the Japs would repeat the same shout in an effort to confuse and attract some men towards them.

Frederick Palmer of No. 5 Commando was wounded in the Maungdaw fight:

I was wounded on two occasions. First, when on patrol with No. 2 Troop of No. 5 Commando in the Maungdaw area when a bullet wound in my left leg put me out of action for two months. I remember being carried on a makeshift stretcher by six Burmese for three or four miles to No. 5 Commando base and HQ at the beach. Freddie Hoyle was the Admin Officer and Sam Hartley was RQMS. Colonel Nonweiler was the Brigadier at that time, and he was on board his command ship about a mile offshore. There were three or four wounded already on the beach. There was a lad in Commando HQ Admin named Fred Musson, a regular soldier, and he fastened a rope around his waist and swam out to the Brigadier's ship, which was a small fishing boat. Using this rope, the wounded were pulled from the shore to the boat and then taken to a field unit at a place called Nela. After a short stay there I went on to Chittagong, strapped to the wings of a Tiger Moth-type plane. I didn't know about all this until it was over as they had given me a jab to put me out for the flight.

Denis Crowden was also at Alethangyaw:

Our first joust with the Japs was not far from the beach, where we were dug in the traditional box formation we used in Burma, on the grounds that you never knew which way the Japs would come from. The villagers dug in too. One night when one of our troops went out to look for Jap long-range guns which had been giving us hell, they walked right into the Japs advancing on three sides of our box. Battle commenced and among our wounded was one chap who had been wounded thirteen times and lay there groaning all night until we could retrieve him at first light. Both sides suffered heavy casualties and I had to lead my section out to bring in the dead and wounded.

I shall never forget how the order was passed verbally round our box then stopped at me. Some of the dead had already stiffened and looked grotesque. In my ignorance, at 23 years of age, I tried to straighten out their limbs, but the only way to do that was to break them and I wasn't going to do that to my friends. A few dead Japs were there too. The Japs usually took their dead away but this time they had had enough and didn't waste any time on that though they did sever one or two arms from their dead to remove forms of identification. When we pulled out, my troop had to stay another night in another location. We were plied with rum so we were trigger-happy and nearly wiped out a herd of cattle in the dead of night.

We were exhausted but before we could return to an area of safety we were called upon to rescue some gunners who had been cut off by the Japs. To find them we went over swampy land in amphibious vehicles, called DUKWs. Lieutenant Noble took his section in while the section I was in formed a bridgehead. Those who went in were

244

badly cut up. A particular friend of mine was wounded and unfortunately tried to sit up and was promptly shot again. He was pulled out but seemed to have no will to live and he had lost both legs.

Lieutenant Noble pulled out three of the wounded single-handed, under fire. He was very brave. When they returned to our bridgehead they came through at the point I was covering. Lieutenant Noble couldn't speak, he was in shock and the wireless operator who was with him, although not wounded, had all the webbing holding his equipment shot away. One saw some strange wounds, such as a groove under the bottom lip, or a neat hole in one cheek and a much bigger hole where it came out through the back of the head . . . terrible sights, really.

Victor Stevenson of No. 1 Commando also recalls the conditions of soldiering in Burma:

Certain things made South-East Asia different . . . and none of them were good. Solid bamboo, steamy jungle, mosquitoes, leeches. The first cut you to pieces, the others ate you alive. We all had malaria, dysentery, rotten jungle sores, prickly heat. I suppose we complained but I don't remember it. These were simply the occupational hazards of everyone caught up at the sharp end in Burma, quite apart from the daring of the Nips.

Colonel Nonweiler's half-brigade returned to India where No. 44 Commando had elephants on the unit strength for a time, and then moved to Ceylon where Nos 42 and 1 Commando arrived to join them in September 1944. Charles Hustwick of the Signals was there as well:

From Bombay we went by train to a camp just outside Poona, which was to be our home for a little while to become acclimatised. At long last we were all together; the other Commando, No. 5 and No. 44 (Royal Marine) Commando were already encamped there. This was the first time I had made any contact with Marine Commandos. They were not volunteers like us and their outlook on life generally was quite different.

Still, after a while both the Army and Marines buried their differences and got on remarkably well. The battles which took place later in Burma proved that. After a period of acclimatisation we moved south to Belgaum near the border with Portuguese Goa for jungle training. We camped astride a river which was alive with water-snakes, though few of us took any notice, everyone enjoyed the swimming and in fact we had a gala. We had a chap called Ron Roberts, an ex-London policeman and Olympic swimmer, so we won most of the events. Learning to live in the jungle was hard; one had to learn how to deal with the mosquitoes, snakes (which were abundant), scorpions, leeches, in fact, anything that moved.

By November 1944 these units had begun raiding again along the Arakan coast, all units participating in a long series of attacks. Half a troop of No. 42 Commando went ashore on Elizabeth Island, south of Akyab, on 30 November, charged with the task of taking one prisoner of war (if possible) for the Japanese soldier was notoriously reluctant to surrender, and would often kill himself rather than fall into Allied hands. The 42 patrol killed ten Japanese soldiers who charged into their position, shouting and firing, and withdrew with the loss of one man . . . and without a prisoner.

On 10 November, Nos 1 and 42 began nightly patrols down the coast from their base at Teknaf and by the end of the month had been ashore eleven times. John Ferguson went on these raids:

On the Teknaf Peninsula about thirty of us used to embark in two LCAs about 02:00 hours every morning and get into a position just behind the twelve-foot swell where the huge breakers thundered down. The LCAs anchored just this side of the breakers and we jumped in and made our way shoreward and carried out an unopposed landing. How nobody was drowned in the breakers is really incredible.

After the landings we made our way back to base, about five miles. Our clothes soon dried in the sun later in the day. This was carried out every morning for a week, and we took it to be part of our normal training but not so! A few weeks later our small party was kitted up and we went to the southern tip of Teknaf and embarked in two MTBs, where to my great surprise and pleasure we met a raiding party of SBS.

The Japanese had erected thirty-foot tall bamboo watch-towers for hundreds of miles down the coast of Burma, and recent aerial photography showed six towers in our area. An SBS reconnaissance party found them to be guarded by a company of Japanese, and our task was to dispose of the towers and as many of the guards as possible. The SBS went ashore in folboats, and myself and some others of our party were selected to go with them in some spare craft. We also had a Carley float fitted with explosives and charges to represent all manner of fire – machine gun, rifle, mortars, etc. – when it was detonated. This float was to be a diversion while the towers were being disposed of.

Anyway, we set off in our folboats, aiming for a break in the surf which pounds the beaches all down the Arakan coast. The advance party of SBS got ashore undetected and put the folboats under cover, but a recce showed that these towers were defended by a whole battalion of Japanese, not a single company as was first thought. So, after discussion it was decided to call off the raid as we could not have got anywhere near the towers with so many defenders to contend with. So it was back to the MTBs, where we launched the Carley float and set it off, the MTBs travelling away at speed. As we passed offshore, we opened up on the Japanese with all our armament. They, of course, replied and passed on information to their other towers, who opened up on us as we sped north . . . an exciting but abortive raid.

On 29 December 1944, command of the Brigade passed to Brigadier Campbell Hardy, DSO, of the Royal Marines, who had a considerable reputation among the Commando forces and Alf Pimblett remembers the Brigadier well:

> One of the things that always comes to my mind is his composure and guts. We were pinned down on a hill on the Myebon Peninsula in the Arakan when he crawled up beside me and said, 'Are you all right?' I said, 'Yes Sir, but scared stiff.' Bullets were flying all about us, but he stood up and said, 'Follow me,' and away the Troop went, over the top of the hill. We killed twenty-four of the enemy in the next half-hour and never had a casualty, thanks to the guts and calmness of a fine soldier and gentleman.
>
> I had occasion to meet him again at Kangaw on Hill 170. Some of the Indian troops were firing at our chaps on the hill, and an officer, Lieutenant Allen Davies, and me, were told to get to them and point out where the chaps were. We both ran like hell across open ground, and lo and behold the Brigadier turned up. We had just lost our Colonel, shot in both knees, and I said to the Brigadier, 'The bastards have got our Colonel.' Realising I had sworn at him, I said I was sorry, but he put his hand on my shoulder and said, 'It's all right, son, heat of the battle.' That's the type of man he was; we would have died for him.

With the Japanese in retreat, No. 3 Commando Brigade expanded its operations, moving on from coastal raids to all-out assaults, beginning on 3 January 1945, with a landing on the island of Akyab. The largest amphibious lift ever seen in Burma was assembled for this operation, but when an RAF reconnaissance plane overflew the island early on the 3rd, the pilot reported back that the place seemed deserted. No. 3 Commando Brigade and 26th Indian Division therefore landed unopposed, though Captain 'Chips' Heron, MC, of No. 5 Commando managed to overtake the retreating enemy at Pauktaw and killed six of them.

Otherwise the snag at Akyab was not the Japs but the mud, as Fred Atter recalls:

Getting ashore was a long exhausting slog through waist-high mud; if the Japs had been on the beach we could not have made it. Some of the troops took *three hours* to cover the 400 yards from their craft to the beach, and staggered ashore exhausted. Others got ashore without their boots or trousers, all sucked off by the mud.

Dr J. K. Paterson was then a Signals Officer in No. 1 Commando:

I was the only officer in the Brigade who spoke Urdu so as a result I was on every 'outing' we had from then on. Very exciting and full of entertainment, but this is not the important thing about my time with 1 Commando. It was a very special unit, from the CO Colonel (later Brigadier) Kenneth Trevor, the second-in-command, Major Jim Davis; the Adjutant Ian Catrell, right through to my Troop funny man Cockney ex-copper, Fusilier Stan Burden. Some are now dead but some I continue to meet, year after year, at reunions, run since 1948 by No.1's orderly room Sergeant Major, Henry Brown.

John Ferguson continues with an account of the landing at Myebon:

Our LCA took us to within 200 yards of the beach and as we got out the sea came up to our chests, but the lower three feet was all thick slime. As we got to the beach some of our comrades were killed when they stood on mines laid just under the surface. We pushed forward and took up position to clean the Japanese from their holes on a ridge. Our Troop officer was wounded as he was preparing for the attack.

The order was given for covering fire as one section advanced, then the covering party moved up. All this time the Sherman tanks were firing, when suddenly, out of the undergrowth on my left, a young boy and girl both about twelve years of age and holding hands, came forward, looked at me, smiled in a startled sort of way, and made their way to the back of our lines, realising that way meant safety. I often wonder what became of these two youngsters. While all this was going on, the headman of one of the villages came running forward to say that some of the villagers were badly wounded half a mile away. We just could not hold up the advance at that moment, so pressed on up the hill as some of the Japanese came out of their foxholes with hands up, although one could never be sure if they had a grenade in a clenched fist, ready to lob at us. Wherever we went there were scores of dead Japanese lying around, but you never knew if they were booby-trapped. Even going over ground or through bushes recently evacuated was a risky business; there was always the possibility of a counter-attack.

The Commando landing at Myebon was supported by tanks of the 9th Lancers which, unable to land across the mud, were put ashore further up the coast, and it took hours of work by Engineers before they could rejoin the Brigade around the Rose, a feature which was attacked and taken at dawn on 13 January.

No. 42 Commando then led the Brigade advance to Myebon village, which was found to be unoccupied, and the Brigade moved on to drive the enemy from the small hills which overlooked the village. During these operations, Lieutenant-Colonel Fellowes of No. 42 Commando was wounded and borne off to the rear, shouting, 'Carry on lads, I'll be back.' That night, 13/14 January, passed quietly and on the following day, the Brigade began to send patrols forward, with No. 1 Commando getting into one sharp fight which required tank support before the Brigade moved on to the village of Kantha. No. 1 Commando, supported by the tanks of the 9th Lancers, took another hill, Point 200, overlooking Kantha, and the Japanese then withdrew. At

Myebon, No. 3 Commando Brigade could chalk up a successful operation, driving the enemy off with 150 killed for the loss to the Brigade of four men killed and twenty-eight wounded.

Frank Atter recalls one incident at Myebon:

No. 5 Commando was in the second wave, and although the landing was somewhat sticky, the tide was not right out, and we were not bogged down in the mud as those who followed us were. We led the advance, and then paused while the Brigade and supporting tanks joined us. Then Brigadier Campbell Hardy planned a series of advances up the peninsula. It was obvious that he knew his job, and we were therefore confident.

I remember at this time, Campbell Hardy noticed Peter Young (our Deputy Brigadier) walking around near us dressed in khaki and wearing red tabs. Campbell Hardy urged him to go to the rear, because if he himself became a casualty, his deputy should be ready to take over. But most of us expected to see Colonel Young up where he always was – at the front, where the action was.

My troop had to advance down a short slope and take a hill on the forward ground. There was a certain amount of fire directed at us, but we moved very quickly through thick cover. The Japanese left the position and we arrived at the top where the situation seemed uncertain. Fire was coming at us from in front and rear and the fire from behind was coming from Garand rifles so Captain Heron, never bothered, simply waved a hand about and said, 'This must be the fog of war.'

After this operation the troops had a few days' rest before sailing up the Daingbon Chaung to land on the mainland, where No. 3 Brigade advanced inland and took up position on a low hill near the town of Kangaw, a hill called Hill 170, that was soon to be the setting for one of the hardest Commando battles of the war.

Peter Young gives the background:

The Japs were pulling out and our task was to get across their line of retreat and make it difficult for them. At Kangaw, No. 1 Commando took Hill 170 and the rest of the Brigade then came up and gradually unrolled to take other hills nearby . . . and then the Japs came up and just hurled themselves at us. They attacked one end of 170 which was held by one Troop of No. 1 Commando and this Troop behaved wonderfully. They massacred the Japs but in the process they got pretty well massacred themselves. We lost over 100 men that day and had wounded being carried past all the time. On the following day we replaced No. 1 with 5 and later that day, when I visited Robin Stewart, the CO of 5, he said that he thought that if we gave the Japs one more shove they would cave in.

I told him that the Brigadier had said there were to be no more counter-attacks as we had done six already. However, I added, 'If you do want to do it, I shall support you.' Robin was one of those chaps who didn't give a bugger, so, without thinking of his commission, he gave them another shove – and they were all dead . . . the lot. There they were, all lying on the ground, dead. You couldn't step on the ground without treading on dead or dying Japanese. I've never seen anything like it, ever. They had great gashes in them, great head wounds. We had killed over 300 and found only two or three with enough breath left to croak. I captured one Japanese soldier, the only one we took alive on Hill 170, the only one remotely human. He only had his heel missing, but we got him back to hospital.

He survived, although the Sikhs wanted to cut his throat. We took one prisoner at Hill 170 and the battle went on for days. Afterwards we got a nice letter from 'up top' saying we had won the decisive battle of the Arakan campaign, but of course it's all forgotten now. Nobody knows or cares about what happened in Burma.

What happened in Burma was one of the great Commando battles of the war. No. 1 occupied the lower, southern slopes of Hill 170 before being held up by machine-gun fire. No. 42 Commando then came up and took the land between 170 and a small *chaung*, while No. 44 Commando advanced past 170 on to another hill feature, codenamed Pinner, which they occupied without difficulty. This done, No. 44 failed to dig in adequately and was unprepared when the Japanese put in a furious series of counter-attacks, preceded and interspersed with artillery fire from field guns manhandled close to the Commando lines and fired in at point-blank range. No. 44 took heavy casualties before the Japanese withdrew, after which the unit pulled back behind Hill 170 which had now fallen to No. 1 Commando.

The Brigade stayed on or around Hill 170 for the next ten days, while the Japanese continued to shell it intermittently and infiltrate its positions each night with small, aggressive, probing patrols. The more experienced Commando soldiers could sense that something big and menacing was building up in the dense jungle to their front, but the relative calm continued until 06:00 hours on 31 January, when the Japanese hit 170 with everything they had.

Charles Hustwick recalls what followed:

The enemy made a fierce attack on No. 1 Commando, who fought bravely, hand-to-hand with the Japs. Shelling was continuous all the time we were up there and there were many casualties within the whole Brigade. Many shells fired by the Japs failed to explode, the lads getting up and cheering at each dud.

Having held the line for some ten days, we were about to be relieved when a heavy artillery concentration was put down on Hill 170 and the fiercest battle of the campaign was fought for twenty-four hours in an area of about one hundred square yards. The loss to the enemy was well over 300 killed and goodness knows how many wounded. The hill was finally cleared the following day. The back slopes of the hill were covered with enemy dead. They were dwarf-like and armed with long rifles and French-style long bayonets – really ugly creatures.

It was here that Lieutenant Knowland, of No. 1 Commando, a reinforcement from England, won a posthumous VC – he was last seen firing a two-inch mortar from the hip. Casualties in our Commando were heavy among the Bren gunners. Twelve men were hit behind one vital Bren as they went up to keep it firing, one after the other. By the evening after about twenty-four hours' hectic fighting which at one time involved the Headquarters of 1 Commando, the enemy onslaught ceased. A strike by Thunderbolt aircraft inflicted heavy casualties on the now retreating enemy. Several dead Commandos were found well forward, among the Jap dead. I have no idea what 1 Commando's final casualties were, but the price of victory had not been small.

Henry Brown recalls Hill 170:

I was the Senior Administrative Warrant Officer, and just as I had done in North Africa, I went into Kangaw and set up a small base, just me and my typewriter on the lower slopes of Hill 170 along with Dave Reid of the Orderly Room staff. From our position, low down on the hill, we could see several incidents. One I will never forget was the sight of a Jap, running naked along the field in front of the hill where all the action was then taking place. As we discovered a few moments later, he was carrying an explosive charge round his waist and dived under one of the three tanks which had struggled through the paddy to the forward slopes of the hill. They could advance no further because of the marshy ground and the Jap blew himself up and put the tank out of action.

We had all heard of Japanese suicide squads and had now seen them at work. The battle of Hill 170 lasted many days, but on the night of 31 January/1 February, they made their last great attack, and casualties were indeed heavy. Our Bren gunners on the hill spotted the new Jap attack and commenced firing. This stopped the Japs in their tracks but they then decided to come across the fields directly in front of my small hovel, so there I was, in front of the troops (by mistake, I might add), and wondering quite vividly what my fate would be. Fortunately, the Bren gunners were spot-on and this attack was halted halfway across the field. I breathed easily once more.

Kangaw was certainly some battle and our success prompted the Corps Commander, Lieutenant General Christison, to issue a special Order of the Day, praising the action of 3 Commando Brigade.

Des Crowden of No. 5 Commando continues the story:

The hill was known as 170 because it was that height in feet. It was also known as Brighton, but it was nothing like Brighton. The whole Commando Brigade was earmarked for this one with sundry other troops, plus Air Force and Navy support. The beaches and surroundings were hit by American bombers from Ceylon and shelled to hell by the Navy. The landing craft were lowered and circled round the mother ship until every one was down, then they formed up in line abreast and headed for the shore. Before long the water was spouting up around the landing craft. I comforted myself by thinking it was our naval fire falling short, but of course it was the Japs. They had survived the bombing, or some of them had.

Anyway, the Navy's gunners were more accurate, as we were to discover later. Our Commando was the second to land. The beaches out there are steep and we were up to our armpits in water. Mines and small arms fire harassed us as well as the load we had to carry – all our usual equipment plus ammo, grenades, extra food, as well as petrol cans full of drinking water. Once ashore, you had to scramble through the mangrove swamps. By then the first casualties were coming back to the beach, much envied by the rest of us, I might add. We reached the hill and the first task was to dig in again in box formation. The ground was very hard and at least one chap was shot dead while we were digging in.

Food varied between bully beef and tinned soup, and we had solidified smokeless fuel, which we lit in the bottom of our trench or foxhole. The Medical Corps set up on the same hill and did all kinds of wonderful things while the battle raged all round them. Patrols were sent out to nearby hills and Jap long-range guns continually shelled us unless one of our spotter planes was in the air – they were a godsend.

The Japs decided that they liked this hill and they attacked us in strength and overran about an eighth of it. By the time they were forced to retire they had lost over 300 men and many more were wounded. The night before they finally retreated, my troop, No. 4 of 5 Commando, were at the sharp end, almost shoulder to shoulder in a box and under attack, but none of the Japs got through. The following morning, one of those ridiculous things happened; mail arrived on the hill from the UK . . . and two hard-boiled eggs apiece. We looked through this pile of mail, took out our own and passed the rest on, knowing that many letters would never be claimed.

The support from the RAF and the Navy was fantastic. The RAF were bombing and strafing with Hurricanes, and at one point I thought they were dropping leaflets, but one of our planes had been hit with small arms fire, had blown up and was dropping in small pieces. We got plenty of Jap souvenirs on this trip and I understand that a Jap officer's sword was sent to the family of the pilot of this plane. The Navy were shelling the enemy through the trees above our heads and their OPs were on the hill with us and their direction was magnificent.

Then we were ready to finish it off. One of our sergeants took some men along the foot of the hill while the rest of us crawled towards Japs along the top. One Sergeant-Major filled up a native's basket with hand grenades and did a solo attack. He was badly wounded but was dragged out and lives to this day. He was decorated. An officer of No. 1 Commando fired on the Japs till he was killed and he got a posthumous VC. Progress anywhere along the hill had to be in single file, and the one up front was usually killed or wounded.

When it was my turn to lead, I saw a group of Japs retreating, carrying their wounded. I let fly with my Tommy-gun and signalled my colleagues to move up. It was looking better now and soon it was all over. The trenches we approached were full of dead or wounded Japs, many wearing green berets they had taken from our dead. We also found a wounded Naval OP officer who, it turned out, had been seconded to us when we were in Madagascar. I should think he was glad to see the back of us.

We suffered a lot of casualties and were glad when Indian troops moved in to take over. Every month for the past three months, a draw had taken place in each troop, and the winner's name went into the hat. When not in action the whole Commando were on parade to watch the final draw, for the outright winner got a month's leave back in Blighty. Believe it or not, the final draw took place on this bloody hill. The winner, who was in my Troop, had to run across open ground to reach a landing craft on the nearby *chaung* and head home.

Frank Atter of 5 Commando:

Until the last Japanese attack, most of the danger was from very accurate shellfire. At first we thought the attack was for a short spell just after dawn. Their guns, mostly 75s, were brought very close to the hill, and a really massive barrage was directed at us. I know the guns were close because the two explosions of detonation and the explosion of the shells seemed almost simultaneous. Later, the barrage continued at a greater distance, but still with the accuracy that Japanese artillery were noted for, and the 75s were joined by heavier guns. Our own 25-pounders gave excellent support, as did the tanks, which were in territory unsuitable for them. Water was not in plentiful supply, apart from salt water from the *chaung*.

Then 5 Commando moved forward to a hill in front. Nothing happened there except the occasional shelling until one night we heard the noise of a real battle. This was the big attack on 1 Commando, and it was obvious it was serious. We were told to make our own way to Hill 170 by subsections, and we went back to our old positions but I can tell you very little about the battle. My only real duty was to take ammunition up to those who were involved. I never realised before how fast you could run carrying heavy ammunition boxes, but when you are being shot at it does concentrate somewhat.

The tactics employed against No. 44 Commando – intense close-range artillery fire, followed by massed infantry assaults – were repeated on a rising scale of violence against No. 1 Commando on Hill 170. The main Japanese infantry assault came in against 4 Troop of No. 1 Commando, holding the north edge of 170, reinforced when possible by troops from Nos 42 and 5 Commando. No. 1 Commando – perhaps 250 men – disputed its position on 170 throughout the day with counter-attack following counter-attack as the British and the Japanese fought for the hill.

On 1 February the Japanese destroyed three tanks which had become bogged in the marsh below the western slopes of 170, and then mounted a second major offensive against No. 1, overrunning the first line of trenches before they were stopped. British Commandos and Japanese infantry were locked in battle at close quarters, much of it hand-to-hand, bayonet-to-bayonet. The Japanese manhandled their artillery pieces forward to pound the Commando trenches over open sights, the Commandos engaging the Japanese gunners with Brens and mortars.

At one Bren position, twelve gunners were killed or wounded one after the other, but another man always came crawling out from cover to take up the fight, while men in nearby trenches lobbed over full magazines to keep the Bren in action.

Ted Coker was a Bren gunner in No. 1 Commando:

There was the grim day when we finally knocked them off the hill. I remember moving up a track to relieve one of our Troops (there were seven Troops in No. 1 – I was in No. 6). We met our blokes being led and carried out, looking absolutely shell-shocked, and I remember thinking, this is one we won't get out of. Anyway, we managed to get to our forward positions.

I had a No. 2 on my Bren with me, but after about an hour he was killed and I understand mine was the only Bren to keep going. It's funny what you remember about your thoughts at the time. I kept thinking, Thank Christ for 1st and 2nd IA. When I was training on the Bren, the instructors were forever drumming into us our 1st IA and 2nd IA. IA is Immediate Action, what you do when the gun stops firing and I used to think, how the hell can you have 1st and 2nd IAs! But on this day, on Hill 170, I was so glad I had done both blindfolded in training, as it no doubt saved my life and helped 6 Troop take part in that particular victory.

I was lying in a shallow trench, and an officer and some others were managing to get magazines to me to keep me going, and I thought, why must they keep hitting me in the back, throwing those loaded mags at me. To give you some idea of the ferocity of that day, our people counted over 370 dead Japs in front or around our position the next morning and we had lost far too many bloody good blokes. You can't describe it properly, you can't make anyone who wasn't there understand what it was like.

Ted Coker won the Military Medal on Hill 170.

By mid-afternoon on 1 February, the heart of the fight had settled round the 24 surviving men of 4 Troop, now commanded by the newly commissioned Lieutenant George Knowland, late of No. 3 Commando. They beat off one attack by 300 Japanese infantry, Knowland leaving his trench to move about the position, throwing grenades, sharing out the remaining ammunition, cheering his men on, taking over the Bren when yet another gun-crew were shot down.

Knowland then engaged a second attack, firing into the advancing Japanese line with a 2-inch mortar and a Bren, picking up a rifle and then a Tommy-gun to spray their still-advancing ranks, now only thirty feet away. He was killed just before this attack petered out, when another desperate counter-attack by 4 Troop, aided by gunfire from the support craft on the *chaung,* beat the Japanese off yet again.

The fight for 170 went on all that day and well into the night. The Japanese clung to that part of the hill they had captured, digging in and bringing up machine guns. Counter-attacks by 3 Troop of No. 1 and reinforcements from Nos 5 and 42 Commando failed to shift them.

John Ferguson:

We had been moved to the forward edge of Hill 170. There were hundreds of Japanese at the base of the swamp and many more coming in through the swamps. While throwing hand grenades, I could hear them shouting, 'Cease fire, don't shoot,' and thought 'I'll give you bloody cease firing.' Later, during the grenade throwing, a burst of gunfire at close range severely damaged my left shoulder and put my arm out of action, but somehow it was possible to carry on throwing grenades. Then a further burst hit me in the chest, and down I went, poleaxed, with blood flowing over my chest. There is still a bullet in there, close to my heart. I got another grenade out and tried to get up again but all strength had gone. The last thing I remember was saying to someone, 'Make sure that the pin is still in position,' then oblivion.

The Indian Navy sloops anchored in the *chaung,* the last surviving tank from the 19th Lancers and strafing aircraft came in to help No. 1, but this was an infantry battle, fought with machine guns and rifles, bayonets and grenades, by exhausted men on either side hauling themselves up and forward for one more effort, one more attack, across ground already littered with dead and wounded. As darkness fell on 1 February, the battle spluttered out, fading into occasional bursts of machine-gun fire, the crump of mortar bombs, a splutter of rifle shots. That night the Japanese withdrew, and at dawn, as Peter Young has related, No. 5 Commando was allowed to advance and take possession of the ground.

CSM Joe Edmans of No. 1 Commando gives his account of Kangaw:

The type of enemy we were now fighting was different from the half-hearted Italians and the methodical Germans we fought in North Africa. The Japs had snipers tied in trees, used wounded men to draw you into the open, shouting in English 'Johnny', or 'Joe, where are you?' or 'Help, help, I am wounded over here,' hoping you would go out to pick him up. Can you imagine dense jungle, pitch-black, and every now and then these voices coming out of the dark? The least little movement outside your foxhole, a snake or some other jungle creature moving around, and you thought, 'Here they come, crawling towards me.' You had to be fully alert and on top of the job, with a steady nerve.

The northern end of 170 was held by 4 Troop with No. 1 Troop and the rest of the Commando spread along the top. My Troop, No. 6, was next to No. 4. At the bottom of the hill was HQ and along from them were two support tanks. Private Beaney and I were crouching in our trench at the dawn 'Stand-To', looking through the morning mist to see if we could see anything moving. Suddenly, there was a terrific explosion from the bottom of the hill. I found out later that this was our tanks being blown up by a Japanese suicide squad.

Then, from out of the trees across the paddy fields came a Japanese officer, waving his sword and running towards us. He did not get far and was soon brought down. An officer of 42 Commando at the bottom of the hill dashed out to try and get the sword, but was hit in the leg and had to get back to his trench. Another lad tried and he was more successful. At the northern end of the hill the sound of the firing became fierce. Then we got the news that 4 Troop at the northern end had been overrun. Our section was then ordered to go down the right-hand side of the hill to clear any enemy.

So off we went, Sergeant Roberts, Beaney, Dearden, Ruffell, Sweeney, McFall, Hobbs – all in single file, with bullets whistling through the trees. Keeping very low, we were moving down the side of the hill now and the fighting to our left was getting fierce. Suddenly, Dearden, who was in front of me, was fatally wounded. We carried on down the hill and Sergeant Roberts was hit, but he crawled back up the hill. We consolidated our position and Sweeney and McFall set up the Bren, facing up the hill in the direction of the Japs. Just a short distance from the bottom of the hill, out in the paddy field, was a bamboo hut. On seeing this, Hobbs ran across the open ground to the hut.

Hobbs disappeared from view but we heard a burst from his Tommy-gun. Then he came running back to say that he had killed four Japs who had been hiding, probably waiting for us. He then dashed across the open ground to go back to the hut, but a Jap sniper had seen him, and as he ran back across the paddy field he was hit in the jaw. He came dashing back, holding his jaw which was pouring with blood, and went up the hill to the medics.

Our Bren team was giving the odd burst towards the Japs, then down came a grenade which failed to go off, a couple more came down, and one went off, wounding the two Bren gunners. We realised that we were at a disadvantage being at the bottom of the hill, so we started on our way up, when we heard a moaning sound. Looking back towards the hut, we saw Beaney had been wounded and was lying in the open. A couple of lads went back but as soon as they stepped into the open, all hell was let loose. Beaney kept on shouting and we tossed a couple of smoke grenades for cover but as soon as the smoke came, down came the automatic fire. We tried to get to him several times but to no avail. We sent word back to HQ and were told not to try any more as the casualties were heavy.

A Royal Marine sergeant came down to see if he could

help but the fire being put down by the Japs in front of Beaney was fierce, so we went up the hill to place ourselves in a better position. On reaching the top we heard that Sergeant Lander, who had been with No. 1 since 1940, had been killed by a sniper. At the top of the hill we got in our trenches and waited, while at the northern end, 2 Section of 6 Troop, under Captain Evill, were given the job of trying to clear the Japs off that end of the hill. Suddenly, the Japs charged up the hill, yelling and shouting; we let them come up so far, then we gave them everything we had. We must have been out-numbered twenty to one but we used Bren gun, Tommy-gun, Garands, Colt .45s, and tossed quite a few grenades. After several attempts they gave up.

By this time we had been reinforced with some of No. 42 and No. 44 Royal Marine Commandos and then, coming through the trees at the bottom of the hill, was No. 5 Commando, who were in reserve and had the job of knocking the Japs off the hill. Lieutenant-Colonel Pollitt used to be our Troop Captain and was a great officer, getting us out of a few tight corners while we were in North Africa. They came along the bottom, fanned out and went into the Japs, firing as they went. Suddenly one of the lads was engulfed in smoke and came running up the hill. A bullet had hit one of his phosphorus grenades and he was in agony.

The fighting carried on for some time, then eventually it died down and things went quiet. We stayed in our trenches till the next morning in case they decided to make another attack, but they never came, and we were relieved by an Indian Division. While the troops were moving to the boats, I went round the hill, first to the side that we went down, and once again further down, to where Beaney lay; he had been killed with a bayonet.

The 3rd Commando Brigade lost forty-five men killed and ninety wounded on Hill 170. Lieutenant George Knowland received a posthumous VC and Lieutenant-General Christison, commanding 15th Indian Corps, issued a special Order of the Day:

'3 Commando Brigade, for indifference to personal danger, for ruthless pursuit in success and for resourceful determination in adversity, has been an inspiration to all their comrades-in-arms. The battle of Kangaw has been the decisive battle of the Arakan campaign and was won due to the magnificent courage shown by 3 Commando Brigade on Hill 170.'

Kangaw was the final Commando battle. No. 3 Commando Brigade was withdrawn to Akyab and then to India, where it began to train for Operation Zipper, the invasion of Malaya. On 6 August 1945, the US Air Force dropped the first atom bomb on Hiroshima; three days later another bomb fell on the city of Nagasaki . . . and on 15 August the Second World War came to an end.

EPILOGUE

DISBANDMENT, 1945–6

When the Second World War ended, Nos 1 and 4 Commando Brigades stayed on in Germany after the surrender, helping to restore order during the early days of the Allied occupation. No. 1 Commando Brigade returned to Sussex in July 1945 and began to train for operations in the Far East. No. 2 Commando Brigade had arrived from Italy in mid-June, and No. 4 Commando Brigade finally came home in November.

After the Japanese surrender in August, No. 3 Commando Brigade was sent to Hong Kong, where it arrived on 12 September in time to take the formal surrender of the Japanese garrison. The future of the Army Commando units was already being discussed in high places, and the decision was announced to the men of No. 1 Commando Brigade by General Robert Laycock on 25 October 1945.

'It has fallen to my lot to tell the Commandos, who have fought with such distinction in Norway and the islands of the north, in France, in Belgium, in Holland, and in Germany, in Africa and Egypt, in Crete and Syria, in Sicily and Italy, on the shores and islands of the Adriatic, and in the jungles of the Arakan and Burma, it is with great regret that I must tell you today, that you are to be disbanded.'

The Army Commando disbandment began the following month. Many wartime soldiers returned to civilian life, while the professional soldiers went back to their parent units to continue their military careers. The Headquarters of the UK-based

Commando Brigades were gone by the end of the month, and the other elements of the wartime Commando structure, the Basic Training Centre at Achnacarry, and the Holding Operational Commando at Wrexham, soon followed.

The Holding Operational Commando was finally disbanded in early 1946. Since the ending of the war in Europe, the Holding Operational Commando had been receiving back Commando soldiers released from prison camps and hospitals, and getting them fit and retrained before they returned to their units, but these men were no longer needed.

Fortunately, before the end of 1945, it was decided that the British Forces would retain a Commando Brigade, drawn – somewhat to the chagrin of the Army Commandos – from the ranks of the Royal Marines. This Brigade, No. 3 Commando Brigade, Royal Marines, began to form in Hong Kong in the autumn of 1945, while the wartime No. 3 Commando Brigade began to break up. Nos 1 and 5 Commando lost a steady stream of demobilised men and were combined into No. 1/5 Commando, which finally disbanded in January 1947.

The Army Commandos of the Second World War have stayed together down the decades since the end of hostilities under the umbrella of the Commando Association, formed at Achnacarry by Lieutenant-Colonel Charles Vaughan in 1943 and, although time is thinning their numbers now, the Association is still alive and vigorous. Henry Brown, of the Independent Companies and No. 1 Commando, was their Secretary for over forty years until his recent retirement.

No. 3 Commando Brigade, Royal Marines, has carried the Commando tradition on since 1945, serving with distinction in every operational theatre. Their history records only one year from 1945 to the present day when men or units of this Commando Brigade were not in action somewhere in the world.

Nor was 1945 the end of the Army Commandos. At the end of the 1970s, when the Royal Marines Commandos expanded into Commando Groups, Army Commando units from the Royal Artillery and the Royal Engineers were raised to support the infantry of Nos 40, 42 and 45 Commando. These army units sailed with the Brigade to retake the Falkland

Islands in 1982 and, as this book is written, over 1,000 soldiers of the British Army wear the green beret, having passed the All Arms Commando Course at the Commando Training Centre at Lympstone in Devon.

So the traditions created on the beaches of Dieppe and the hills of the Arakan, at St Nazaire and D-Day and a thousand other fights still survived. The Commando spirit, created and fostered by the men whose stories have appeared in this book, lives on to inspire a new generation of soldiers who wear the green beret.

'They performed whatsoever the King commanded.'

GLOSSARY

ALC	Assault Landing Craft
CCS	Casualty Clearing Station
CO	Commanding Officer
CSM	Company Sergeant Major
FOO	Forward Observation Officer
HE	High Explosive
HMS/M	His Majesty's Submarine
LCA	Landing Craft, Assault
LCI	Landing Craft, Infantry
LCG	Landing Craft, Guns
LCT	Landing Craft, Tank
LMG	Light Machine Gun
LRDG	Long Range Desert Group
LSI	Landing Ship, Infantry
LST	Landing Ship, Tank
MG	Machine Gun
MGB	Motor Gun Boat
ML	Motor Launch
MMG	Medium Machine Gun
MT	Motorised Transport
MTB	Motor Torpedo Boat
OC	Officer Commanding
OP	Observation Post
OR	Other Ranks
RSM	Regimental Sergeant Major
RTU	Returned To Unit
RQMS	Regimental Quarter Master Sergeant
SGB	Steam Gun Boat
TSM	Troop Sergeant Major